FORBIDDEN WIFE

FORBIDDEN WIFE

The Life and Trials of Lady Augusta Murray

JULIA ABEL SMITH

First published 2020

The History Press
97 St George's Place, Cheltenham,
Gloucestershire, GL50 3QB
www.thehistorypress.co.uk

British Library Cataloguing in Publication Data.
A catalogue record for this book is available from the British Library.

ISBN 978 0 7509 9333 3

Typesetting by Geethik Technologies
Printed and bound in Great Britain by TJ International Ltd.

In memory of
Charlotte Haslam,
Landmark Trust Historian, colleague and friend
1954–97

Acknowledgements

It is a pleasure to list the many people who have helped me in the preparation of this book. First, I acknowledge with sincere gratitude the permission of Her Majesty Queen Elizabeth II to make use of the relevant material in the Royal Archives at Windsor Castle.

I am deeply indebted to Anne Dunmore, initially for allowing me to look at her family papers, and subsequently for taking such an interest in the project. Her support has been invaluable.

Tessa Spencer at the National Register of Archives of Scotland helped me to find the Hamilton and Adam family papers and I am grateful to the Duke of Hamilton and Keith Adam for letting me examine those documents.

In Cambridge, the staff in the Rare Books Room at the University Library were most helpful, as was Paul Simm at Trinity College, where the Master and Fellows have given me permission to reproduce their portrait of the first Duke of Sussex.

For his help with tracking down references to Lord Archibald Hamilton, I would like to thank Mark Curthoys at the Oxford Dictionary of National Biography. The ODNB is only one of the Oxford University Press online databases that I have been grateful to access through my Essex Library card.

Charles MacRae located the Harrow School archives, where Rita Boswell found what I needed. At Winchester College, Suzanne Foster was similarly helpful. Heather Purvis at Longford Castle pointed me to a plan of the Radnor mausoleum, which showed where and when Lady Augusta's sister was laid to rest.

Peter Hunter's visual memory enabled me to trace the portrait of Lady Augusta's children; Simon Heffer gave me useful advice at an early stage; Alex Kidson of Liverpool Museums answered all my questions on George Romney and James Bettley lent me his books on Winchester College. I am grateful to the Spedding family at Mirehouse in Cumbria for allowing me to study their Stewart family tree. For his help with the D'Este children, I thank Angus Sladen.

Michael Gray translated some of Augusta's writings from French into English; Jonathan Foyle discovered the third Earl of Dunmore's ledger in Lincoln Cathedral and Dido Arthur introduced me to Emma Pound, who gave me information on women's libraries in the eighteenth century.

In America, Gavin Leckie has helped me with the War of Independence. Andrew Watt visited DACOR Bacon House in Washington, where there is a painting of Lady Augusta and her son. DACOR is a private organisation for foreign affairs professionals and I am grateful to them for allowing me to reproduce the portrait.

In Ramsgate, Jaron James took photographs of the 1822 town survey, and the D'Este mausoleum, on which, with the parish church, Margaret Bolton generously shared her knowledge.

In Scotland, Kathy Harley and Richard Ibbetson could not have been more hospitable, going out their way to take me to research appointments. Andrew Widdowson lent me his flat in Edinburgh and Claudia Pleass drove me to Blair Adam on a snowy morning. Catriona Prest had me to stay when I was researching in Kent and while working at the National Archives in Kew I stayed on numerous occasions with Peter and Joanna Wolton. I am grateful to them all.

Brian Mooney has given me unstinting direction in planning and writing and I sincerely thank him.

While any mistakes are mine, a number of people have kindly read the draft: John Martin Robinson, Mary Wolton, Edmund Abel Smith, Diana Heffer, Gail Mooney and Charles Abel Smith.

In the steps of Augusta, my family have accompanied me with grace and enthusiasm to Dunmore, Edinburgh, Teignmouth, Ramsgate, Rome, New York and Virginia. However, I hope that my children, Marina, Nicholas and Edmund, will forgive me for keeping them waiting in uncomfortably high temperatures outside the John D. Rockefeller Jr. Library in Williamsburg. My husband, Charles, has been my mainstay.

Contents

Family Trees

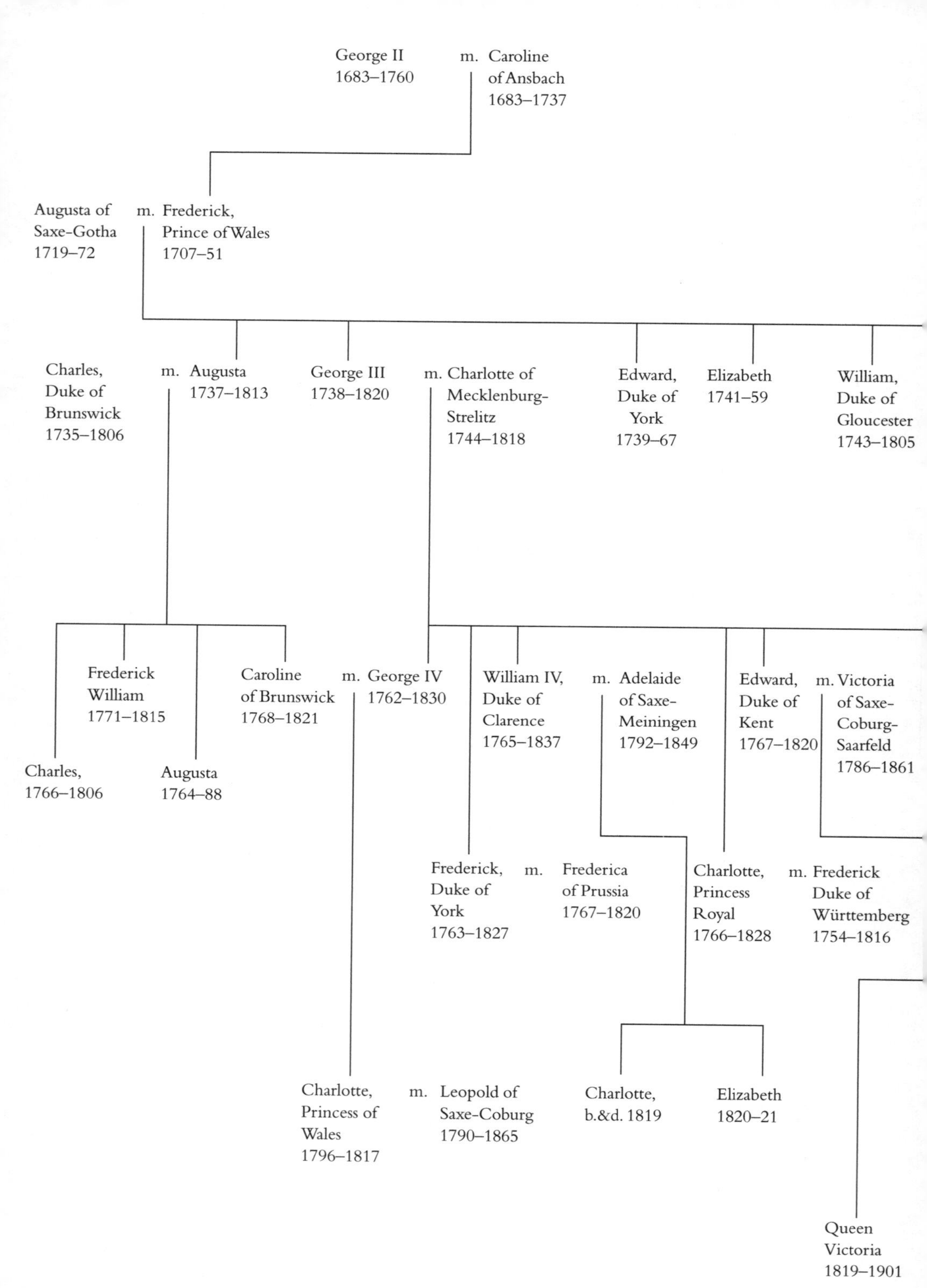

The Royal Family Tree.

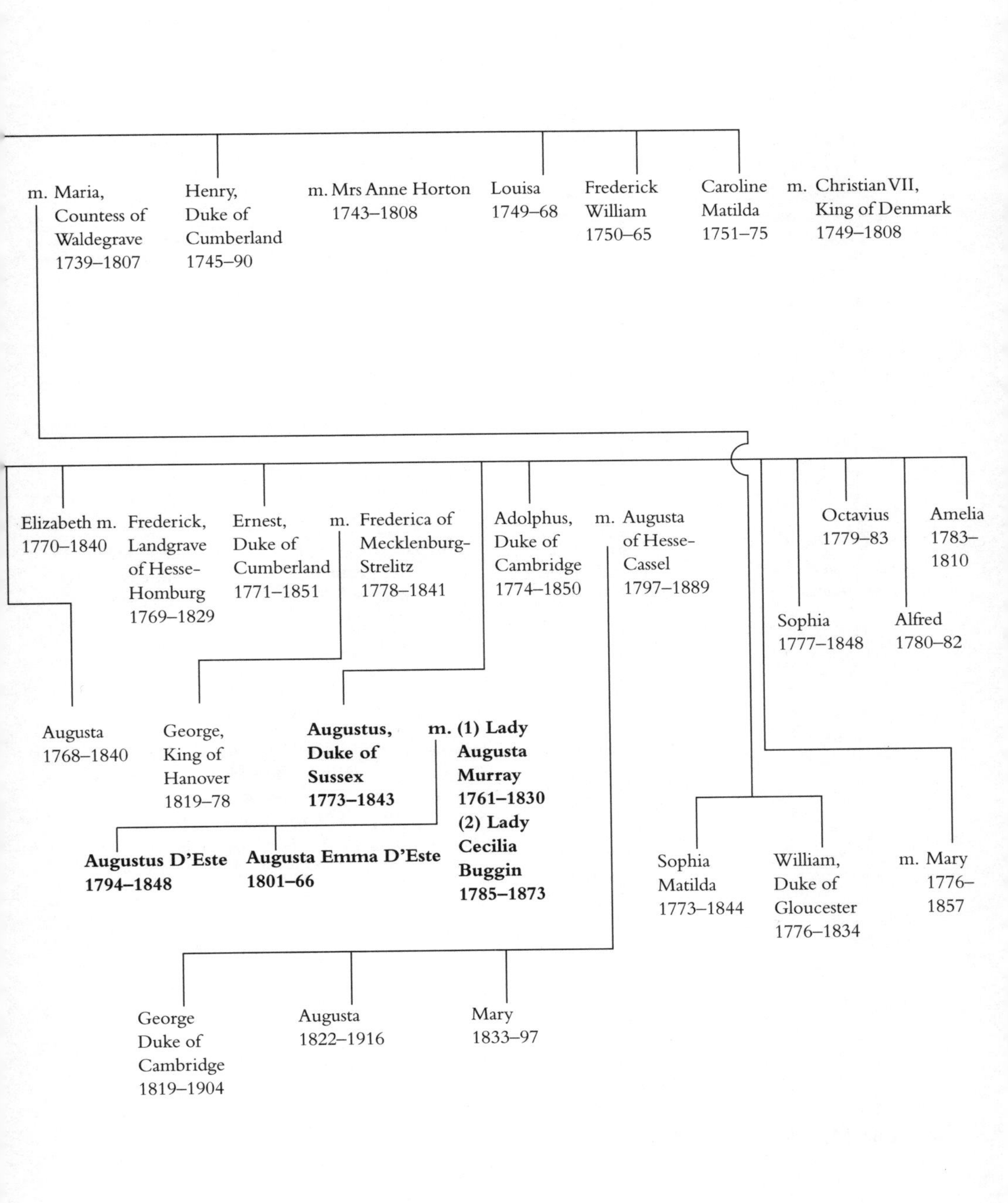

m. Maria, Countess of Waldegrave 1739–1807
Henry, Duke of Cumberland 1745–90
m. Mrs Anne Horton 1743–1808
Louisa 1749–68
Frederick William 1750–65
Caroline Matilda 1751–75
m. Christian VII, King of Denmark 1749–1808
Elizabeth m. 1770–1840
Frederick, Landgrave of Hesse-Homburg 1769–1829
Ernest, Duke of Cumberland 1771–1851
m. Frederica of Mecklenburg-Strelitz 1778–1841
Adolphus, Duke of Cambridge 1774–1850
m. Augusta of Hesse-Cassel 1797–1889
Octavius 1779–83
Amelia 1783–1810
Sophia 1777–1848
Alfred 1780–82
Augusta 1768–1840
George, King of Hanover 1819–78
Augustus, Duke of Sussex 1773–1843
m. (1) Lady Augusta Murray 1761–1830
(2) Lady Cecilia Buggin 1785–1873
Augustus D'Este 1794–1848
Augusta Emma D'Este 1801–66
Sophia Matilda 1773–1844
William, Duke of Gloucester 1776–1834
m. Mary 1776–1857
George Duke of Cambridge 1819–1904
Augusta 1822–1916
Mary 1833–97

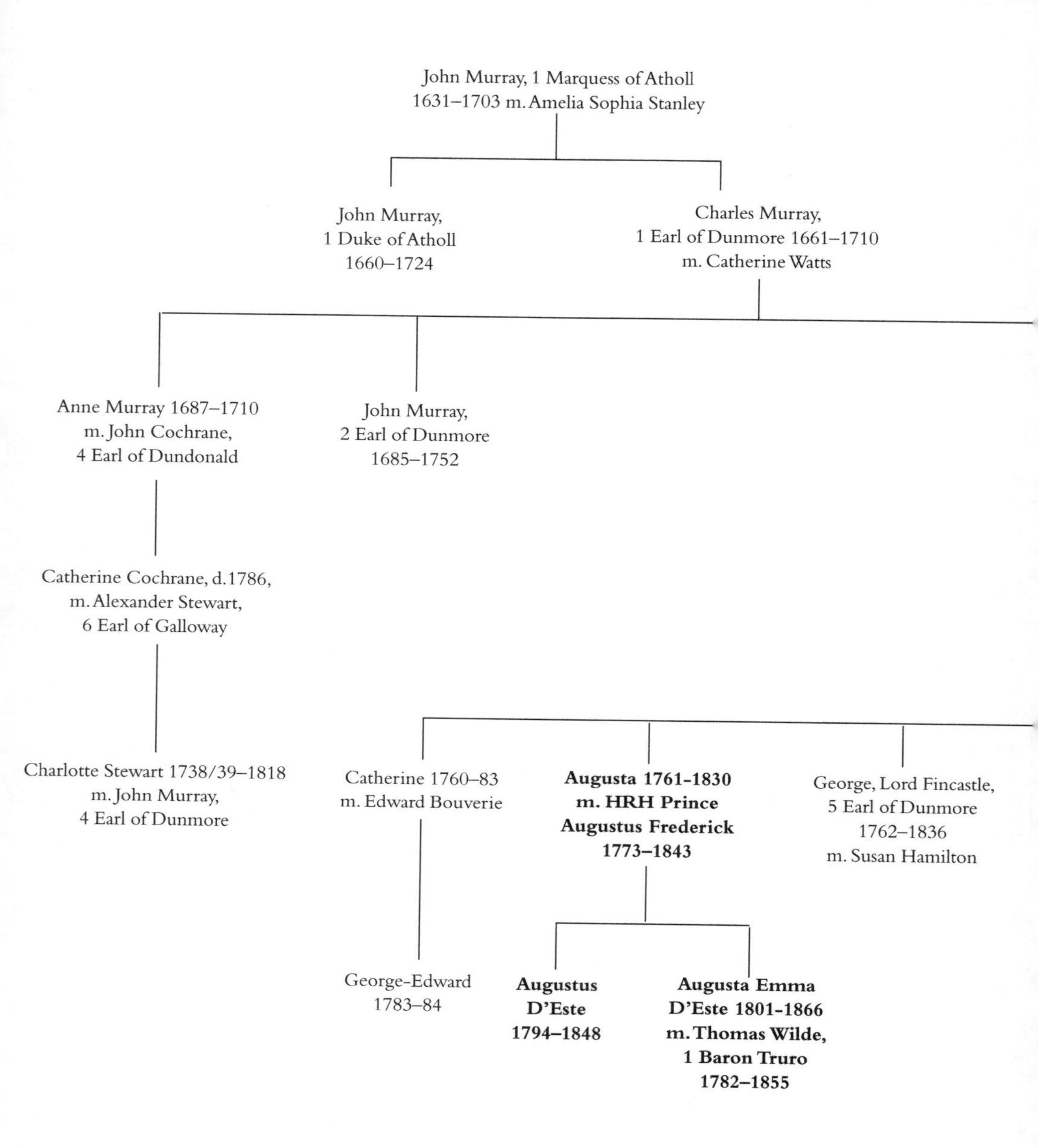

The Murray Family Tree.

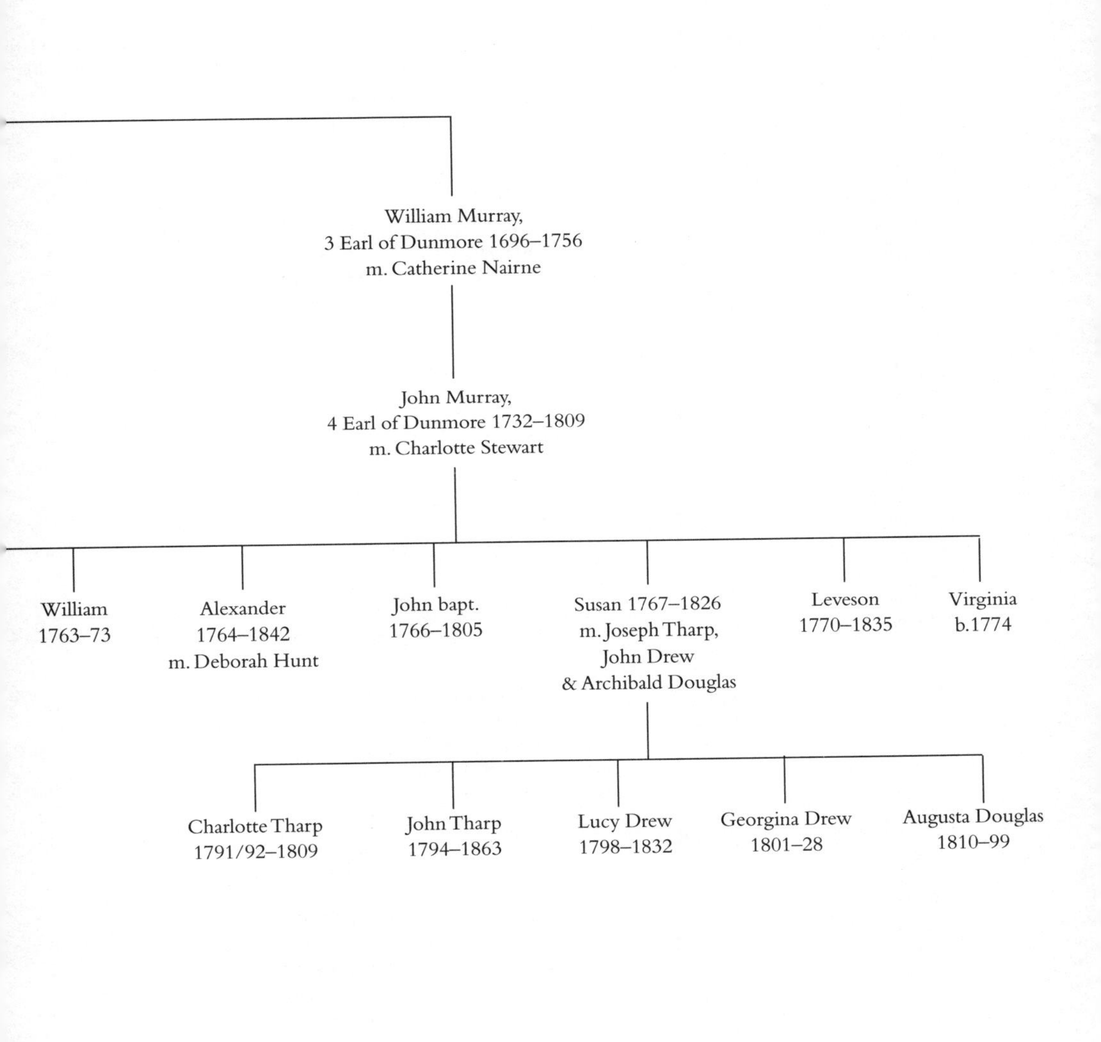
William Murray,
3 Earl of Dunmore 1696–1756
m. Catherine Nairne
John Murray,
4 Earl of Dunmore 1732–1809
m. Charlotte Stewart
William
1763–73
Alexander
1764–1842
m. Deborah Hunt
John bapt.
1766–1805
Susan 1767–1826
m. Joseph Tharp,
John Drew
& Archibald Douglas
Leveson
1770–1835
Virginia
b.1774
Charlotte Tharp
1791/92–1809
John Tharp
1794–1863
Lucy Drew
1798–1832
Georgina Drew
1801–28
Augusta Douglas
1810–99

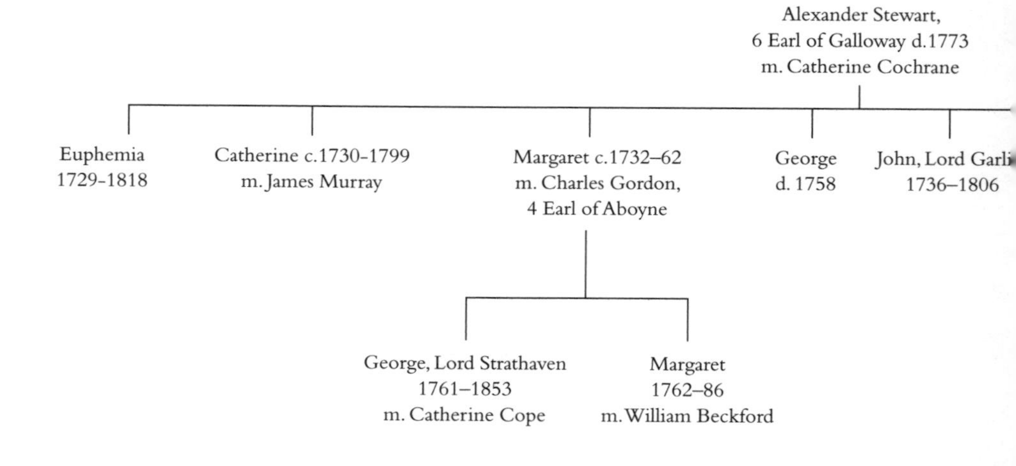

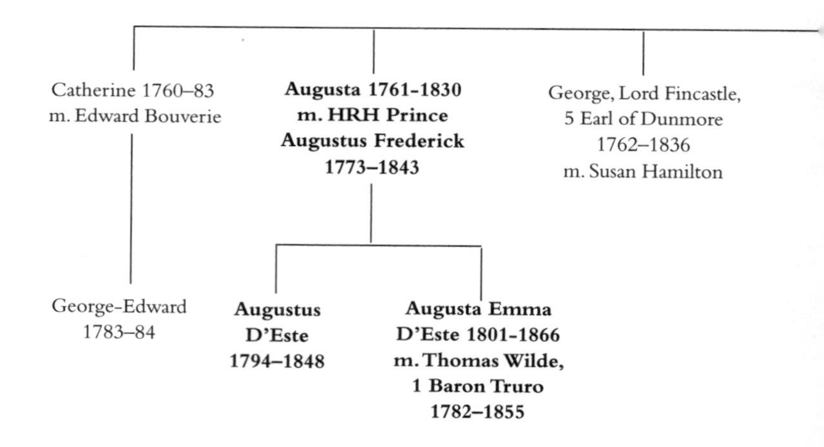

The Stewart Family Tree.

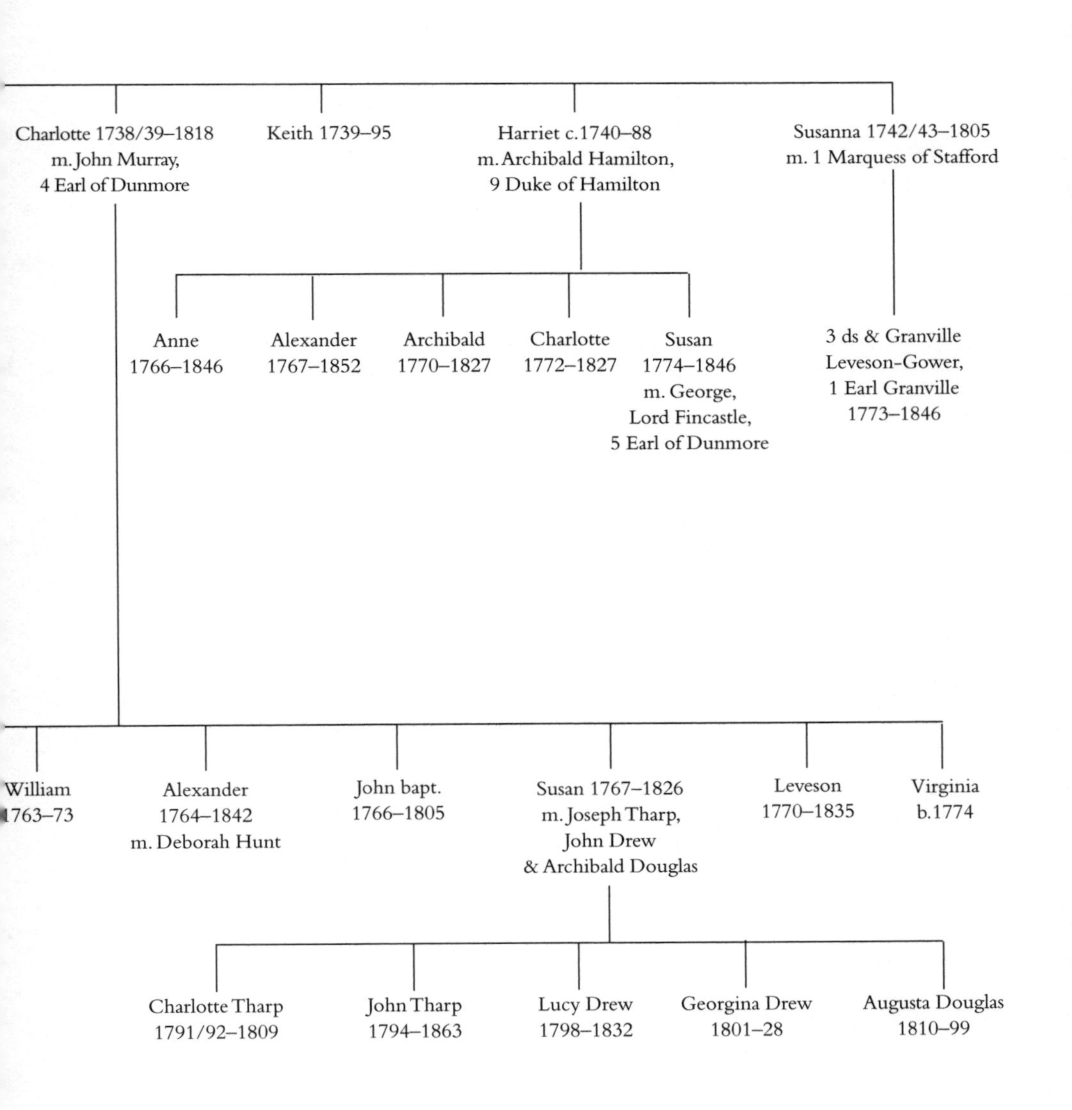

Charlotte 1738/39–1818
m. John Murray,
4 Earl of Dunmore
Keith 1739–95
Harriet c.1740–88
m. Archibald Hamilton,
9 Duke of Hamilton
Susanna 1742/43–1805
m. 1 Marquess of Stafford
Anne
1766–1846
Alexander
1767–1852
Archibald
1770–1827
Charlotte
1772–1827
Susan
1774–1846
m. George,
Lord Fincastle,
5 Earl of Dunmore
3 ds & Granville
Leveson-Gower,
1 Earl Granville
1773–1846
William
1763–73
Alexander
1764–1842
m. Deborah Hunt
John bapt.
1766–1805
Susan 1767–1826
m. Joseph Tharp,
John Drew
& Archibald Douglas
Leveson
1770–1835
Virginia
b.1774
Charlotte Tharp
1791/92–1809
John Tharp
1794–1863
Lucy Drew
1798–1832
Georgina Drew
1801–28
Augusta Douglas
1810–99

Introduction

I discovered Lady Augusta Murray while researching a tropical fruit. I was working as the information officer for the Landmark Trust, a charity that rescues buildings in distress and gives them a future by letting them for holidays. The Trust's Historian, Charlotte Haslam, and I worked at 21 Dean's Yard, a neo-Tudor house of five storeys beside Westminster Abbey. It had been the home of the Chapter Clerk and its interior was decorated with Gothic wallpaper from Watts & Co., the ecclesiastical purveyors nearby. Church calm prevailed: Victorian prints hung on the walls and a grandfather clock ticked steadily in the hall. From our dining room on the third floor we had a bird's eye view of the abbey entrance and enjoyed watching congregations gather for state occasions, but my introduction to the tropical fruit was far away below stairs.

Charlotte's office was in the former servants' hall and there she asked me to revise the history album of one of our Scottish buildings: The Pineapple, an eighteenth-century folly near Stirling. Forty-five feet high, it towers above the centre of the walled garden built by Lady Augusta Murray's father, the 4th Earl of Dunmore. The fruit is a lapidary version of the *Jamaica Queen* cultivar and from its windows he and his family could admire the garden below.[1] It is one of the most famous follies in Britain, yet its architect remains unknown. Charlotte had given me a challenging assignment and I looked forward to searching for architectural drawings and plans; surely I could find a reference to the designer in family correspondence, diaries or bank accounts?

I started work in my sunny office over the porch, where my desk faced Church House, just visible through the London plane trees. Once I watched an unexpected but entertaining fixture: an episcopal hockey match. Occasionally a group of boys from Westminster School, larking down the street, would disrupt the peace but Dean's Yard was mostly undisturbed.

It was there I encountered Lady Augusta Murray. The most beguiling of Lord Dunmore's children, she captivated me and the more I researched, the more I wanted to know. Months later I completed The Pineapple history album and although I failed to discover the architect, I could not forget Lord Dunmore's daughter. I gathered all the information I could on her tragic story, cruelly defined by her marriage to the sixth son of King George III, and I discovered material that has revealed unexpected aspects of Augusta's character. Some years later I completed my research by reading the wedding registers at the Westminster Archives Centre, one street away from Dean's Yard where it had all begun.

Part I

1

My Prince – My Lover, and Now, Indeed, My Husband

In the evening of 4 April 1793, preparations were being made for a clandestine ceremony in Rome. The wedding of the son of the King of England to the daughter of the Governor of the Bahamas would not only be concealed, it would also be illegal. That night His Royal Highness Prince Augustus Frederick was married to Lady Augusta Murray without witnesses. The rector of a small parish in Norfolk read the service in the bride's lodgings: a striking contrast to the wedding of the groom's parents, which was celebrated by the Archbishop of Canterbury in the Chapel Royal at St James's Palace on 8 September 1761.

The couple had known each other for only three months but they believed their destiny was entwined. He was Augustus, she was Augusta, and moreover they shared a birthday. They were deeply in love but the consequences of their rash union would be terrible. It was the worst miscalculation of the Prince's life, but while eventually he found redemption, Augusta's destiny was changed beyond anything she could imagine. From an eighteenth-century socialite she became a nineteenth-century reject.

Their wedding nearly did not take place. The previous night both the Prince and Augusta had considered suicide. All evening she had waited for her lover but he did not appear. Instead the Reverend William Gunn, the Anglican rector who was to marry them, came to clarify the impediments to their proposed nuptials. When he left she confided in her journal, 'All my hopes of happiness are fled; where can I fly, where can I go without misery being my constant companion; Mr Gunn will not, cannot marry us.'[1]

The Prince lay awake in his residence on the Via del Corso nearby. At four in the morning he wrote to her trying to make amends, 'Such has been my desperate state last night that I was unable to come to you my dearest Augusta, or do anything whatever … My torments and anxieties are so great that with the best principles in the world one might forget oneself.'[2] Augusta was not in a mood to look kindly on his excuses. She too had suffered 'torments and anxieties' and her patience was exhausted. She tied together every one of his daily letters and returned them, absolving him from his promises.

When his valet brought in the parcel the Prince responded immediately. He told her that if he had received the package the night before 'it would have encouraged me to have put my criminal purpose [suicide] in execution'. She had also contemplated ending her life and he told her that, 'If you attempt any thing of the sort I will follow, good God, I am distracted, Angels of Heaven assist me, what an agony I am in … Augusta, revoke your wish of dying.'

Augustus had not eaten for more than two days. Etiolated and delirious, he scribbled another letter to Augusta:

> Death is certainly better than this, which, if in 48 hours it [their wedding] has not taken place, must follow; for, by all that is holy, till when I am married I will eat nothing, and if I am not to be married the promise will die with me. I am resolute; nothing in the world shall alter my determination. If Gunn will not marry me I will die … I would rather see none of my family than [be] deprived [of] you … I will sooner drop than give you up … I am half dead. Good God! What will become of me; I shall go mad most undoubtedly … What a dreadful situation I am in; and how can I be otherwise, when she for whom I was taking care of myself will not have me? Life is a burden; but if Augusta will yield, this night I will be hers … If you will allow me, soon after seven I will be at your house, and not care a word for what any one says, but go directly to our room.[3]

As the day advanced, Prince Augustus became more rational. Despite suffering several asthmatic attacks, he made some plans; whatever happened, they would force Mr Gunn to marry them in Augusta's rooms at nine o'clock that night. They would disguise their intentions and confuse the poor rector: Augusta would send for him with a pretext and the Prince would be waiting. He told her, 'I will be with you, and the ceremony must be performed tonight or I shall die ... Call me and I will come, nothing shall detain me, I care not what they say to me, what they do, provided I am yours ... your friend, your lover and your husband.' Obediently, Augusta wrote a disingenuous note to the clergyman. She would be happy to see him after he had paid the Prince a call and she would be alone because her mother and sister were going to a party.

When William Gunn arrived at the Prince's apartment, he was told that His Royal Highness was asleep. Puzzled, the rector set off to keep his appointment with Lady Augusta. Like many British travellers, she was staying in the Piazza di Spagna, the 'Strangers' Quarter', where her mother had taken rooms in the Hotel Sarmiento. Lady Dunmore's servant, Monticelli, admitted Gunn and, as expected, he found Augusta alone.

A moment later the Prince startled him, coming out of a side room laughing. A prayer book was open at *The Solemnization of Matrimony* and the rector saw that he had been tricked. Turning to the Prince, he asked, 'Why do you use me ungenerously? I have always treated you with openness and sincerity?' Summoning every argument at his disposal, Gunn tried to dissuade the couple from their purpose. He accepted their current despair but explained that if they defied the terms of the Royal Marriages Act by marrying without the King's consent, their future would be worse. Gunn forecast disgrace and misery for Augusta if they persisted in marrying against a law instigated by the King himself and implored the Prince to consider Augusta's situation, asking him to respect her 'in a higher degree'.

William Gunn also knew that Augusta's seniority would not help her 'situation'. While both she and Augustus were born on 27 January, the rector knew that she was older than the Prince. Had he known the precise difference in their ages, he would have been even less willing to marry them. At a time when it was frowned upon for a woman to have a younger husband, Augusta was a shocking twelve years older than her fiancé. She was a mature 32 while he was only 20.[4]

Gunn turned once more to Augustus, who was light-headed with hunger and beyond reason. In tears, Augusta placed the prayer book in the rector's hands and reminded him of the betrothal promises that she and the

Prince had exchanged. Gunn told them to release each other immediately from such bonds, which were nothing more than self-imposed. Augusta then heard somebody on the stairs and rushed from the room. Gunn took advantage of her absence to remind the Prince of 'your Family, your Rank, your Country, think of your Father, your Mother, and what it is you wish to have done'. He told Augustus that in 1772 the King had passed the Royal Marriages Act to prevent just such a wedding as the one now proposed. The Prince had neither asked, nor received, his father's permission to marry Augusta and Gunn knew that if he married them, he himself would also be committing a crime.

When Augusta re-entered the room the prayer book was once again thrust into Gunn's hands and once again he demurred. He suggested marrying them when the Prince came of age the next January but Augustus would not listen. Expecting to be summoned to England imminently, he said that he would not leave Italy without Augusta as his wife and promised recklessly that if they were united, the marriage would remain unconsummated until he was 21, when the ceremony could be repeated.

The rector was defeated. He married the Prince and Lady Augusta with grave misgiving and in his distress left out part of the ceremony. Retaining the wedding certificate, he ensured that both bride and groom were sworn to secrecy. The couple, ecstatic in their relief and joy, tried to express their gratitude but Mr Gunn's conscience was troubled: he knew he had broken the law. He allowed the newlyweds a kiss before insisting that he and the Prince should leave. Augusta stood aside and against his will, the bridegroom was led away.

She flew to her desk and wrote:

> My dearest, and now really adored husband, you are but this moment gone; the sacred words I have heard still vibrating in my ears – still reaching my heart. Oh my prince – my lover, and now, indeed, my husband, how I bless the dear man who has made me yours; what a precious – what a holy ceremony; how solemn the charges – how dear, and yet how aweful![5]

Once home, her husband also poured out his feelings: 'This moment I am come from Augusta. She is mine to all eternity. God has given me her. She is to depend upon me, and no one else.'[6] For Augusta the day was 'ever sacred' and she wrote, 'Oh moment that I must record with letters of gold: you are written on the tablets of my heart, you have changed my destiny.'[7] As she wrote those words, she could not know how much her marriage would change her destiny: its consequences would prove a tragedy for this warm-hearted and well-meaning young woman.

2

Fine Sprightly, Sweet Girls

Twenty years earlier, the little port of Cowes was bustling. Beneath a steep hill, scattered with cottages, villas and a church, the quay was bounded by Henry VIII's castle at one end and bristling shipyards crowding the mouth of the River Medina at the other. Business was brisk in the shops, sailors gathered at tavern doors, porters wheeled trunks and boxes and the pilot made preparations. The busy scene presaged a ship's departure: the *Duchess of Gordon* was about to leave for New York on 19 November 1773.

Provisions, luggage and cargo were stowed below and finally the *Duchess* was ready to receive her passengers. A tender ferried a mother and her six children to the ship and when everyone had embarked, the crew raised the sails and heaved up the anchor. The *Duchess of Gordon* sailed past the Needles, which rose from the waves like rotten molars, and the pilot descended, his job done. Twelve-year-old Augusta was on her way to America, where the family would take up residence with her father, now the Governor of Virginia.

Her older sister, Catherine, and her brother, George, Lord Fincastle, were with her. Her younger siblings Alexander, John and Susan were also aboard but two of Augusta's brothers were absent. Six months before, William had died aged 9 and 2-year-old Leveson had been left at home in the care of his paternal grandmother.

After forty-four days, the *Duchess of Gordon* docked on 2 January 1774.[1] Augusta's arrival in New York harbour coincided with one of the most significant periods in American history. The British American colonies resented being taxed without parliamentary representation and their relationship with Britain was deteriorating. A couple of weeks before, 'The Incident', known today as the Boston Tea Party, had taken place in Massachusetts.

On the night of 16 December 1773 a small band of colonists, disguised as Native Americans, boarded three ships in Boston harbour. Their mission was to ransack the cargoes of East India Company tea, a commodity detrimental to the American market, but forced onto it by the British Tea Act. The colonists tore open every chest and poured the contents overboard. The British Government reacted by closing the harbour until the requisite duty had been paid on the lost tea. This measure ensured that the commercial life of Boston, a town reliant on shipping, was brought to a standstill; with their prosperity threatened, the citizens and merchants began to plot.

Meanwhile, Lady Dunmore and her children recovered from their passage in New York and waited for the weather to improve before continuing their journey south. A New Yorker, known for criticising newcomers, was charmed. 'Lady Dunmore is here,' he wrote:

> [she is] a very elegant woman ... Her daughters are fine sprightly, sweet girls. Goodness of heart flushes from them in every look. How is it possible, said that honest soul, our Governor, to me, how is it possible my Lord Dunmore could so long deprive himself of those pleasures he must enjoy in such a family? When you see them you will feel the full force of this observation.[2]

This was unmerited criticism; Lord Dunmore had missed his wife and children and the combination of her husband's entreaties and her slender means had encouraged Charlotte Dunmore to pack up and move to the New World.

The Earl of Dunmore had taken the governorship because he needed money. When he married Lady Charlotte Stewart, a younger daughter of the 6th Earl of Galloway, in 1759 he had been a rich man, having inherited a spectacular legacy from his uncle. Unaccustomed as he was to such wealth, Lord Dunmore had spent it too freely. He built the walled garden at Dunmore and topped it with the extravagant pineapple, and he bought the Glenfinart estate on the western shore of Loch Long. The earl was also profligate in his dress and one lavish waistcoat, copiously embellished with gold lace, caused a stir amongst his friends in Edinburgh.[3]

When staying in the Scottish capital, the family occupied the suite of rooms in the royal palace at Holyrood that Queen Anne had granted her old friend and Master of the Horse, the 1st Earl of Dunmore. Landed families often wintered in Edinburgh, so when Augusta was born on 27 January 1761, the event probably took place at Holyrood. Three months after her birth, Augusta's father became a Representative Peer for Scotland, one of the sixteen Scottish peers elected to sit in the House of Lords under the terms of the Act of Union.

The appointment required him to live near Westminster when parliament was sitting and he moved his family to a large house in Lower Berkeley Street (now called Fitzhardinge Street) between Manchester and Portman Squares. The earl enjoyed his new status and he and the countess moved in London circles with friends such as the future prime minister, Lord Shelburne, and Lord Weymouth, the heir to Longleat. In keeping with his rank, Dunmore commissioned Sir Joshua Reynolds to paint his portrait in full length, a pose reserved for royalty and the nobility. Reynolds was one of London's most costly artists and the painting remained in his studio, unpaid for; today it belongs to the National Portrait Gallery in Edinburgh and dominates any room in which it is hung. By the time that Augusta's younger sister, Susan, was born in 1767, Lord Dunmore had run up debts of £7,000 and had to ask his cousin, the Duke of Atholl, for a loan of £2,000. He explained that he could repay it only if he acquired a position yielding a substantial income.

The earl's prospects brightened when his sister-in-law, Lady Susanna Stewart, married Granville Leveson-Gower, a politician favoured by the King. With the patronage of his new relation, Dunmore was selected as Governor in Chief of the province of New York, whereby he was granted the much-needed salary of £2,000, which came with the possibility of American land grants. Like many other Scots who took colonial office, Dunmore's estates were not enough to support him and the appointment was a pecuniary relief. He was dismayed at leaving his wife, described by Lady Sarah Lennox as 'charming and Scotch', and his delightful children, that a friend had called 'the finest he ever saw'.[4]

In 1771, after a year in New York, Dunmore was assigned as Royal Governor of Virginia. For most of the eighteenth century, governors of Virginia stayed in London and their lieutenants performed the role in Williamsburg. As the King's representative in the colony, the lieutenant governor was in charge of matters civil, military, judicial, fiscal and religious. In 1768 however, against the background of uneasy relations between America and Britain, and mindful of the colony's economic importance, the government attempted to woo the people of Virginia by appointing a full royal governor, Lord Botetourt, who resided in Williamsburg. When Botetourt died unexpectedly in 1770, the post was offered to the Earl of Dunmore.

He had not been pleased, protesting, 'Damn Virginia. Did I ever seek it? Why is it forced on me? I asked for New York – New York I took, and they robbed me of it without my consent.' He was reluctant to take up the post because he thought that Virginia was remote and unhealthy. Lord Botetourt had died of a fever after two years in office and Dunmore was unhappy about exposing his wife and children to the South, which was humid and insalubrious in summer.

The thought of leaving New York was anathema, but Virginia, a larger and more prosperous colony, offered Dunmore a better salary and therefore he accepted the post. Moreover, of all the American colonies, Virginia was in a league of its own. Protestant pilgrims, fleeing Episcopalian Anglicanism, had settled in New England, whereas aristocratic landowners, who had crossed the Atlantic to make money and to escape the Puritan ascendancy in England after the execution of Charles I, populated Virginia. Gentlemen, inhabiting elegant tideway houses on plantations up and down the James and York rivers, grew tobacco, a lucrative business dependent initially on indented and later on slave labour. When Dunmore reached Williamsburg in 1772, the town's population comprised 52 per cent black and 48 per cent white people, the former working on plantations and in domestic service.

As he had feared, soon after his arrival the earl became ill. Home leave to recover his health was conditional on resigning his post, something he could not afford to do. Consequently, in May 1773 Dunmore decided to stay and despatched his secretary to escort the gubernatorial family to Williamsburg.

3

Welcome to Williamsburg

After a month in New York, the countess, her children and ten servants set out for Virginia. They went by carriage to Philadelphia, the largest city in the British American colonies, and on to Annapolis, capital of Maryland. On the quay they boarded the governor's schooner, tactfully named *Lady Gower* after the wife of Lord Dunmore's patron, who had played such an important part in helping procure his appointment. Sailing down the Chesapeake Bay past the mouths of the Potomac and Rappahannock rivers, after three days they entered the York River and made their way towards the south bank. On 26 February 1774 *Lady Gower* docked at Yorktown, one of Virginia's busiest deep-water ports and soon to become famous as the site of Lord Cornwallis's surrender at the end of the War of American Independence.

The arrival of the governor's family was almost as momentous as a royal visit. Awed and fascinated, the tobacco farmers and slave owners, many of them recent immigrants from England and Scotland, crowded the riverbank. Town officials had arranged a cannon salute to greet Lady Dunmore but despite their careful plans a distressing accident with gunpowder marred what should have been a dignified and joyful ceremony. The *Virginia Gazette* described the horror:

> Mr. Thomas Archer, and Mr. Benjamin Minnis, being extremely active in managing the cannon, but by ramming the rod too violently against the iron within, it occasioned a kind of friction ... which communicated to the powder, and the above gentlemen being very near the gun when it went off ... received considerable damage; the arms, face, and

> eyes, of Mr. Archer, being bruised in a most dreadful manner. Mr Minnis was much hurt in the thigh, and otherwise terribly wounded. Captain Lilly was also bruised about the eye, though slightly. Two Negroes that assisted were dreadfully mangled, one of them having lost three fingers off his right hand; the other is so much burnt in the face, and his eyes are so much hurt, that is thought he will never recover their use. Fortunately, none of their lives are despaired of.[1]

The incident did not bode well.

Departing in a state of shock, the governor's family crossed Yorktown Creek. The last 12 miles of their journey to Williamsburg took them over marshes and through woods of oak, maple and pine.

The capital of Virginia rejoiced at the prospect of a royal governor, his wife (herself the daughter of an earl) and their six children living in the Governor's Palace. Earlier in the month, John Byrd, a student at William and Mary College, told his father that the town was making preparations 'for the reception of Lady Dunmore, fireworks, with great illuminations, for which I understand there is a large subscription made'.[2] Now the waiting was over.

At seven o'clock in the evening crowds of well-wishers, calling out 'Welcome to Williamsburg', met the governor's carriage, which was emblazoned with the arms of the colony of Virginia on one side and those of the Earl of Dunmore on the other. It entered the town accompanied by children and youths. On Duke of Gloucester Street, the town's principal thoroughfare, windows were illuminated and that evening, throughout the town, gentlemen raised their glasses to 'the Governor of Virginia and his Lady just arrived' and 'Their Majesties', and more tellingly, they raised their glasses to 'Success to American Trade and Commerce'.

The carriages containing Lady Dunmore, her children and attendants turned into Palace Green, an open space bordered by catalpa trees, and drew up by the governor's residence at the end. Augusta stepped down after her mother and Catherine; Susan followed her and the boys descended from another carriage. Lord Dunmore had not seen his family for over four years and the *Virginia Gazette* celebrated their reunion in lines dedicated to his wife:

> Hail, noble Charlotte! Welcome to the plain,
> Where your lov'd Lord presides o'er the domain:

But who can speak the rapture that he proves,
To see at once six pledges of your loves?

Your lovely offspring crowd to his embrace,
While he with joy their growing beauties trace;
And while the father in his bosom glows,
The tears of pleasure from each cherub flows;
All eager pressing round about his knees,
In sweet contest, their father most to please.
O charming group! So blooming, and so fair,
In virtue rear'd by thy maternal care.[3]

Augusta, the second of the 'six pledges' of her parents' love, was now 13 years old and overjoyed to see her father.

Her new home, the scene of so much imagined and real delight, was one of the handsomest houses in the colony. After the Dunmores' departure the palace became a hospital for soldiers wounded at the battle of Yorktown and in December 1781 it caught fire. However, in 1934 it was opened to the public having been rebuilt from its foundations and restored to its original appearance with Rockefeller funding. Today, the Colonial Williamsburg Foundation presents it as the eighteenth-century residence of the last royal governors and it appears once again as the home that Augusta would recognise.

The palace is 'of special importance to America, as the first great classical mansion of Virginia'.[4] It had been built in the Queen Anne style: a symmetrical red brick house of two storeys, with dormer windows in the steeply pitched slate roof. A glazed lantern, topped by a cupola and weather vane, surmounted the roof balcony and tall chimneys on either side enhanced its silhouette. The entrance hall doubled as an armoury and the walls were decorated with shields, pistols and swords, while a display of muskets with fixed bayonets radiated from the ceiling. The royal coat of arms reminded the visitor of the governor's vice-regal status.

Augusta's bedroom was on the first floor, across the landing from her parents' suite, and her brothers slept on the floor above. When she looked round the twenty-five rooms, although much was new and strange, Augusta recognised some items from home: hexagonal plates with the family coat of arms and portraits by Sir Peter Lely.[5] She was pleased to learn that dancing was a favourite pastime in Virginia and admired the ballroom at the back of the house. Coronation portraits of King George III and Queen Charlotte, painted by Allan Ramsay, her father's acquaintance in Edinburgh, hung on its walls. Charlotte's small figure was draped in ermine and blue velvet and her left hand lay on her crown, which was placed on a matching blue velvet cushion. George III, staring into the distance, was dressed in a gorgeous golden suit, flowing ermine and the collar of the Order of the Garter; like his wife, he stood on a thick turkey carpet. The painted presence of Their Majesties was another powerful reminder of the royal authority vested in her father.

From the supper room beyond the ballroom, double doors led into the garden, which Lord Botetourt described as 'well planted and watered by beautiful Rills, and the whole in every respect just as I could wish'.[6] At the side of the flower gardens, terraces ran down to a canal and there was a maze and an icehouse. Beyond the garden 150 cattle grazed in the Governor's Park, where Lord Dunmore took his morning walk; in the summer he cooled down in the hexagonal bathhouse.

Augusta's home was the centre of administration for the governor of Virginia. Visitors to the house, planters, soldiers, sea captains, officials and messengers passed through a sequence of spaces, culminating in an audience with the governor. They came down Palace Green, through the wrought-iron gates into the courtyard and up the steps to the front door. From the impressive hall they were shown into the adjacent parlour, where they waited before being escorted upstairs and admitted to her father's private office, the 'great Room' lined with gilded leather.

While her husband was administering the colony of Virginia, Lady Dunmore did not neglect her daughters' education. A girl from Augusta's background was expected to excel in the gentler arts and she learnt needle-work, drawing and dancing. She was fluent in French and although she told Prince Augustus later that she regretted her lack of musical accomplish-ment, there was plenty of opportunity for her to practise in Williamsburg. There was a harpsichord and piano as well as three organs and other musical instruments in the palace. Her father encouraged her to read and she sought sanctuary in his 'valuable Library consisting of upwards of 1,300 volumes' opposite her bedroom.[7]

Her brothers were enrolled at the College of William and Mary, Virginia's venerable seat of learning. Indeed its existence had been a factor in Lord

Dunmore's decision to bring his family to America, and in the Wren Building (a colonial version of London's Chelsea Hospital) the boys learnt mathematics, geography, the classics and 'penmanship'.

William and Mary College was located at the west end of Duke of Gloucester Street. At the east end was the Capitol, which housed Virginia's highest court, and the legislative assemblies. Copying the Westminster formula, the Capitol was divided into two parts: the King's side comprised the General Court and the Council Chamber, or meeting place of the upper house. The debating chamber of the lower house, or House of Burgesses, was on the other side and one of its most distinguished members was Colonel George Washington, the senior burgess for Fairfax County.

As a young girl, Lady Augusta Murray met the man who would become the first President of the United States. Colonel Washington and Lord Dunmore were united in their zeal for investing in land and allocation of land title was in the governor's gift. The year before Augusta arrived, a land-surveying expedition planned by her father and Washington was cancelled when Washington's stepdaughter died of epilepsy. It is unclear whether their friendliness was based on their mutual interest in acquiring land or whether it was political expediency on Washington's part, probably both, but it appears that, until their relationship was affected by revolutionary events, there was a degree of warmth between the two men.

In July 1772 Washington had hoped to receive the governor at Mount Vernon, his home in Fairfax County, and told him that he had looked in vain 'every hour for eight or ten days for your Lordship's Yacht' sailing up the River Potomac.[8] In December 1773 he sent the governor a barrel of hawthorn berries and like Dunmore, he shared a love of pineapples. When he was in Barbados in 1751, Washington confessed that of all the fruits he found there 'none pleases my taste as do's the Pine'.[9]

When in Williamsburg for meetings of the General Assembly, the colonel was often a guest at Lord Dunmore's table. On 16 May 1774 he dined at the palace for the first time since the arrival of the governor's family and we can imagine Augusta's father proudly introducing his wife and six children to George and Martha Washington. However, when the colonel dined and spent the evening at the palace a few days later, political events in Virginia had caught up with the 'incident' in Boston harbour.

On the morning of 16 May, Washington had been present in the House of Burgesses when it resolved to set aside 1 June as a time for fasting and prayer for a successful outcome to the altercation between Boston and London. Later at the palace he did not allow civil disobedience in a distant port to spoil a good dinner. The next morning, according to his diary, Washington 'Rid out with the Govr. to his Farm and Breakfasted with him there'.[10]

It was only the next day that the significance of the 'Boston Tea Party' became obvious.

On 17 May Lord Dunmore learnt of the Williamsburg burgesses' proposal for the day of prayer and fasting. Furious, he commanded them to assemble immediately in the Council Chamber where, gripping their resolution, he thundered, 'I have in my hand a paper published by order of your House, conceived in such terms as reflect highly upon His Majesty and the Parliament of Great Britain; which makes it necessary for me to dissolve you; and you are dissolved accordingly.'[11] Lord Dunmore failed to intimidate the burgesses. They merely reassembled at the Raleigh Tavern and formed the Virginia Association, agreeing that deputies from the colonies of British America should 'meet in general congress, at such place annually as shall be thought most convenient; there to deliberate on those general measures which the united interests of America may from time to time require'.[12] The fissure in Virginia's relationship with Britain was widening.

The timing of Dunmore's dissolution was unfortunate because the House of Burgesses had arranged a subscription ball to welcome Lady Dunmore the next night. Everyone was determined not to lose face and the burgesses continued with their plans for the dance. As Washington's biographer, Douglas Southall Freeman, has written, it was:

> an extraordinary, a paradoxical, an amusing and, withal, an enjoyable affair: the hosts were to be put to the bother and expense of a canvas and a new election for no other reason than they had decided to have a fast day; all the same, as gentlemen, and at £1 per capita, they bowed low to the wife of the man who had dissolved their House.[13]

In the Capitol the burgesses received Lady Dunmore graciously as the highest-ranking lady in North America and she was welcomed and fêted by the best of Virginia society: the Byrds, the Lees and the Jeffersons. The countess appreciated their courtesies for she loved a party and was an accomplished dancer.

There was one burgess however, who had been unable to attend the ball. While George Washington was dancing at the Capitol, hundreds of miles away on the banks of the River Ohio an uneasy land surveyor, Colonel William Preston, was writing him a letter. The British Government's undertaking, under the terms of the Royal Proclamation of 1763, to protect Native American land rights west of the Appalachian Mountains was another reason for American colonists' disquiet with the mother country. Virginian tobacco planters were in constant need of 'plenty of cheap land to replace the acres wasted by soil-exhaustion and soil-erosion, the marks of inefficient agriculture' and Native American tribes had resented the settlers' incursions on their lands south of the Ohio for many years.[14] Tales of torture, scalps and abduction did nothing to calm the nerves of the white settlers and their surveyors. In his letter, Preston told Washington of the recent disappearance of three of his party and his fear of the Native American, who were hindering his business. Contrary to the Proclamation, Lord Dunmore supported the Virginian settlers. He was also concerned by the dispute further up river between Virginia and Pennsylvania over the area around Fort Pitt (present day Pittsburgh). On 10 June he instructed his lieutenants in the frontier counties to start raising militia to act against the towns of the Shawnee tribe across the Ohio.

Charlotte Dunmore was now expecting another child. As her pregnancy progressed, her husband was preparing to lead a detachment of 1,400 men from Williamsburg across the Appalachians to participate in the campaign known today as 'Dunmore's War'. The governor departed for the Ohio River with the approbation of the Virginians, but it was an anxious time for his wife and children left at home. He arrived at Fort Fincastle (present day Wheeling) to the south-west of Fort Pitt on 30 September 1774. A few days later, the Shawnee were routed and the governor began to negotiate with the defeated tribe at Camp Charlotte, a new fort, which he named after his wife. By a treaty of friendship, Cornstalk, the Shawnee Chief, renounced his tribe's hunting rights south of the Ohio, leaving the way free for future Virginian settlements.[15] Returning home a hero on 4 December, John Dunmore discovered that Charlotte had given birth the day before.

The *Virginia Gazette* reported that, 'Last Saturday morning the Rt. Hon. the Countess of Dunmore was safely delivered of a daughter, at the Palace. Her Ladyship continues in a very favourable situation, and the young Virginian is in perfect health.' For Augusta the joy was twofold. Her father had returned safely from a military campaign and her mother had survived a process no less perilous: that of giving birth.

In 1775 Williamsburg celebrated Queen Charlotte's birthday on 19 January and began with the christening of the governor's daughter at Bruton parish church on the corner of Palace Street. The baby received the name 'Virginia', as requested by the General Assembly and happily agreed by the governor; indeed the victorious expedition to the Ohio had elevated Lord Dunmore's standing to such an extent that no other name would have been acceptable. Fifty years later, Lady Dunmore told John Quincy Adams, America's Minister Plenipotentiary to Great Britain, that George Washington held Virginia at the font.[16]

The festivities continued that night with a birthday ball at the palace. It was a splendid occasion but not for the faint-hearted. The kitchens were instructed to cater generously to sustain the dancers' stamina. Five meats were served, glass *épergnes* were filled with candied fruits and sugared nuts, and a choice of desserts (pastries, syllabubs and jellies) were displayed on crystal stands down the middle of two tables in the Supper Room. At midnight the musicians struck up again after supper and the dancing continued. Lord Dunmore requested Scottish reels, and the cotillions, rigadoons and gavottes did not cease until nine o'clock the next morning, when the musicians packed up their instruments and the last guests departed. It had been a spectacular success and although nobody knew it at the time, the celebration for Queen Charlotte's birthday would be the last ball hosted by a royal governor at the palace in Williamsburg.

Later in 1775 the governor and his family sailed down the James River to Norfolk, where Augusta had another opportunity to dance. Norfolk, an important trading city with warehouses lining the quay, returned one burgess to the General Assembly of Virginia. Years later an 'Old Burgess' recalled the sensation that the governor's wife and his daughters caused on the dance floor:

> the fiddles struck up; and there went my Lady Dunmore in the minuet, sailing about the room in her great, fine, hoop-petticoat, (her new fashioned air balloon as I called it) and Col. Moseley after her, wig and all. Indeed he did his best to overtake her I believe; but the little puss was too cunning for him this time, and kept turning and doubling upon him so often, that she flung him out several times ... Bless her heart, how

> cleverly she managed her hoop – now this way, now that – everybody was delighted. Indeed we all agreed that she was a lady sure enough, and that we had never seen dancing before.

It was high praise from a resident of Virginia, a colony that prided itself on its prowess on the dance floor.

After Lady Dunmore's display, the mayor danced a minuet with Lady Catherine, then the 'Old Burgess' recalled Captain Montagu taking out 'Lady Susan' and 'the little jade made a mighty pretty cheese with her hoop'.[17] Susan was then aged only 6, so the 'little jade' was probably Augusta. George Montagu was a 24-year-old naval captain with a *distingué* presence and an elegant Roman nose.

Soon after Augusta's 14th birthday in 1775, an event in Richmond provoked her father to authorise a manoeuvre that resulted in his family fleeing America. Discontent over Westminster's measures for taxing the colonies continued to fester and at the Second Revolutionary Virginia Convention in March, Patrick Henry, an orator of exceptional power known as the 'firebrand', proposed assembling and training a revolutionary militia. He concluded his call to arms with, 'Almighty God – I know not what course others may take; but as for me – give me liberty, or give me death!' With his young family living at the palace, Lord Dunmore felt increasingly vulnerable, both politically and personally, and the prospect of rebellion horrified him. His next step however, inflamed the colony and hastened more than any other its progress towards revolution.

The 'Powder Incident' took place between three and four o'clock in the morning of 21 April 1775 at the magazine on Duke of Gloucester Street. Surrounded by a protective wall, it was an octagonal brick building designed to hold a substantial arsenal with everything necessary to wage a minor battle: guns, bayonets, pistols and gunpowder, all imported from England for the protection of the colony of Virginia.

Lord Dunmore instructed Captain Henry Collins, commander of HMS *Magdalen*, to seize the gunpowder and remove it to his armed schooner moored in the James River. Silently, a detachment of marines crept up to the magazine, loaded the barrels of gunpowder into the governor's wagon and, undetected, drove it through the quiet streets. Nobody raised the alarm but with daylight came the discovery that the people of Virginia could not defend themselves. Alarmed and exasperated, the citizens cried 'To the Palace'.

The family heard angry noises outside. A party of gentlemen, members of Williamsburg's municipal council, then arrived requesting clarification for the clearing of the magazine. While the noise from the crowd increased, Augusta could see the back of her father addressing the throng from the first floor balcony of his office. He told them that if the powder were needed it would be delivered in half an hour and that it was now in a secure place. His explanation did not satisfy the crowd and Augusta heard more shouts and threats before the people dispersed.

Lord Dunmore was now gravely concerned for the safety of his wife, children and 4-month-old baby, Virginia. As he wrote to Lord Dartmouth, the Secretary of State for America, he was obliged to shut himself in 'and make a Garrison of my House, expecting every Moment to be attacked'.[18] He instructed the household to arm itself and weaponry, previously displayed in the entrance hall, was made available. The governor's home was now a fortress. Augusta's visits, excursions and outings to the shops ceased and armed servants accompanied her in the garden. Thus imprisoned, the helpless family and their servants became more and more afraid.

The 'Powder Incident' had given the counties of Virginia an excuse to raise their militias. The people began to arm themselves and volunteers gathered in the capital. Meanwhile, on 3 May the Hanover County militia, under the control of Patrick Henry, never one to exercise restraint, advanced to within a few miles of Williamsburg, and in the governor's words 'encamped with all the Appearances of actual War' trying to cut off any help that might come to His Excellency from HMS *Fowey* lying off Yorktown.[19] Henry demanded financial restitution from the governor for the powder. Dunmore arranged for £330, the estimated value of the powder, to be sent to Henry to avoid an attack on Williamsburg and more precisely the palace. Tension mounted when the governor arranged for cannon to be planted in front of the palace and, despite Henry's best efforts, a group of marines marched from Yorktown to guard the governor's residence.

Lord Dunmore began to make secret preparations for the evacuation of his family and explained to the children that they must go with their mother to Yorktown, where they would be escorted to the man-of-war waiting at anchor. It was a terrible leave-taking. Augusta's father was left alone in his fortified home at the mercy of the rebels, while his frightened family drove to Yorktown. Augusta recalled her first journey from Yorktown to Williamsburg, full of excitement and anticipation. Now she was departing by stealth in an unmarked carriage. Arriving at Yorktown that night, they were rowed out to HMS *Fowey*. Safely on board, Augusta discovered that the ship's captain was her dancing partner in Norfolk, George Montagu.

Meanwhile, Lord Dunmore had received orders from London to submit a proposition called 'The Olive Branch' to the General Assembly and he summoned a meeting at the Capitol on 12 May. Williamsburg became tranquil and the marines, nicknamed 'Montagu's boiled crabs', left the palace. Lady Dunmore and the children were able to return, according to the *Virginia Gazette* 'to the great joy of the inhabitants … who have the most unfeigned regard for Her Ladyship, and wish her long to live amongst us'. On 13 May the newspaper, in a blacker mood, discussed 'the danger arising to the colony by the loss of the public powder, and of the conduct of the Governor, which threatens altogether calamities of the greatest magnitude, and most fatal consequences to this colony'. The governor's correspondence was intercepted and often published, and a number of loyalists began to leave the colony. After nearly a month, Lord Dunmore realised that his position was untenable and he could not guarantee the welfare of his family in Williamsburg.

Before dawn on 8 June 1775 Augusta was awoken and told to dress. The family assembled downstairs with the baby and her nurse and the small group moved silently through the peaceful house to the ballroom and left by the back door. In the garden they avoided the gravel paths and hurried down the grass verges to the carriages waiting at the back to take them to safety. By two o'clock in the morning the last royal governor of Virginia and his family had left the palace forever.

The *Virginia Gazette* of 10 June announced their departure and printed the following message left by the governor for the Assembly:

> Being now fully persuaded that my person, and those of my family likewise, are in constant danger of falling sacrifices to the blind and immeasurable fury which has so unaccountably seized upon the minds and understanding of great numbers of the people, and apprehending that at length some among them may work themselves up to that pitch of daringness and atrociousness as to fall upon me in the defenceless state in which they know I am in the city of Williamsburg, and perpetrate acts that would plunge this country into the most horrid calamities, and

> render the breach with the mother country irreparable; I have thought it prudent for myself, and serviceable for the country, that I remove to a place of safety, conformable to which I have fixed my residence, for the present, on board His Majesty's ship, the Fowey, lying at York.

Finally, he expressed the vain hope that he would be visited on board by some of their members.

Augusta's stay in America, which had started with good will and a hearty welcome from the people of Williamsburg, ended with a midnight flight and her father's ignominy. Virginia had venerated the goose and her goslings, but by the summer of 1775 it could not endure the gander; the only prudent option was for Lady Dunmore and her children to return to Britain. On 29 June they boarded the *Magdalen* and Lord Dunmore, aboard the *Fowey*, accompanied his wife and children down river as far as Chesapeake Bay. Before sailing through the Virginia Capes and into the Atlantic, Lady Dunmore and the children bade the governor a final farewell from the *Magdalen*'s deck and, with a dip of the flag, Captain Montagu turned back towards Yorktown. As America receded, Augusta's spirits sank.

Without the support of his family, the governor was left to fulfil his duties in a rebellious and hostile land. He concentrated on bringing Virginia to heel. In one of 'his diabolical schemes', Lord Dunmore managed to unite both patriots and loyalists against him by issuing an inflammatory proclamation. On 7 November 1775 he offered freedom to any rebel-owned slave willing to fight for the King. In so doing, he incensed his former dinner companion, George Washington. The day after Christmas, Washington wrote to Richard Henry Lee, one of Virginia's delegates to the Continental Congress, telling him that if:

> that Man is not crushed before Spring, he will become the most formidable Enemy America has – his strength will Increase as a Snow ball by Rolling; and faster, if some expedient cannot be hit upon to convince the Slaves and Servants of the impotency of his designs ... I do not think that forcing his Lordship on Ship board is sufficient; nothing less than depriving him of life or liberty will secure peace to Virginia.[20]

Lord Dunmore's attempts to reclaim Virginia with the assistance of his so-called 'Ethiopian Regiment' were unsuccessful. Threatening further incursions from HMS *Fowey*, the governor continued to menace Virginia until he was defeated not only by the rebel army, but also by starvation and sickness in his own ranks. Unlamented by most Virginians, he eventually sailed to New York where he took part in the battle of Long Island. In November 1776 Lord Dunmore, one of the most hated British officials, left America. With hopes of regaining Virginia temporarily dashed, he returned to England, with his life and liberty intact, just before Augusta turned 16.

From 1774 to the middle of 1775 she had lived in Williamsburg as the daughter of Virginia's last royal governor. In an era when girls of her age rarely went abroad, Augusta's unique experience gave her a worldliness and confidence that set her apart from her peers at home. Later she could recall that she had met some of the chief protagonists in America's break with the mother country: a cruel and very bloody civil war, which caused immense upheaval and lasted eight years. She could look back to some of the earliest events in a campaign that changed Britain's relationship with its former colony forever, for she had watched the beginning of the end of the British Empire in America.

4

Not Entirely Ill Made, But in Truth Nothing Resembling a Venus

When the Countess of Dunmore returned from America in the autumn of 1775, she took a house in Twickenham. The fashionable and elegant Thameside village had been popular with the Scottish since Charles I had granted Ham House to William Murray, 1st Earl of Dysart.[1] It was a two-hour carriage ride from London and Lady Dunmore could let their house in Lower Berkeley Street. Augusta's new home, Colne Lodge, was a villa surrounded by pleasure grounds on the bank of the River Colne, which here emptied into the Thames.

We know little about Augusta's life in the six years after she left Virginia. In September 1781, when British troops were defending Yorktown during the final campaign of the American War of Independence, William Beckford informs us that Augusta attended his coming of age celebrations. She had family connections with Beckford, who was half Scottish. His mother was a Hamilton and a close friend of Augusta's aunt, Euphemia.

The Beckford festivities were held in Wiltshire. Augusta travelled there with her cousin, Lady Margaret Gordon, whose engagement to William, Mrs Beckford and Euphemia had been plotting. Beckford's late father had been a Jamaican sugar baron of stupendous wealth and the opulence of his son's gala befitted the indulgence of William's youth. He had studied architecture with the King's tutor, William Chambers, and piano with Mozart.

In a letter to his cousin Beckford described the preparations for the revels as 'perpetual bustle' with his home exhibiting 'an appearance little better than Bartholomew Fair'.[2] Fonthill Splendens, his father's Palladian house, stood in a park with a lake, woods and groves, temples, a grotto and a pagoda. Such was the backdrop to the *fête-champêtre*. 'As soon as the arch which formed the entrance of the temporary square was lighted up and the whole range of tents illuminated,' William's letter continued, 'the Lord Chancellor Thurlow [his guardian], Lady Dunmore, her daughters and a great many of our friends and relatives, walked all over the lawn and hill, the crowd dividing to give us passage.'[3]

Everyone was enchanted. Bonfires were lit and fireworks, set to music, flashed in the sky and shimmered on the water below. Over three days and three nights, 10,000 guests – family and friends, neighbours and tenants – found themselves in another world. Even Lord Shelburne of Bowood, a Wiltshire neighbour and Lord Dunmore's old friend, who had avoided social gatherings since the death of his wife, attended the Fonthill Elysium.

At Christmas Augusta and Catherine returned for another party, wholly different from September's extravaganza. This time it was an intimate group. The Reverend Samuel Henley, professor of moral philosophy at the College of William and Mary in Williamsburg, accompanied Augusta's young cousins and Beckford's, Alexander and Archibald Hamilton. Beckford's art teacher, Alexander Cozens, was there, as well as 13-year-old William Courtenay and Louisa Beckford, the wife of William's cousin. Tension and sulks resulting from her host's liaisons with both William and Louisa might have spoilt the party, but Augusta had a magical time in the best tradition of Fonthill hospitality: generous and glamorous, exuberant and exotic.

It was bitterly cold outside the house at Splendens, but inside Beckford created a world of the 'most extravagant intensity' for his guests. He arranged music to be sung at intervals by concealed castrati, decorated the rooms with an abundance of hothouse flowers and provided outlandish cuisine at every meal. Philip James de Loutherbourg, the painter and scene designer, produced light effects: 'volcanic eruptions and moonlit glades' by 'passing painted lenses and fabrics across powerful lanterns strategically sited'.[4] It was a sybaritic start to 1782.

To mark William Beckford's coming of age, George Romney had painted his portrait and Lady Gower commissioned the same artist to do Augusta's picture when she reached 21. Augusta's aunt Susanna was an important patron of Romney, and his celebrated work, *The Gower Family* of 1776–77, features her four children dancing to the music of a tambourine played by their elder half-sister, Lady Anne.

Augusta's first sitting took place on 28 March 1782 at Romney's studio in Cavendish Square and the artist required ten more visits before the picture was completed a year later. In his book on Romney, Arthur Chamberlain described the half-length portrait, sadly untraced, as one of the artist's 'most frankly classical performances. The lady's dark hair is unpowdered, and falls in natural ringlets on the shoulders. The dress, with its simple, flowing lines, is one of Romney's own devising, with little likeness to anything his fair sitters would wear outside the studio'.[5] Romney often used the style of Augusta's robe, which is similar to that worn by Anne in *The Gower Family*.

He depicts Augusta sitting by a table, looking up at the statuette she has been drawing, with her attention focused on her subject. She appears unaffected, holding her portfolio and a crayon in her right hand and her sketch in her left. The ability to draw was necessary for a cultivated young woman and Romney chose the arrangement of Augusta's portrait to suggest his sitter's artistic accomplishment. Her face, refined and serene, has its own beauty.

In 1786, three years after the portrait was finished, Lady Gower settled Romney's bill for £42. The gap between her niece's final sitting and payment was probably deliberate. The commission was ostensibly executed to celebrate Augusta's coming of age, but there may have been an underlying motive. Fashionable parties, including eligible young men, enjoyed visiting artists' studios, and Romney's painting rooms were a popular destination. A strategically positioned work in progress of a lovely young woman served two purposes: the portrait advertised the artist's skill but could also excite interest from a potential husband. Marriage to a gentleman of means was the ambition of every girl of Augusta's background and her aunt had approached George Romney with this goal in mind.

At the same time as sitting for Romney, Augusta penned her own likeness, *Mon Portrait*, in one of her commonplace books.[6] It is written in an honest and self-deprecating way and was not intended for anyone else to read. Here is a girl who does not take herself too seriously with an engaging way of laughing at herself. The description of her appearance matches Romney's painting and is worth quoting:

> I shall say that men have called me fair; I am not so, but the sum of all my parts has its effect … my complexion is not bad, my eyes will pass,

> my brow is charming, my nose, it has been said, is after the Grecian style, though I cannot see it myself. As for my mouth, I have not the least idea; my waist is fine, but no miracle. I am tall, not entirely ill made, but in truth nothing resembling a Venus.

Augusta hopes that the man she eventually marries will value her for what she is and not expect perfection:

> on the other hand my head and heart are far loftier than I seem to suggest, or than people would imagine. Behind the mindless mask, I think, I reflect, I observe, and the best of it is, it is not the trivial which occupies my mind – though it is hard to credit, for when I am in company my conversation turns on trifles. The reason for this contradiction is that I prefer to seem foolish rather than making a show of wit, or tiresome remarks.

Intelligent and perceptive, she knew that prospective husbands found overtly clever women both unattractive and threatening so she concealed her intellect, behind 'the mindless mask' preferring 'to seem foolish'. She appeared to take little interest in food; she did not care what her 'neighbour at table was eating' and affected not to notice 'the dress the next woman was wearing'. She concluded by declaring her 'genuine affection for all my family – domestic harmony is a wonderful sight to behold. I love my brother as myself, and Catherine better still.'[7]

Augusta's brother had been named in honour of Lady's Dunmore's brother, George Stewart, who had died at the siege of Ticonderoga. Further in her commonplace book Augusta portrays her own brother, George Fincastle, as her 'My Memnon', comparing him to the brave King of Ethiopia, who fought in the Trojan War. Her delightful vignette shows the respect she had for his sensitivity and intellect:

> this young man was twenty years old, well to do, in good health, not unattractive, and a fine wit. Moreover he was a philosopher, not after the Paris fashion, but a disciple of Rousseau, he thought, pondered much, took heed of suffering, took no pleasure in distress, so that joy and happiness were for him practically one and the same thing. His intention was to take everywhere with him the wisdom he had thought to disguise by the

> study of philosophy. He had an honest soul, and any dishonest pleasure held no charm for him. He was a man of reason, and wished to spread reason everywhere.[8]

The family was fond of nicknames: George was 'Fin', short for Fincastle, and two of Augusta's other brothers were 'Alex' and 'Jack' while Catherine was 'Cat', Augusta herself was 'Goosy' and Virginia later became known as 'the Virgin'. They were united, cheerful and loyal.

In the spring of 1782 Catherine and Augusta threw themselves into the London season, the period that coincided with parliamentary sessions from late October until Christmas and from February to the summer recess at the end of May. As a member of the 'ton', the exclusive coterie of aristocratic and artistic guests, whose presence assured the success of any social gathering of pretension, Augusta had a social engagement most days during the season.

She told Lady Gower, in a letter that was probably written in January 1782, that she hoped to attend the drawing room assembly at court the next day if her gown were ready in time. Drawing rooms were held at St James's Palace on Thursday afternoons and Sunday mornings after divine service at the Chapel Royal.[9] The King and Queen would receive new members of society, ambassadors and senior officials and then mix freely with their other guests. Anybody well dressed could attend. Ladies' court dress entailed a heavy hooped skirt with a train, and a headdress of ostrich feathers, sometimes dyed to match the dress and often interlaced with diamonds. Augusta expected the drawing room to be 'as crowded as at the [Queen's] Birthday for there was no court Sunday on account of the Kings not being well, he has violent bleedings at his nose, for which he has been blooded several times'.[10]

We know from Augusta's *Portrait* that 'some malicious tongues' had linked her name with a potential husband. This may have been Colonel Banastre Tarleton, whose flamboyance and self-regard Joshua Reynolds depicted in an outstanding portrait that year. Tarleton had recently returned as a war hero from the battle of Yorktown and Augusta was seduced by his martial glamour. At Lady Stormont's ball where 'the bon ton men were last night assembled', she told Lady Gower that she had never seen 'such a number of handsome women, and all well drest'. She danced every *contredanse* and Colonel Tarleton was one of her partners. Obviously smitten, she wrote excitedly 'nous sommes aimés des les premiers momens, and he desired to be presented to us; his bravery, his enterprising spirit, and his merit m'avait deja prevence en sa faveur … how the dear creature came to be charmed with me, cannot so well be explained.'[11] Augusta's relationship with him was short-lived because the attentions of the 'dear creature' amounted to no more than flattery and flirtation. Soon he would scandalise society by embarking on a five-year affair with the beautiful actress Mary Robinson. Painted by both Romney and Reynolds, Robinson was known as 'Perdita' after famously performing the part in *The Winter's Tale*. Tired of Tarleton's overtures to her daughter, she eventually left him.

Far away from London, Augusta found solace from rejection at her home in Scotland. In 1754 the trustees of young John Murray had acquired the Elphinstone estate in Stirlingshire. Augusta's father renamed it 'Dunmore' and the family lived in the Elphinstones' early sixteenth-century tower house, which commanded a ridge of land sloping towards the south bank of the River Forth. The walled garden nearby was crowned with the beautifully executed, enormous, stone pineapple dated 1761, the same year as Augusta's birth. It would, however, be misleading to believe that this fruity folly was in some way a commemoration or celebration of Augusta. Lord Dunmore was hoping for an heir and when a second girl was born, Lord Shelburne was quick to sympathise. Mischievously he begged 'leave with you and my lady as they do with Princes to congratulate and to condole, upon the birth of a daughter, I wish all your friends had as good reason to go to bed as you have'.[12] It therefore appears to be no more than coincidence that the date carved on the keystones beneath The Pineapple is the same as Augusta's birth.

In England the kitchen garden was mainly cultivated for table produce. It was a place of work, where the gardeners were rarely disturbed by their employers. Scottish walled gardens, on the other hand, were of high status and contained ornamental flower borders as well as fruit and vegetables. They were places of resort, enjoyed and admired by the family, and Augusta, suffering from unrequited love, found consolation in her father's walled garden at Dunmore.

Wandering between the flowerbeds 'enamelled with the brightest colours', she wrote a 'Fable', probably dedicated to Banastre Tarleton.[13] Reflecting sadly on the events of her life, she wrote:

> I was growing sad, I was weeping, I was also sighing, but without knowing why, when I heard a plaintive voice which chimed with the melancholy of my heart. The poor creature aroused my interest, I looked round to find whence came these sounds; imagine my astonishment when I saw it was a Butterfly, who thus told his sorry tale.

The butterfly's story, in which he visits myriad flowers but finds repose with none, is an allegory for Augusta and her admirers. The rose might represent feckless Tarleton:

> I saw the Rose, which embodied a thousand charms, offered a thousand delights. I was inhaling the pleasure of being at her side; the cruel creature admired the sheen of my wings, but was unmoved by their beauty; I was about to alight on her but the fickle flower entertained instead the fly … loved the cricket – I was heartbroken and left her.

Among the plants, Augusta mentions myrtle, orange blossom and jasmine, as well as aloe and eglantine. The butterfly in her fable calls on a 'heavenly Violet' and a tulip of imperial magnificence 'adorned with the rich dyes of India – gold shone around her petals, Asiatic purple lent them new brilliance' but 'she gave no scent'. The melancholy tale concludes with the words, 'Strike up the hymn of Condolence, my dear Companions, And leave off these songs of Joy, for a broken heart shuns noisy laughter.' However, she and Catherine were themselves often the cause of heartbreak in others. The writer of a love poem to the 'fair Murrays' adored them 'in vain', extolled their 'sweetness' and easy elegance and with percipience in Augusta's case, supposed that their 'dignity & charms' would one day 'grace a Monarch or a Prince's arms'.[14]

It was not a monarch or a prince, but Edward Bouverie, the fourth son of the Earl of Radnor, who married Catherine on 24 May 1782. Poor Augusta, her sister's wedding was a double blow. In the same month that Tarleton attached himself so publicly to Mary Robinson, Catherine's marriage deprived Augusta of her sibling and oldest friend. There was no one now to whom she could turn when she was unhappy and the loss of her childhood companion was made worse because Bouverie irritated her.

Augusta's family sustained a number of bereavements in the 1780s, the first of which caused terrible distress. Newspapers regularly carried reports of women who had been injured when their clothes caught alight from sparks, candles or night-lamps and in December 1782 Catherine was badly burnt when her clothes caught fire. Getting dressed was a lengthy process for ladies such as Catherine and Augusta and required the help of one and sometimes two maids. First on was the shift, then an under petticoat; boned stays raised the bosom and maintained a neat waist, panniers or hip pads gave the gown its form, and then another petticoat was placed on top. A light kerchief, or fichu, was worn around the neck for modesty and a decorated or plain stomacher filled the front bodice. Before the gown itself came the gown petticoat, in either matching or contrasting material, and to complete the outfit, for effect only it should be said, was a muslin apron.[15] In case of fire, it was impossible to throw off these constricting layers quickly and sometimes women were burnt to death.

Moved by Catherine's fortitude, Augusta saluted her sister's bravery and patience in verse:

A cheek, a little pal'd with langour's hue,
An Eye that beaming with the rays of sense,
Speaks to the Soul an artless eloquence,
And seems a look of gratitude to throw
On those whose feelings share the sufferer's woe
And last her lips, whose blushes well display
The glowing colour of the ruby's ray,
Where patience dwells, refusing to complain,
With resignation that can smile at pain.[16]

Worse was to come. On 7 July 1783 Catherine died in Brighton. She was 23 and had been married just over a year. Until now the date of Catherine's death has been unclear. Family documents state that she died a decade later but a letter from Augusta to Aunt Susanna dated 'Wednesday 30th' contains an important clue.[17] Augusta wrote, 'My beloved is no more, I have lost my friend, my sister, I have lost a great deal in my Catherine.'[18] She tried to cheer herself by remembering that God had taken Catherine to Himself and 'by doing so has released her from sickness, pain, and many troubles'. She was so distressed that she put the affairs of heart aside, not wishing 'now to be greatly married, I have forgotten former ambitious schemes, I cannot share them with Catherine, they lose their whole relish.'

Catherine, who may have died in childbirth, left a baby boy, George-Edward.[19] Doubtless on his account, Augusta resolved to keep in touch with Edward Bouverie as 'Catherine would have wished it, and I shall make it my study to remain well with him as I am convinced that if she sees our actions she will like her Augusta for it … yet I think of Longford, and the cold grave; – Oh my heart grows damp – I grow sorrowful.'

From this we know that Catherine's body was taken to Longford Castle in Wiltshire, the seat of her father-in-law, the Earl of Radnor. A burial plan shows that on 13 July 1783 her coffin was placed in the family mausoleum at Britford church, peacefully situated in the water meadows between Longford and Salisbury Cathedral.[20] Her death tested the faith of Augusta, who knew she must accept that 'the dispensations of Heaven are wise' and 'submit to the decrees of an all gracious maker'. At times, however, she found Heaven's dispensations hard to bear.

The second tragedy of the 1780s was the death of Lady Margaret Gordon. Aunt Euphemia's plans had come to fruition when Margaret married William Beckford by special licence at Euphemia's London house in 1783.[21] After an incident at Powderham Castle involving William Courtenay and broadcast by the tutor, sexual scandal hovered over Beckford and he was no longer welcome in British society. He took Margaret to live in Switzerland, where she gave birth to their second daughter on 11 May 1786. Euphemia rushed out to assist her niece, who was in the throes of puerperal fever and did not recognise her aunt when she arrived on 26 May. When she died later that evening the wheel had come full circle: Margaret herself had been left a motherless baby. Now she was dead, leaving a baby girl and a 1-year-old daughter. Beckford was obliged to stay in Switzerland and Euphemia took charge of her two tiny nieces, returned to London and delivered them into the care of Beckford's mother.[22] It was a devastating tragedy; William had lost his wife and at the same time his two little daughters were removed from his care.

In March 1786 Augusta's family received some happier news. Aunt Susanna's husband, Lord Gower, was created Marquess of Stafford. A supporter of the King and William Pitt the Younger, Stafford had once been considered for the role of prime minister and now, as Lord Keeper of the Privy Seal, he was well positioned to forward the interests of his extended family. The Earl of Dunmore had finally accepted that he was powerless to do anything to regain Virginia and he needed employment elsewhere. Through Stafford's patronage, he was offered the governorship of the Bahamas. The remote posting was not to Lord Dunmore's taste but financial reasons forced him to accept the job and he sailed for Nassau on 28 August 1787. Augusta did not see him again for nearly ten years.

5

Those Scrapes Which a Young Man May Very Easily Fall Into

When Lord Dunmore left England, Prince Augustus Frederick was beginning his second year at the University of Göttingen in Hanover. He spent his youth on the Continent, where the climates of Italy and the south of France benefited his asthma, and did not return to England permanently until 1804. When Augustus first came home, he was cultured and well travelled. He was also nursing a secret that threatened to destroy his relationship with his father, the King.

Apart from Princes Octavius and Alfred, both of whom died young, Augustus is the least known of George III's nine sons. We are familiar with the Prince of Wales, who became Regent, then King George IV. Full of panache, he was a significant art collector and spent lavishly on Carlton House, Buckingham Palace, Windsor Castle and the Royal Pavilion at Brighton. George IV was also the first monarch to visit Scotland since Charles I. We remember William IV, the 'Sailor King' and the only member of the Royal Family to visit New York when it was in British hands. He married charitable-minded Princess Adelaide and gave his royal assent to the Reform Bill of 1832. Prince Frederick was the 'Grand Old Duke of York', who 'had 10,000 men', and another soldier brother, Edward, Duke of Kent, is memorable as the father of Queen Victoria. Further down the family tree the collective memory dims. History may have largely forgotten Augustus Frederick but his Continental upbringing made him the most enlightened royal sibling.

Like George III's other children, Augustus spent his early years in the nursery at the Queen's House (extended and renamed Buckingham

Palace by George IV) where the royal governess, Lady Charlotte Finch, was an advocate of creative play. Her small charges did geographical jigsaws, used flash cards as aids for arithmetic and learnt the alphabet with pictorial ivory counters. 'T', for example, was for 'Twite', a small bird in the finch family, so perhaps Lady Charlotte herself chose the pictures. In June 1773 Lady Mary Coke visited her friend, the governess, and wrote in her journal that she had seen 'His Majesty's two youngest sons, and I think they promise to be the handsomest of all the children. Prince Augustus is quite a little angel.'[1]

From the royal nursery Augustus progressed to Kew Green, where he shared a house with his older brother, Ernest, and younger brother, Adolphus. On 28 June 1786, when Augustus was 13, the sheltered trio embarked in the royal yacht, *Augusta*, to pursue their education at university. His second brother, Prince Frederick, had recommended Göttingen, telling the King that it offered 'less dissipation and diversion' than Lüneburg where Prince Edward had studied. Located on the River Leine, the walls of Göttingen enclosed a town hall, a market, red-tiled houses and numerous churches. The university, established by the boys' great-grandfather King George II, already enjoyed a reputation for academic excellence. Its research library in the Paulinerkirche was famous for the breadth of its book collection, the display of antique sculpture casts and its generous lending policy. Having enrolled as students, the brothers began their studies and Augustus told his father that he was taking lessons in 'Religion, History of the Empire, Mathematics and Latin'. While determined to make the best of his new life, he admitted to feeling homesick but told the King stoutly, 'were I not deprived of the sight of my family I am completely happy'.[2]

Everyone at home missed Augustus. Within a week of his departure his favourite sister, Princess Elizabeth, told him that 'my dear Augustus little knows how much he is loved by those he has left in England, you are very, very often the topick of conversation, & when I do not talk of you, you are constantly in my thoughts'.[3] Queen Charlotte sent him news of the family, the Court, and her own pursuits. In later years she often described the progress of her works at Frogmore, her 'little paradise' in the park at Windsor.

Her correspondence was filled with the tenderness that mothers feel for delicate children; she sent him kindly counsel and soon after his departure expressed the hope that:

> you are quite settled at Göttingen and have begun your instructions, in which I do flatter myself you will try to give all possible attention for your own sake as well as out of affection to the best of Fathers who puts you in a way of obtaining every advantage possible by placing you where you are ... you lay now the foundation for your present and future happiness & the satisfaction of well spent time is a blessing of which nothing can deprive us of, as it rejoices us in prosperity & supports us in adversity. I hope that all our little indolences are left at Kew & never to appear in Germany.

Touchingly, she signed her letter, 'Everybody in this house sends love & respect to you, indeed you are much thought of by everybody, but by none more than my dear Augustus your very affectionate mother and friend, Charlotte.'[4] The Prince of Wales sent Augustus gifts and took the opportunity to tease his brothers in his accompanying letter, 'I should be very glad to see you, as you know I always loved you very much ... I have sent you some little trifling presents ... I have also taken the liberty of sending Ernest & Adolphus some few little things, if they be alive but as I suppose by their silence they are no longer in this world.'[5]

Augustus corresponded with all the family but Princess Elizabeth had to remind him gently to observe sibling hierarchy to maintain harmony at home. Her letter of 21 July 1786 indicates that the Princess Royal was feeling left out. Elizabeth told Augustus:

> As I shall not show this letter to any body, I must give you one piece of advice which is, happy as I am in receiving letters from you, at the same time though you told me I am your favourite, & promised me to write often to me, do my dear Augustus write sometimes to Princess Royal, for I am sure that I should be very unhappy to think that I ever should be the cause of your receiving reproaches from the Queen or any part of the family.[6]

Aware of the potential for his eldest daughter's distress, the King asked Augustus in his letter of the same day 'considering how much your eldest sister loves you would it not have been better that one of the others had remained without a letter from you than her; I am certain it hurts her though she has not said so.'[7]

When Augustus departed, the King told him to write once a week. Initially his father responded despite the attempt on his life by Margaret Nicholson, a lunatic, who tried to stab him as he descended from his carriage on 2 August 1786. George III took a close interest in his sons' education and offered plenty of advice. Six days before Christmas, he told Augustus, who had recently been ill, that:

> Your letters contain such religious sentiments that I do not doubt but your conduct will ever be agreeable to them. I trust by this time your health is so thoroughly re-established that you will be enabled with more constancy to pursue your studies and that I shall consequently hear that your progress is as I could wish. Indeed I have sent you so early into the right road for obtaining knowledge that I shall be much disappointed if you do not strive to gain the advantages I have placed in your reach. I know your good sense and spirit must sufficiently point out to you that if you are to advance in the world you must make yourself fit for it, otherwise the more conspicuous your situation the more contemptible will you appear.

He signed his letter 'your most affectionate father George R'.[8]

Towards the end of the next year, 1787, the King received good reports of Augustus's examination results but was concerned to hear that his son had been unwell again and had put on weight. The ascetic monarch, convinced that his son's illness had been caused 'by too good an appetite and too little walking', advised 'abstinence and exercise'.[9] The rosy cheeks, depicted in early portraits of the sturdy and serious little boy, gave no indication of the asthma attacks that disrupted the Prince's teenage years. The 'violent pains' in his chest were sometimes so severe that his brothers could not bear to witness his suffering. He endured being blooded, blistered and cupped – unpleasant and painful procedures – and as his ailments intensified his projected career in the Navy seemed more and more unlikely.

A few months later King George was also unwell and the Princess Royal related to Augustus an episode that had unnerved all the family. She said that their father's illness 'was very disagreeable and indeed alarming for the time that it lasted; the spasm beginning at three in the morning, and continuing till eight o'clock in the evening, he is thank God perfectly recovered; but is advised by Sir George Baker to drink the Cheltenham Waters which are particularly good for all bilious complaints; we are to go to Cheltenham on the twelfth.'[10] In early July 1788 the Queen told Augustus that 'it is supposed that the dryness & heat of the season has occasioned these violent attacks for everybody has been troubled with this complaint'.[11]

On 13 July the King himself wrote Augustus a cheerful letter from Cheltenham. 'I am much recovered,' he said 'and doubt [not] that the efficacy of the waters ... the salubrity of the air, the change of scene ... and above all the exercise of riding and good mutton will do what may at present be wanting.'[12] The Cheltenham waters provided a temporary cure and on her return Queen Charlotte informed Augustus happily that 'never did school boys enjoy their holidays equal to what we have done our little excursion'.[13]

After Augustus sustained another dangerous bout of asthma, his father wrote to him with the sympathy of a fellow invalid. The King had suffered more stomach spasms in mid October. At the end of the month he told his son that as the doctor 'thinks you should after so many attacks avoid a cold winter; I sent my rough draft that no time might be lost in preparing for your going to a mild climate for the winter; I am grieved to part you from your brothers, and to interrupt your studies, but the first object I want you to acquire is health; I am certain your own good sense will make you grasp at every advancement of information you can obtain not detrimental to your health.'[14] It was the first of many occasions when Augustus would escape the Hanoverian winter.

Bidding his brothers farewell, he travelled to the south of France where the sea breezes and sunshine benefited his lungs. Hyères was a pretty Provençal town with a church tower surmounted by an ironwork campanile typical of the region, but there was nothing for a lonely 15-year-old to do. With 'few families of any distinction' and accompanied only by his physician, his gentlemen and a tutor, the Prince missed his brothers and friends in Göttingen. He was therefore grateful when the French court arranged for the 'Commander of the Sea Forces' to show him Toulon, the home of the French navy. He saw 'the Port and Place where the ships lay' and 'went aboard the largest ship ever yet built *Le Commerce de Marseille*'.[15]

At the beginning of December 1788 Augustus received a severe shock. In a surprise letter from his brother, Frederick, he learnt that the King was suffering from a period of insanity and that no one knew whether he would recover from this 'melancholy situation'. His 'complaint which is a total loss of rationality has apparently been coming upon him for some time but now is grown to such a pitch that he is a complete lunatic. I can easily conceive how much you will be affected with this account, it is a dreadful thing indeed and totally unexpected.'[16] Frederick was right, Augustus was seriously affected and wanted only to go home and share the burden of 'this unhappy business' with his family. What horrors were they enduring? Had his father deteriorated since Frederick's letter was written? What form had the lunacy taken?

For the time being his questions remained unanswered. It was impossible for Augustus to return to England; apart from the practical considerations, he was not strong enough to undertake such a perilous journey in midwinter. Alone in a foreign country, frantic with worry and filled with misgivings, the young man's emotions can only be imagined. Early in 1789 he received better news when Princess Augusta Sophia told him that their 'dear father' was improving and that the country was suffering from an exceptionally cold winter. She also relayed some dreadful news from Paris: 'people have been found dead in the streets for want of fuel and bread'.[17]

In mid February Princess Elizabeth reported that the King 'is amazingly recovered within this fortnight' and that the royal household was now 'the happiest in the world'.[18] Despite his recuperation, the King became an unreliable correspondent and never again wrote regularly to his sixth son. All Augustus's brothers, except the Prince of Wales, spent time abroad and the King's failure to correspond with them and apparent lack of care distressed them all. Like many boys, Augustus craved paternal approbation and longed to hear from his father. After 1788 he was continuously disappointed.

The Queen, however, continued to write. On Augustus's return to Hanover in the summer of 1789, she told him enthusiastically, 'I want words to express my feelings upon your returning in so much better health to Göttingen.'[19] The Royal Family was going to Weymouth, where she hoped the sea air and the 'addition of dissipation' would restore the King's strength and, no doubt, her own. On 14 July 1789, a miserably cold day on the Dorset coast, the British Royal Family enjoyed a sailing excursion in Weymouth Bay. Across the English Channel, insurgents in Paris were storming the Bastille.

The situation in the French capital deteriorated quickly and when Augustus's medical advisers prescribed a second winter in a warm climate, the Prince informed the King that he could not return to Hyères because 'the present political state of France renders travelling to strangers hazardous'.[20] Consequently Italy was selected as his next winter destination.

Augustus hated leaving Göttingen again. He told his father bravely that 'it cost me a tear to forsake my brothers and that town but considering that the physicians thought it better for my health I am happy to make the journey'.[21] The journey to Italy over the narrow and vertiginous Alpine passes held no attraction for him. His coach soon became restrictive and irksome: axles and spokes splintered with regularity and the change of horses delayed the wearisome process, travelling mile after mile on rough roads. The quality of the inns was inconsistent and evenings spent in the company of his gentlemen taxed his patience. His attendants disliked the itinerant way of life as much as their charge, and the continual upheaval lowered the party's spirits. Disagreements, which tainted the atmosphere and made everyone restive, often broke out among the all-male entourage.

Once they had arrived in Florence, the mood of the party improved. Leopold, the Grand Duke of Tuscany, welcomed Augustus in the friendliest manner at the Pitti Palace, his Renaissance residence. Behind the palace, wooded gardens, with a grotto, an amphitheatre, statuary and fountains, extended across the Boboli Hill, culminating with fine views over the city. Two of Leopold's sons, Archdukes Charles and Alexander Leopold, were the same age as Augustus and finding himself in the middle of a large family again, he relaxed and his health improved, although he broke his collarbone romping with the boys. In February 1790 the Grand Duke's brother died and he became Holy Roman Emperor, an appointment that necessitated moving to Vienna. His hospitable wife, Maria Luisa of Spain, who treated Augustus like her own son and had arranged parties and visits for him, invited him to prolong his stay in Florence. Postponing a proposed visit to Rome, he accepted her invitation with pleasure.

In June he was back in Göttingen, where he was joyfully reunited with Ernest and Adolphus. Augustus would complete his studies that autumn and was impatient to settle his future. He needed a plan and, encouraged by his renewed strength, he reconsidered the possibility of becoming a midshipman. In January he had dined on HMS *Leander*, a ship of the line anchored at Livorno, the Mediterranean port that the British called 'Leghorn'. Descriptions of the home fleet preparing for war, Augustus told his father, had roused his sense of patriotism; indeed, 'the blood of a British subject boils within me ... The Family of Brunswick have always been renowned for their courage; I wish also to show mine, but in a manner most useful for my country.'[22] The Queen told him that she would do everything possible to promote his cause but doubted that the King had given much consideration to his absent son's career.

In August the Prince became seriously ill and by the end of September he was resigned to an immediate future of convalescence. Unable to breathe lying down, he had been blooded and blistered without complaint while the promotion of his brother, William, to rear admiral highlighted his incapacity. Increasingly desperate for any kind of direction, in the summer of 1791 Augustus suggested to his father that he should enter the Church. As naval service was out of the question, he believed that the quiet life of a cleric would keep him away from the danger of politics. His proposal showed a desire to be worthy of his father and to lead a purposeful life, but to his distress and frustration, he did not receive a response.

The next week, prompted by Prince Frederick's forthcoming marriage to Princess Frederica of Prussia, Augustus turned to matters of the heart. In a letter to the King he wished the couple every joy but the impending union emphasised his loneliness. He told his father that, 'There is certainly no happiness in this world so great as that reaped by the union of two hearts which reciprocally love another,' and continued, 'There are few who are happy in this state because there are few who know how to make a right choice for themselves.'[23] Determined not to fall into such a trap, he suggested searching foreign courts, just as his father and brother had done, for 'an object worthy of my affections and capable of making me happy.' Acknowledging that his father would 'doubtless smile at seeing a person of my age thinking already to establish himself', at 18 years old, Augustus knew that he was susceptible to attractive women and that if he were to become a clergyman, it would be 'the best and only way of keeping out of those scrapes which a young man may very easily fall into'. It was an admirable demonstration of self-knowledge.

Undeterred by his father's silence, he continued to send him ideas for his future. Augustus had everything mapped out: first he would recover, second he would find a suitable wife, and third he would enlist at one of the universities as preparation for entering the Church of England. His sensible proposals provoked no paternal reaction.

On his way to Naples for the winter, Augustus visited Rome. The Pope received him graciously and expressed gratitude for the consideration shown to Catholics in Britain. The Prince was popular wherever he went and Lady Knight, a correct and rather stuffy widow, reported favourably on his visit. She told a friend that Augustus was tall with a fine figure and behaved with 'good humour and ease and seems in perfect health'.[24] By December 1791 he was in Naples as the guest of Sir William Hamilton, the British envoy-extraordinary to the Court of King Ferdinand.

Prince Augustus became more and more disillusioned. It was now not weeks nor months since he had received a letter from his father, it was years. Just after Christmas, feeling homesick, he wrote to the King with restraint, 'It is not with some little eagerness that I await your Majesty's orders,' but once more received no response.[25] When Augustus left Naples for Rome, he was universally lamented. Sir William wrote that, 'his manner is so simple, amiable, and obliging ... He speaks French and Italian perfectly. In short, I shall be much mistaken if our Royal Master and Mistress do not find a lasting comfort in Prince Augustus.'[26] If the King found any pleasure in reports such as this, he did not show it.

After wandering in Venice and Milan, the Prince reached Vevey at the end of June. He had left England exactly six years before and having heard nothing from his father, he lost patience. His fortitude had been admirable but now he had had enough. Aged 19, tired of being treated like a child by his entourage, bored of being on the road and exasperated with his attendants, he fumed at his father in a letter of 26 June 1792:

> My journey is intended for my health but ... it does me more harm than good. I am unhappy and that is the cause of my present indisposition. The two gentlemen who are with me though they conceal their illness, are both unwell nay very seriously indisposed. To be constantly surrounded by melancholy faces, with people who suffer, whose temper is soured by their sufferings is more than I can support and makes me truly miserable. Their indisposition prevents my enjoying many parties on account of their not being able to accompany me ... I know my situation and the inconveniences attending my rank which I never make any difficulty to submit but I think a line may be drawn now, especially as I feel myself of an age to begin to act for myself. My wishes are not unreasonable Sir.[27]

Again he did not receive a response.

Queen Charlotte missed her son just as much as he missed his mother. His teenage years, a time of personal and physical change, had been spent abroad and she worried that she might no longer recognise him. Consequently, the miniature he had sent her was a source of 'inexpressible pleasure … it is constantly in my pocket & frequently taken out to be looked at both by myself & other people & everybody does still trace the good old countenance which makes me very happy.'

She continued lovingly:

> I am glad & heartily rejoice to hear that you are well & liked by everybody for your very proper conduct wherever you appear, let this encourage you my dear Augustus to pursue the way you are in, by experience you know that one cannot well enjoy life without health, & your sufferings have given you time to reflect upon the necessity to employ your time well, I therefore trust to your good understanding that you will enjoy life in a reasonable way & never launch out in extremes, the sense of religion you possess will I hope assist you in every step you take & reason will convince you that nothing should ever be undertaken both in public or private life without well considering the consequences thereof which is necessary for every body to do, but particularly in your situation, for what would be trifling in another person's conduct, becomes censurable in … persons of rank who are to serve as examples to others.[28]

Her carefully worded counsel, imparted with the best of maternal motives, was soon to be forgotten.

By mid November 1792, the Prince had reached Rome. His request to search for a suitable wife had been unacknowledged, but as an affectionate young man who enjoyed female company, Augustus was impatient to immerse himself in Roman society. Uncertain of his future and no longer able to contain himself, he cast aside his mother's advice, forgot the consequences, and launched out into extremes that neither Queen Charlotte, nor Augustus himself, could ever have imagined. He had tried unceasingly to do the right thing and behave in a way commensurate with his rank, but his father had persistently ignored him.

6

We are the Ton

In late summer 1787 Augusta's family dispersed. Fincastle went to Cheltenham and Lord Dunmore left for the Bahamas. Susan had a bad cough and at the beginning of September 1787 Augusta told Lady Stafford that 'my poor dear Father has been gone near a week … and I attribute [a] great part of S's malady to all these departs'.[1] Soon after her 20th birthday, Susan had become engaged to the son of a West Indian sugar nabob, Joseph Tharp, who had departed with Lord Dunmore. Augusta explained to her aunt that Joseph was, 'going to Jamaica before his marriage which scheme we approve of, because his father has written to say, he wishes to settle with him when he comes of age, enfin, pour arranger ensemble les états de leurs affaires'.[2]

Within a month of the departures, Augusta was baffled to find herself in Paris. She told Lady Stafford, 'I fancy you will be as astonished to receive a letter from me dated from France, and Paris too, as I am almost at finding myself here,' and said that their visit was to please her future brother-in-law.[3] Tharp's reason for their stay, however, remains a mystery.

The betrothal appeared to satisfy everyone except Augusta: Joseph was to marry the daughter of an earl, and Susan, with no fortune of her own, would live in luxury; Tharp's father, John, owned 2,800 slaves across eleven plantations in Jamaica. Augusta described John Tharp as 'an artful, silent, plodding, ill-natured & unjust man', while Joseph was 'a weak, wavering, good tempered, silly fool, & almost as dangerous to live with as [his father]; these are the men [Susan] is doomed to live with, I am sorry for it, for she is an honest & good girl.'[4] Augusta was in no doubt that Susan's alliance would demean her.

When Joseph became engaged, his father put him in charge of a remote plantation to learn estate management. The paternal plan was a disaster. Unwillingly uprooted from London where he enjoyed life as a captain in the Life Guards, Joseph arrived in Kingston with bad grace. Isolation in a backcountry plantation was anathema and soon his worried father was writing to a neighbour, 'It is said he tipples with low company and leaves his bed hot with the perfumes of Arabia. If this be true you should try and correct such a disgraceful and most abominable practice.'

While Joseph was abusing slaves in Jamaica, his fiancée was in Paris. Offering a plausible explanation for the family's presence in France bothered Augusta and she asked Lady Stafford for 'a reason pointed out by you to give for our jaunt here … as we cannot give Mr Thorpe's to the world we must think of something else'.[5] Did Joseph's jealousy make them cross the Channel? Did he fear that, while he was in Jamaica, competition in London might rob him of his blue-blooded bride?

Augusta's sunny disposition ensured that she was a pleasant companion in the French capital, but she too would have liked to be engaged. Her Romney portrait had failed to procure a husband and her younger sister's forthcoming marriage highlighted Augusta's unwelcome celibacy. Paris in September 1787 was, however, congenial. Augusta and her family were based between the Ile de la Cité and the Louvre, staying at the Hôtel de Luxembourg, where past guests included Horace Walpole and Lord Chesterfield. Once again Lord Stafford's connections proved invaluable. His nephew, the Duke of Dorset, was the British ambassador and introduced them to Parisian society. Notwithstanding the duke's relationship with Lady Stafford, Augusta blithely informed her aunt that while popular with the French, he was detested by the English. The duke, who was conducting an affair with the Duchess of Devonshire, was regarded as a philanderer. Augusta's Hamilton cousins, Charlotte and Susan, 'very fine girls', were also in Paris, finishing their education in the care of aunt Euphemia.

Although there were plenty of English in the city that September, most of the French had not yet returned from their country houses. Soon after their arrival, Arthur Dillon, the worldly but benign primate of France, invited Lady Dunmore and her daughters to stay at his château in Picardy where he kept a pack of staghounds.[6] Augusta's host had been born at St Germain-en-Laye, the son of Earl Dillon, an Irish Jacobite, who commanded the Dillon regiment in the French Army. Arthur Dillon had had a successful church career: Bishop of Évreux, Archbishop of Toulouse, and Duke-Archbishop of Narbonne, Commander of the Order of the Holy Ghost and President of the States of Languedoc. Although his income was enormous, while in Paris he preferred the hospitality of his widowed niece and reputed lover, Madame de Rothe. (Another niece was the letter writer Lady Frances Jerningham.) On Augusta's return to Paris, she told Aunt Susanna, 'We are this day come from the Archevèque de Narbonne's, he is a charming man, very lively … so that his acquaintance is a very desirable one; I own, I rather like the french way of living, & his society is a very good one, so that we all liked the expedition.'[7]

Although the cost of travel was a consideration, not long afterwards they set off to Compiègne to stay with their Dunmore kinsman, the Duc de La Trémoille, at Attichy. They were among the last to enjoy the famous water works in the duc's park, which along with his château were destroyed by revolutionaries two years later. En route to Attichy, they visited Ermenonville, the Marquis de Girardin's celebrated park, laid out in the English Garden style. Famous for its temples and grottoes, cascade and lake, its main attraction was the small island where poplars shaded Jean-Jacques Rousseau's tomb. Everything at Ermenonville charmed Augusta and she took notes on what she saw, but no folly in France or England could match The Pineapple at Dunmore.

Back in Paris, the beau monde opened its doors to Augusta and she became 'excessively employed'. Toast of the French court, she was presented to the 'best society' in a swirl of parties and visits to the opera. Her vivacity made her popular wherever she went. Modestly she attributed the praise she received to the French 'love of what is new' and admitted after supper with the Duchesse de La Valliére that 'the French are as fond of novelty as the Prince of Wales's set in London, and indeed all the women were so ugly that tho' I am tired of my own face I am not astonished as their liking it better than those of their own ladies'.[8] Augusta was delighted to be at the centre of French society. She went to parties at the Palais Royal, the home of the Duc d'Orleans, she socialised with the Duc de Biron, nephew of Louis XV's distinguished military leader, and she enjoyed the company of the Spanish Ambassador to France.

She had also been presented to the glamorous Polignacs, friends of the French Queen. Amid the social engagements, it was however, impossible to ignore the unease and disquiet in the city, especially when the

Polignacs were burnt in effigy on 5 October. Prussia's recent invasion of the Netherlands threatened the security of France and wherever Augusta went, the conversation was dominated by one topic. The French 'all talk of War, they pretend to be cautious before us, but it is not in their nature to be silent, so we saw their grand despair at the news that the Duke of Brunswick had taken the Hague'.[9]

She told Aunt Susanna that the French blamed their Queen. It was generally thought that, as the sister of the Holy Roman Emperor, she had sued for peace and had thereby 'disgraced them by preventing a War, so very necessary to their honour'.[10] Marie Antoinette was doubly inculpated because the French believed that her uncontrolled spending had ruined their finances, although any reasonable person knew that the economy of France was in 'un état pitoyable' and prayed for peace. Apart from the torrid political situation, the Queen was facing domestic problems. Her husband, Louis XVI, was suffering from depression and both of them were mourning the loss of their baby, Madame Sophie, who had died in June aged 11 months.

In the autumn Augusta wrote to her aunt that 'the Queen has sent to tell us, that as soon as Madme de Lamballe is returned to Versailles, we must meet her at her house'.[11] Augusta had already met the royal favourite, Marie Thérèse Louise of Savoy, Princesse de Lamballe, at the Duke of Queensberry's and at Lady Melbourne's when she had been in England that summer. The Princesse was 'charmingly good natured, & unaffected' and appeared 'to like England very much'.[12] When she returned to France she was warmly hospitable and Augusta could write, 'We were at Versailles New Year's Day, Madme de Lamballe makes her house almost ours, we dined & supped there two days following, Madme de Polignac nous a montré bien des provenances, the Queen was delightful.'[13]

Mary Wollstonecraft, an early campaigner for women's rights, endorsed Augusta's opinion. In Wollstonecraft's *View of the French Revolution,* she wrote:

> besides the advantages of birth and station, [the Queen] possessed a very fine person; and her lovely face, sparkling with vivacity, hid the want of intelligence. Her complexion was dazzling clear; and, when she was pleased, her manners were bewitching; for she happily mingled the most insinuating voluptuous softness and affability, with an air of grandeur, bordering on pride, that rendered the contrast more striking.[14]

Élisabeth Vigée Le Brun's portrait of Marie Antoinette, in which her younger son gestures sadly at Sophie's empty cradle, shows us what the Queen looked like when Augusta met her. The pinnacle of European fashion, she wears a low-cut red velvet dress trimmed with lace and sable and a matching red velvet headpiece, a *pouf*, or gauze ring, also trimmed with lace frills and fur, as well as copious ostrich feathers.

Knowledge of fashion at the French court was essential to anyone with pretensions to style and Augusta felt duty-bound to keep her aunt and Leveson-Gower cousins up to date. She tried to persuade Mrs John Pitt, a wealthy widow who was returning to England in the autumn, to take her cousins 'two bonnets à la Napolitaine' or poke bonnets. However, Mrs Pitt, unwilling to be encumbered with extra hatboxes, did not oblige and early in 1788 Augusta sent her cousins other examples of current headwear. She hoped that they liked the *poufs* and explained that 'those feathers are quite new, Mlle Bertin only has them.' The prices charged by Rose Bertin, the Queen's couturier, reflected her exclusivity; depending on the number of feathers, her *poufs* cost between 86 and 120 livres, the equivalent of about £520 and £780 today.

Augusta was concerned that her cousins understood 'how the head things were to be pinned on' and asked Lady Stafford to tell her daughters that the French put on the feathers 'rather forward'. Augusta also advised them that 'velvets are very much worn, as much upon the head as upon the body ... bonnets in the morning, & the hair not at all over the forehead; even high up at the sides'.

Apart from the Hamilton girls – Charlotte who 'promises to be handsome, and Susan to be tall, and shewy' – Augusta saw another cousin in Paris. Dashing Lord Strathaven, son of her late aunt Margaret, had joined them by early January 1788. He told a friend that 'I found Lady Dunmore here upon my arrival, which has made Paris much more pleasant to me than it would otherwise have been, as she knows everybody.'[15] He won universalacclaim at the French court. The Queen herself enjoyed his company and admired his sprightly Scottish reeling. Augusta told Aunt Susanna that 'he is always with us, & my mother dotes upon him', but if Lady Dunmore hoped that her nephew would make a suitable husband for Augusta, she was destined to be disappointed.[16] Family politics could be savage and Lady Stafford, busily encouraging the two daughters of Sir Charles Cope, had other plans for George Strathaven. In 1791 he married Catherine, the younger Cope daughter, while Lord Stafford's nephew married her older sister.

There seemed little hope in Augusta finding a French husband. She knew that young men there married at 19, although it did 'not prevent their making love'. Moreover, they did not compare well with her compatriots; she was 'quite sick of these half sort of men, they have such large frizzed out heads upon such little bodies, they are so bowing yet so vain that it is impossible after having lived in England to like them'.[17]

Whatever her feelings about Frenchmen, Augusta's birth and vitality had enthralled Parisian society and on 5 January 1788 she could inform her aunt that 'we are the ton … I would not tell it to anybody but you, the saying those things looks silly, therefore I only own it to you to show you dans peu de mots, the good footing we are upon'.[18] Although she remained unmarried, just before leaving England, she had received a declaration of love from an eligible, although much younger, cousin.

7

Rather Too Free with the World

The Countess of Dunmore and her daughters returned from Paris in the summer of 1788. On 7 July Susan was married at St George's, Hanover Square and embarked on a European honeymoon. The fragmentation of the family continued with the departure of Alexander to the Turks Islands, where he was to be the King's Agent and Collector of Customs. On 26 November, the day he left, there was a family bereavement. Aunt Harriet, Lady Dunmore's sister and mother of the Hamilton cousins, died in Bath. To add to Augusta's sadness, the household in London was now reduced and she was left with only Virginia and her mother for company.

When Lady Dunmore went to Italy to visit Susan in the autumn of 1789, Augusta stayed at home to look after Virginia, who was in poor health and had a painful knee. She proposed taking her sister to the seaside at Ramsgate knowing that their mother, an advocate of the curative properties of both salt and fresh water, would approve. Harrogate's chalybeate waters had fortified the weakened countess in 1765 after she had produced five children in as many years. Taking her mother's lead, Augusta was also a lifelong aficionado of the healing properties of water and was disappointed when Lady Stafford vetoed the Ramsgate idea. Instead, Augusta sent for Sir Lucas Pepys, Physician Extraordinary to the King, who prescribed bathing in 'the cold bath in Town, to keep her knee strong', after which Augusta could tell her aunt that 'all my fusses about her are at end'.[1]

Plain and pockmarked, Virginia was easy to ignore when guest lists were drawn up and a letter Augusta wrote to Lady Stafford's son, her eye-catching and popular cousin, Lord Granville, reveals the consideration she showed her youngest sister. Aware that Virginia was going to miss another party, Augusta took up her pen with purpose and informed Granville that she knew 'that the best method of pleasing a woman is not to refuse her requests'. Augusta firmly proceeded 'to beg you will get Virginia invited to the Hope ball'. In 1793, Granville, the blond boy in Romney's *Gower Family*, would embark on a long affair with the Duchess of Devonshire's sister, a woman twelve years his senior. He was one of the most captivating young men in London and it is likely that his hostess granted his wish and that Virginia went to the ball.[2]

When Lady Stafford was at Trentham, her husband's country seat in Staffordshire, she relied on Augusta to send updates from the capital. On 8 October 1789 Augusta told her aunt that 'l'etat de la France est affreux'.[3] Two days later she relayed disturbing news to Trentham. With no bread to eat, the 'poissardes (who are the fishwomen of the Halles) assembled, marched in a body to Versailles, disarmed the guards, & brought the King & Queen prisoners to Paris; after insulting them a great while, calling them le Boulanger, et la Boulangère, they confined them in the Louvre ... As the Louvre was not at all fitted, or prepared for this reception, they were obliged to get an old couch upon which the Queen lay that night.' Augusta learnt that Marie Antoinette was so traumatised by this treatment that she had poisoned herself, but on 12 October could tell her aunt that 'it is only a report'.[4]

The French Revolution evoked fear and anxiety in the British establishment. Twice in the eighteenth century the Jacobites had attempted to overthrow the Hanoverians and replace them with Stuart kings, whom they regarded as rightful monarchs. In 1745 Prince Charles Edward Stuart's army had reached as far south as Derby on its way to take London and had turned back to Scotland only because the help promised by France never materialised.

In Rome, when Prince Charles Edward died in January 1788, his brother began styling himself as 'King Henry IX of Great Britain' although he had not been recognised by the Pope or the Catholic courts of Europe. He was the last of his line and the Jacobite threat was long over but in December 1788 King George III again became ill and did not recover his senses for ten weeks. Concerned for her husband's health and alarmed by the events in Paris, Queen Charlotte told Augustus that:

> France furnishes greater but melancholy news. I often think that this cannot be the 18th century in which we live at present for Ancient History can hardly produce anything more barbarous & cruel than our neighbours in France. The hand of providence who never forsakes the just, will certainly support the innocent against a lawless people, & may the present misfortunes of that country bring them back to those principles which they have of late so totally forsaken.[5]

The winter of 1788 had been particularly severe; the Thames had frozen and the price of coal and flour had risen significantly. Many in London and elsewhere believed that it would take little for the French revolutionaries to infect the poor and disaffected in Britain.

Augusta's next letter to Lady Stafford touched on events closer to home. In August 1790 she took Virginia to Cheltenham to seek another cure. A spring of saline and chalybeate mineral water had been discovered there at the beginning of the eighteenth century and after the King and Queen's visit in 1788, the town was basking in royal approbation. Augusta found the surrounding countryside 'divine' but yearned for a husband to share it with: 'I often wish some good match would come down & with his enlivening presence add gaiety to the lovely scene.'[6]

A year later, in the autumn of 1791, while Augusta remained unmarried, Susan was nearing the conclusion of her first pregnancy. Describing the anticipation and excitement in Lower Berkeley Street to Lady Stafford, Augusta said, 'we have so much business with nursing our dearest Susan, & we are so bustled … that when we all meet, we all speak at once, & we are in a very grand heat of confusion'. The expectant mother was blooming. Susan was 'comme une maison, & it becomes her so extremely that really she looks a very fine figure, & a very handsome woman'.[7] It was an easy decision to name Susan's child 'Charlotte' after her maternal grandmother, Joseph Tharp's mother having died some years before.

Why was Augusta herself not yet a mother? Why had this attractive young woman not found a husband of her own? Augusta was warm-hearted and undoubtedly flirtatious but surely coquettishness was a condonable offence and an affectionate nature more appealing than superciliousness? Phillipina Knight was horrified that Augusta had been brought up 'with a mixture of Scotch and American education' and condemned her for being 'rather too free with the world'.[8] Augusta was more confident than some of her demure contemporaries and by comparison perhaps, she appeared unabashed, speaking her mind without reserve. Her spirited personality did not perhaps chime with society's view of appropriate female behaviour at the end of the eighteenth century.

However much Augusta longed for a husband, she knew that when the nuptial knot was fastened, her independence would vanish. Lady Chudleigh's epigram, *To the Ladies*, addressed the intrinsic servility of marriage and her 'caveat' to women resonated with Augusta, who copied every line into her commonplace book:

> Wife and servant are the same,
> But only differ in the name:
> For when that fatal knot is tied,
> Which nothing, nothing can divide:
> When she the word obey has said,
> And man by law supreme has made,
> Then all that's kind is laid aside,
> And nothing left but state and pride:
> Fierce as an Eastern Prince he grows,
> And all his innate rigour shows:
> Then but to look, to laugh, or speak,
> Will the nuptial contract break.
> Like mutes she signs alone must make,
> And never any freedom take:
> But still be governed by a nod,
> And fear her husband as a God:
> Him still must serve, him still obey,
> And nothing act, and nothing say,
> But what her haughty lord thinks fit,
> Who with the power, has all the wit.
> Then shun, oh! shun that wretched state,
> And all the fawning flatt'rers hate:
> Value your selves, and men despise,
> You must be proud, if you'll be wise.[9]

Although Mary Chudleigh had written the poem in 1703, Augusta knew that its conclusions were relevant eighty years later.

Mindful of the poem's theme, she memorised the last two lines. Augusta valued her independent personality and although not wealthy, she was nevertheless the daughter of an earl and proud of her lineage. She could never be a submissive wife but hoped one day she might be marry a man whose intellect she respected. She read widely, spoke fluent French and was well informed about current affairs. She was also attractive. Despite these attributes, by the end of 1791 although Augusta had had plenty of admirers, none of these myrmidons had made her his wife. She was however, unwilling to compromise.

8

I Half of You, You, Half of Me

At Waddesdon Manor in Buckinghamshire there is an early portrait of Augusta's most faithful lover. Everything in the Morning Room appears to be gilded: the French furniture, the doors, and the over mantel. All the pictures – Dutch landscapes and English portraits – are framed in gilt and hung against gold damask. Visitors today might find the opulence oppressive but at the end of the nineteenth century this was *Le Goût Rothschild* at its most uninhibited. In 1891 Baron Ferdinand de Rothschild purchased a pair of oval portraits by Thomas Gainsborough for the newly completed room and hung them either side of the bulbous escritoire that dominates the end wall. The portraits feature two handsome young brothers and, unusually, Gainsborough has signed them both.

The left portrait of Alexander, the future tenth Duke of Hamilton, is suffused with hauteur but the matching one of his younger brother, Archibald, is altogether different. The baron paid £4,410 for the portrait of the younger boy, almost four times what he paid for the one of his older brother.[1] It was an enormous sum but Rothschild's extravagance is justified; 16-year-old Archibald is enchanting. He wears a pale blue satin jacket with slashed sleeves and a tasselled 'Van Dyke' collar and his long curly hair rests on his steep shoulders. He smiles diffidently at the viewer, the sweetness of his character apparent in his gentle eyes. While Gainsborough was busy capturing his subject in paint, Archibald captivated the painter. Alexander, on the other hand, appears to grant the painter a favour by sitting for him and stares coldly over his right shoulder. Which of these two declared his devotion to his first cousin, Lady Augusta Murray, in 1787? It was, of course, Archibald.

Augusta's mother and Archibald's mother were sisters and he was born in 1770, the third child of Lady Harriet Stewart and Lord Archibald Hamilton, later the ninth Duke of Hamilton. After attending Eton and Christ Church, he studied law at Lincoln's Inn, but was hindered by deafness.[2] He and Augusta both attended William Beckford's Christmas party at Fonthill in 1781 and he fell in love with her when he was 17.

In April 1790 Archibald wrote a poem about Augusta's admirers 'long in plenty', who hoped 'Her heart with kindness to engage'. He knew he was not the only man to love her and her insouciant treatment of her devotees meant that she increased the number of the 'gen'ral herd', while contriving 'To like her old ones, none the less'. 'For everyone she put away,' he wrote, she attracted two more. He concluded his verses by exclaiming, 'No form so pleasing to mine eye/No Woman I could love so long.'[3]

When Lady Dunmore planned to take Augusta and Virginia to Italy in the summer of 1792, Archibald's father was to accompany them. By then the connection between the cousins had gone beyond a mere love affair. Archibald had sent her a ring of two interlocking links, 'alike compleat of gold' and in a touching poem he told her that he and she were like the two parts of the ring:

> I half of you, you, half of me;
> And when to foreign climes you roam,
> Know that you've left one half at home.[4]

When they exchanged portraits (probably miniatures) she also gave him a ring and it appears that they became unofficially engaged. He was devastated when she departed on 31 July and the day before wrote eight verses 'uttering curses on to morrow' and reminding her that:

> With me, you gone – all hopes, all joys are past
> But still remain the horrors of despair.

Moreover, he resolved that when she had 're-crossed the main', they would 'separate no more' intimating that as soon as she returned they would be married.[5] Augusta loved Archibald deeply but she had reservations. While acknowledging his 'many engaging qualities', generosity and courage, she questioned what sort of a husband he would make when he was old and bad tempered. When his ardour had cooled, how would he then behave? A committed Christian herself, she was also concerned by his lack of faith but hoped that her time abroad would resolve her feelings.

Once across the Channel, eighteenth-century tourists bound for Italy often travelled to Paris, then via Lyon and the River Rhône, to Marseilles. Embarking at the French Mediterranean port, they sailed down the west coast of Italy to Naples, one of the largest cities in Europe. Incomparably situated on its bay, Naples was a particularly agreeable place: white-painted houses, domes and spires rose up the hill from the coast, which was dominated by the massive walls of the Castel Nuovo. The combination of its climate – sea breezes mitigated the summer heat while it was pleasantly warm in winter – and its social life made the city a popular destination for grand tourists.

When Augusta arrived in September 1792 Naples was enjoying a cultural swansong; excavations were taking place in Herculaneum and Pompeii, and the arts – architecture, science, literature and music – were flourishing.[6] Visitors attended comic operas and alfresco musical entertainments on balmy evenings; further along the bay they could enjoy seaside picnics at Posillipo or hire a sedan chair and inspect Mount Vesuvius. Smoking and volatile, the volcano was a source of fascination to both locals and visitors; its chief aficionado, however, was Lord Archibald's kinsman, Sir William Hamilton. Despite the liberality of Neapolitan society, Sir William's recent marriage to Emma, the daughter of a Cheshire blacksmith, had caused a furore. Unlike many people, Lady Dunmore and her daughters befriended his beautiful new wife. A performance of her notorious 'Attitudes', when, lightly swathed, she struck some of the poses depicted on her husband's classical vases, was unforgettable.

The newly established French Republic brought unforeseen consequences to Augusta and her family during their stay. On 27 November the Reverend Thomas Brand, who was accompanying Lord Bruce, informed his charge's father that, 'The Minister of the French Republic is received, by order of the Court, with almost servile complaisance in the great houses of Belmonte, Butera, &c., and this *citoyenne moitié* was yesterday presented to the Queen.'[7] As Maria Carolina of Naples was the favourite sister of the deposed Marie Antoinette of France, the meeting between the Neapolitan Queen and the French minister was cool.

It was also a volte-face. Two weeks before, thirty guests had excused themselves from the Duke of Miranda's dinner because, 'Lady Dunmore and her daughters, who had twice met the French minister accidentally in their little excursions to Baia and Procida, were to be there, and it was looked upon as a crime to hold any converse with people who had been in such bad company.'[8] Augusta's unlooked-for acquaintance with the French minister was unfortunate, but while staying in Naples she did not make a good impression on Sir William Hamilton and, without giving any reasons, he told a friend in England that he disapproved of her conduct.[9]

After their Neapolitan sojourn, the Murray ladies went to Rome for Christmas. While sightseeing at the church of San Giacomo in December 1792, Augusta met HRH Prince Augustus, the young, handsome, but homesick son of King George III. It was a chance encounter that resulted in cataclysmic repercussions for them both.

9

He Says He Loves Me

Prince Augustus arrived in Rome on 11 November 1792.[1] Two days later he had an audience with Pius VI and told his father that the Pope 'was very polite, and made high encomiums on the way the French [fleeing the Revolution] are treated in England'. He also informed the King that, 'The reception of the French minister at Naples has made great sensation here, and it is even surmised the Court of Rome is also in treaty on the same subject.'[2] The mood in the eternal city was unsettled and the Prince himself morbidly unhappy.

He was accustomed by now to the upheavals of his itinerant way of life but the frequent packing and unpacking with his household establishing him in different places was dispiriting. On 2 December he confided in the Prince of Wales, exclaiming:

> You cannot be a stranger my dear brother to my wish of coming home; after an absence of so many years it not only becomes natural but is alas necessary. I have frequently wrote to His Majesty on this subject, the Physicians have also informed the King … I shall most probably remain here the whole winter [but] what is to become of me then I do not know … That I may return to England then is my only wish and prayer.

Although the King had not written to him for three years, Augustus remained loyal to his father, 'His Majesty has always been good to me that it would be highly unjust and improper in me to complain, but you may well conceive that this silence must make me uneasy.'[3] While waiting for a response he forced himself out and trudged off to explore the area near his apartment on the Via del Corso. When he returned the gloom had shifted and his staff barely recognised their light-hearted charge. An unexpected meeting had transformed him.

He had walked north up the Corso and having admired yet another baroque façade, this time at the Chiesa di San Giacomo, Augustus went inside with few expectations. The marbled magnificence of Roman churches held nothing new for such an experienced tourist; he was familiar with the panoply of the Catholic Church: chapels and altars, candles, statues and frescoes, all suffused with incense, and after a half-hearted visit he emerged from the dark church into the sunshine outside.

Shading his eyes, he nearly collided with a party of three ladies, a mother and her two daughters, one of whom struck him as exceptionally lovely. He recognised them as his compatriots but did not know their names. His interest was immediately piqued and having exchanged smiling courtesies and introductions, the Prince discovered that he had nearly floored the countess of Dunmore and the ladies Augusta and Virginia Murray. Taking care as he picked his way down the church steps, he noticed that one of Augusta's shoes was unfastened. He knelt down and secured the ribbons with a bow. Her mother and sister had already gone inside and, a little surprised, Augusta smiled her thanks before joining them, leaving the young man on the steps. His elegant, yet intimate, gesture not only altered his mood, it changed the course of his life.

The Prince was wintering in Italy for the benefit of his health but Lady Dunmore was there for the sake of economy. If Lord Dunmore had been reticent about asking his family to join him in Williamsburg, there was no question of inviting them to Nassau. Although concerted efforts had been made to eradicate pirates and smugglers, Nassau was not a suitable home for the governor's wife and daughters. After the American War of Independence numerous loyalists had taken refuge there and by 1792 Nassau was populated with cotton merchants, army officers, government officials (mainly Scots) and their slaves. When the small town was extended westwards, the governor took the opportunity to name two of the new roads Augusta Street and Virginia Street.

Italy, on the other hand, was an ideal spot for his daughters and their mother while they reduced their 'pecuniary obligations', and Rome, with its low cost of living, was popular with impoverished Britons. Phillipina Knight, the unpensioned widow of an admiral, and her daughter were staying in a suite of spacious rooms for which she was charged £12 per annum. The equivalent in London would have cost her £200. Food, especially beef and poultry, and the hire of carriages, were also less expensive than in England.

Lady Knight, a slight acquaintance of Lady Dunmore, avoided 'mixed societies' and associated only with other expatriates, whereas Charlotte Dunmore and her daughters embraced Rome's cosmopolitan coterie.[4] It was a heterogeneous group comprising Roman nobility, European royalty, the diplomatic corps and a succession of travellers. Representatives of Rome's aristocracy included Conte Antonio Cicciaporci, who was married to a cousin of Lady Dunmore and came from a family 'whose improprieties were not even veiled by good taste', and the lively and hospitable Princess Santa Croce. The Princess was the mistress of Cardinal de Bernis, the former French chargé d'affaires, who used to entertain 'all strangers at his house with great hospitality; but as his revenues from France have been withheld he now receives company only of an evening'.[5] Once a month Augusta attended convivial *conversazioni* at his palazzo at the bottom of the Corso, evenings where guests could discuss wide-ranging topics, sometimes with the addition of an orchestra, singers or cards. Snacks were on offer and ice cream (eaten in Rome at all times of the day and night) was a popular choice.[6] Other diplomats such as the Portuguese minister, the Venetian emissary, and Count Chernyshev, the former Russian ambassador plenipotentiary at the Court of St James, made agreeable additions to what Lady Knight condemned as the 'gay set'.

Of the European royalty in Augusta's circle, apart from Prince Augustus Frederick there was Prince Stanislaw Poniatowski, the nephew of the last King of Poland, who had lived in Italy since the 1772 Partition of Poland, and the Princess Royal of Sweden, travelling incognito as the Countess of Vasa, was also in Rome. The city was the chief tourist destination for Continental visitors and the goal of every young aristocrat on the Grand Tour. Chance encounters with friends such as the Duchess of Devonshire and Lady Templetown, an amateur sculptress who produced designs of an improving nature for Josiah Wedgwood, were frequent. Augusta kept late hours most evenings enjoying music, cards and dancing, precisely the mode of life frowned upon by Lady Knight, who was 'very apt to think that the present mode of travelling is turned rather to amusement than to improvement'.[7]

While her evenings were social, Augusta spent her days in the pursuit of culture. Expatriates expected tourists to take an interest in Roman civilisation and sightseeing was a serious business for Augusta. She recorded everything that she saw in her journals and her daily excursions were a pleasure rather than a duty, and not only because Prince Augustus accompanied them.[8]

The first of Augusta's journals begins the month after her arrival in Rome, by which time the Prince was already at the centre of her life. Although he had known Augusta for only a few weeks, he had quickly become part of her family circle. Having arrived in the city in the company of dejected gentlemen attendants and uncertain about his future, Augustus was delighted to find himself in the company of three warm-hearted and lively women. Lady Dunmore and her daughters eased the longing he felt for his own mother and sisters. The countess proved kindness itself and soon he was regarding Lady Augusta Murray, personable and affectionate, with more than sisterly affection.

History has unfairly accused Augusta of trapping the Prince, of using the wiles of an older and more experienced woman, but research into her journals reveals that the truth was different. When Augustus fell in love with her, he found an object for his youthful ardour and the intensity of his feelings surprised them both. Within a month of meeting her, the Prince's courtship of Lady Augusta Murray consumed his existence.

As early as 20 December he sent her a prayer by Francis Xavier, translated by Alexander Pope, which opened with the words 'Thou are my God, sole object of my love.'[9] He wrote to her each morning and they met every day in January but two. Their days together followed a pattern. As in England, breakfast was taken around nine or ten o'clock and then the Prince showed the Murray ladies his favourite places in Rome. He took them to Renaissance churches and Baroque palaces. They wandered in the gardens of the villas Borghese and Doria Pamphilj; they inspected classical sites: baths and aqueducts, arches and temples. Augustus, who was interested in antique sculpture, arranged for them to visit the archaeological digs that he helped to finance. After spending the day sightseeing they had dinner about four or five o'clock.

After their excursions Augusta loved to dance in the evenings and took lessons in the tarantella, a traditional folk dance of Southern Italy. However, the Prince preferred her undivided attention at a secluded card table in the houses of friends, where they often played casino or piquet (a card game for two, perfectly suited for intimacy). Later, Lady Knight made it clear that she had disapproved of the 'many vain and sycophantic persons', who shamelessly forwarded the connection between the Prince and Lady Augusta by throwing them together. Mindful of the Royal Marriages Act, Phillipina Knight would have regarded it as high treason to encourage the couple.

Augusta was flattered and enjoyed his attentions but until March she could not believe that his declarations of love were serious and marriage to him did not cross her mind. As her relationship with the Prince developed she sometimes shared her journal with him but initially it was written for her benefit only and the entries underline the pressure that his attention imposed on her. The son of King George III, without the guidance or support of his family, was wooing her intensely but he was in delicate health and Augusta knew that he was the victim of emotions beyond his control.

In the first entry of her journal, dated Sunday, 6 January 1793, the Prince gave Augusta 'a thing which I am always to wear'. At dinner the next night she was sceptical when 'he told me something which might have pleased me if my clairvoyance was not superior to my vanity'. The day after, returning from sitting for her portrait, she found 'a dear little note from the Prince *pour nous consoler*' and in the evening they went to the Princess Santa Croce's, where she found it 'pleasant to couple oneself with an amiable Prince'. On 9 January the Prince added a note in the letter she was writing to her brother, Jack, and two days later after they had had dinner with his friends he took them in his carriage to Lady Templetown's, where he and Augusta played piquet. Seeing Augusta for six days consecutively only increased his affection for her.

In an attempt to cool his passion she told him that her affections lay elsewhere but her openness provoked Augustus to take matters in hand. On 17 January he declared his love to her in a letter and enclosed a ring. Augusta was dazed. First, she had been acquainted with him for less than two months and second, she was in love with someone else: her heart remained with Archibald. She confided in her journal, 'Shocking day, I had a letter from the Prince with a ring, he says he loves me, I do not believe he does, & yet everybody assures me of it.' She knew that people had begun to gossip and the unexpected declaration appalled her.

When the expatriate community organised a subscription dinner to celebrate Queen Charlotte's birthday, Augusta sat on one side of the Prince and the Princess Santa Croce on the other. 'The place of honour embarrassed me but I resigned myself to it,' she wrote sanguinely, and continued. 'The Prince seems to like me much, mais comme al'ordinaire, it appears all seeming to me ... I cannot think he really likes me as he pretends & as his manner may make the world fancy he does.'

She did not believe that he might be in love with her, a woman twelve years his senior, and when Augustus asked for a lock of her hair she thought he was being 'ridiculous' and refused.

Their love affair took place against a background of political instability caused by the French Revolution. Tensions between the Pope and the French had intensified since the Republic had been announced and the French Royal Family imprisoned in the Temple. On 26 December Louis XVI was driven to his trial. Two weeks later the Pope made his feelings about the behaviour of the French towards their Catholic King and Queen so clear that many Frenchmen left Rome.

Unable to serve his country in a military capacity, the Prince kept his father informed about political events abroad and in early January 1793 reported an incident that took place on his doorstep. A group of artists studying at the French Academy, which was located at the Palazzo Mancini on the Corso, decided to aggravate the situation between the new republic and the Pope. The students, Augustus told his father, 'thought it proper to take down ... the old Arms of France. They broke to pieces the statue of Louis XIV ... and ... put up a bust of Brutus. The Pope, being informed ... sent a manifesto to the French Consul declaring he would never suffer the Arms of the French Republic to be put in his States.'[10]

The situation deteriorated when two provocative French officials, wearing the national cockade in their hats and a cap of liberty in their buttonholes, drove down the Corso waving a small tricolour from their carriage. Bystanders began to hiss and a priest tore the flag from their hands. After an exchange of gunfire, one of the officials, Monsieur de Basseville, was stabbed.

Incensed by the two Frenchmen, the Roman mob ran to the French Academy and burnt down its doors but the damage was contained, the palazzo being built of stone. The Prince was stopped in his carriage on his way home and told his father that the crowd 'desired me to cry *Viva il Papa* and upon being told who I was they cried *Viva il Re d'Inghilterra*, to which I joined most heartily and then they let me pass'.[11] Overnight the conflict worsened and the death of de Basseville from his wounds resulted in more riots the next day. Augusta recorded that, 'Guards were placed everywhere, & Rome became tranquil,' although she noted that in a break with their normal programme, they thought it prudent to spend the morning at home.

Later in the month Augusta and Augustus shared a personal event: their birthday on 27 January. Lady Dunmore held a small breakfast party to mark the Prince's 20th birthday but all three Murray ladies quietly acknowledged that it was also a celebration for Augusta, who was 32 that day. Once again Augustus asked her for a lock of her hair and once again she did not comply. Their petty squabble was forgotten when they learnt that all the French had left Naples. There was worse to follow.

Carnival in Rome, usually a rumbustious eight-day gala with horse races down the Corso, dancing, singing and dressing up, was a muted affair that year. On 5 February, while dining with Lady Corbet, a hospitable English expatriate, Augusta and the Prince heard accounts of an act of unconscionable evil witnessed by 20,000 people in the Place de la Révolution. On 21 January Louis XVI had been taken from the Temple and at 10.22 a.m. *Madame la Guillotine* had sliced off his head. Visions of the unhappy Queen held 'in a common prison with common malefactors' were a painful contrast to Augusta's reminiscences of Marie Antoinette sparkling at Versailles. She was horrified that the regicides had refused to allow the King to bid his wife and children farewell.

Lady Corbet's guests departed, overcome with anguish for the French Royal Family, but with the citizens of Paris their indignation knew no bounds. That evening the Prince took Augusta and her family to the home of Princess Santa Croce, where every face and 'every heart bore testimony to the atrociousness of French politics, a melancholy gloom was cast on every countenance, and Louis XVI was lamented and mourned as a good man, an honest man, and a worthy king that villains had cruelly tormented, and shamefully condemned'.

The following morning Augusta rose early. She could not sleep for fretting about the dead King, his unfortunate Queen and their forlorn family. She recalled that on the morning of 21 January, the day of execution, she had been with the son of the King of England at the Palazzo Doria Pamphilj enjoying one of the greatest art collections in Italy. Being in the company of Augustus, a Prince of the Blood, sharpened her response to the events in Paris and she lamented in her journal:

> unhappy King, yours was a change which I hope heaven will make felicity; perhaps you lost an earthly crown to gain an heavenly one ... The Prince read us his [the King's] will, his requests to those cannibals who granted none of them, and his last speech from the scaffold to people, which he still called his, but which ought to have known no appellation given to humanity; when the executioner showed his severed head to the populace, they cried, *vive la nation, vive la République* ... Oh monsters may vengeance be poured on your ... heads, may it make France and her children the execration of all Europe.

Meeting Marie Antoinette had been the zenith of her visit to Paris and she continued despairingly, 'Unhappy Queen what will be your fate, your feelings, and your situation?' Prince Augustus told his father that, 'On such events one dares make no remarks, but it affected me so much that I have been two days ill.'[12]

Augusta noted that most of the French at the Academy, or set up in business, had fled Rome but the riots continued when a few remaining Frenchmen provoked further disorder by displaying republican sentiment. On 22 February 1793 she learnt that, 'That detested, that hated France had declared war against England, Holland, and Denmark; she is already at War with Italy, Austria, & Russia; I am glad of it, may all Europe unite for her destruction.' Augusta's prayer would not be granted for more than twenty-two years when Napoleon's army was defeated at the Battle of Waterloo.

10

I Must Not Will Not Love the Prince

The Prince's declaration of love on 17 January 1793 presented Augusta with a dilemma: she was forced to choose between losing Archibald, or allowing herself to be loved by an ardent Prince whom she could never marry. Archibald's behaviour had bewildered her since she left England. His letters were no longer those of a loving fiancé. When Prince Augustus pronounced his love for her, she admitted in her diary, 'Archd Hamilton je vous aime encore, tho' you behave ill to me, & tho' Susan apologises for the caprice of young men, that apology condemns you more in my eyes than even the coldness of your letters.'[1] The Prince's constant presence and persistent devotion slowly eroded Augusta's allegiance to her old lover.

When she tripped and injured her knee on Ash Wednesday, the Prince's solicitude touched her deeply. The indisposition allowed her a day's reflection and, released from the frenzy of her social life, it dawned on her that the Prince was serious. Two days later, after they had dined with the Bishop of Winchester, Lady Dunmore held a party when 'all society met, Prince Poniatowski, & the Countess of Vasa came to us also, & we spent a very jolly pleasant evening'. She finished by admitting, 'dear Prince I do like you'. One evening when her knee prevented her from going out, the Prince 'came to us during a little moment' and 'quite alone, drank Tea & went away' having shaken off his attendants for the first time. A few moments at the Hotel Sarmiento without the presence of one of his gentlemen was a minor victory for the Prince.

Everything came to a head on 20 February, a day that marked a watershed in Augusta's feelings for her two lovers. She:

> had a letter from the Prince which I liked him for, it mentioned Archibald Hamilton & I alas ventured to read something written by Archd. Oh Archibald why could you not love me why had I not charms, & qualities to make you constant. Or rather why did I read anything of yours, why think of you, why remember you, you who have forgotten me, you care not about your once loved Augusta. – farewell Archibald, your name, your idea, adds melancholy to solitude; adieu, for I still love you. I have cried today over the endeavours I make to forget you, I had nearly abandoned them, but reflection is returned, & tells me what you are, what I am.

While doing her best to forget her cousin – she could not deny her enduring love for him – she continued her feverish comparisons. While the Prince pursued her with declarations, which:

> might persuade any woman but me; how can I be convinced that I who have not attractions of mind or form can captivate a young & handsome Prince, I cannot fancy he loves me; & though he writes it me every morning & tells it me every evening je reste incredule; I like him, I admire his disposition, I am pleased with his person, & perhaps, I may be still more charmed with his character; it requires much to gain my admiration, very little, claims my indulgence; I can excuse every foible, every weakness of humanity, but I can only love what demands approbation, what commands esteem.

Turning back to Archibald, the man she had hoped would make her his wife but who now appeared to have abandoned her, she wrote:

> I have loved you well, for I esteemed you much; you have (in my eyes) character, virtue, honour, & steady principle; – shall I record yr faults, shall I tell that Archibald … but no, I will not, I cannot forget them, they have saddened some moments of my life, & they are well recorded … I will return to the Prince, to that Prince who desires to be called mine, & who is amiable enough not to despise my friendship. I have said that his person was charming & his disposition angelic, his character I have not yet unfolded; & until I have, I dare not trust my pen with the description.

Miserably, she reiterated how much she loved Archibald. The only honourable relationship she could imagine with the doting Prince was marriage, which was impossible. Unlike Dorothea Jordan, the lover of Prince Augustus's brother, William, Augusta would not contemplate becoming a royal mistress. Her self-respect and religious principles forbade it. No longer a young woman, her intractable situation depressed her and on 25 February she wrote 'many envy me, because they think Prince Augustus loves me … I am not made to be any man's mistress I long to be a good man's wife … I must not will not love the Prince.' As time went by she found it more and more difficult to honour her intention: Augustus was so attentive and kind. He was also unusually tall at 6ft 3in and exceptionally handsome, as seen in his portrait by Guy Head.

Head's picture, painted in 1798, depicts the Prince with a thoughtful and unassuming air. He wears Windsor uniform (a family livery the King had introduced to be worn at the Castle), comprising a dark blue tailcoat trimmed with scarlet collar and matching cuffs, and the breast star of the Order of the Garter. His eyes are grey, his mouth small and the soft flesh of his cheeks and jowls is an early indicator of the corpulence of his later years.

Augusta also followed the fashionable practice by having her portrait painted while she was in Rome. Robert Fagan, a resident Irish artist, who also painted her mother, portrayed Augusta sitting beneath a tree with a temple in the landscape behind her. She holds a locket in one hand and the ribbons of her bonnet in the other. Her wavy hair and pearl earrings frame a smile of extraordinary sweetness. She has the Dunmore nose, long and fine, and her large dark eyes twinkle.

In Rome, as in London, the commissioning classes enjoyed visiting artists' studios. One fine but chilly day in February, Augusta joined a party going to the Strada Felice, conveniently close to the Piazza di Spagna. A number of artists resided there including Guy Head and Alexander Day, who painted a miniature of Augusta. First the group visited Hugh Robinson, who was working on portraits of the Duchess of Devonshire and her friend, Lady Elizabeth Foster. At the house of Angelica Kauffman, one of the two female founders of London's Royal Academy of Arts, Augusta listened to a little light music while she viewed the paintings.

In Rome's outstanding art galleries, Augusta could look at historic portraits by some of the best artists in Europe and she noted in her journal all the paintings that she liked. She was 'particularly charmed by a collection of fine pictures' at the Palazzo Doria Pamphilj, where she admired Poussin's landscapes and Caravaggio's beautiful *Magdalen*, startlingly penitent with her jewellery discarded on the flagstones by her side. Later the same day, still full of energy and enthusiasm, Augusta visited the Palazzo Giustiniani, where she saw Raphael's famous *Portrait of Pope Julius II* and a *Venus* by Veronese. The next day she took a break from looking at pictures and 'went out a shopping all morning', but the day after she was back amongst the Old Masters, this time in the Borghese Gallery.

She did not neglect sculpture and called on the English sculptor John Flaxman, who was working on the colossal four-figure group *The Fury of Athamas*, destined for Lord Bristol's house at Ickworth. Flaxman was a member of one of Rome's most prestigious literary institutions. The Academy of Arcadia was founded at the end of the seventeenth century as a reaction to the excesses of the Baroque. Its purpose was to reform Italian poetry by returning to the pastoral simplicity of ancient Greece and admittance to its membership was an honour. When Prince Augustus was enrolled as a member, or Shepherd of Arcadia, on 31 January 1793, Augusta and her family were invited to watch the ceremony.

It was getting dark when they crossed the Tiber and arrived on the Janiculum Hill. The Bosco Parrasio, where the Academy held its meetings, was a sylvan site overshadowed by pines and cypresses. There they joined a torchlight procession snaking up the double flights of steps through the terraced gardens. On the first level a fountain played softly, on the second a grotto formed the backdrop to a water lily pond and at the top there was a small amphitheatre with four rows of stone seats where the 'Shepherds' declaimed in the summer. The gardens culminated in a classical semicircular building, il Serbatoio. Here Augusta watched the acclamation of the Prince as an Arcadian Shepherd 'by the name of Sebato which in Greek signifies Augustus'. Five days later she received a letter telling her that she had been 'chosen a Shepherdess of Arcadia by the name Eristea Tregania'. It was infrequent, although not unheard of, for the Academy to admit a woman.

Prince Augustus was not only a patron of literature in Rome. He was proud of his three-octave vocal range and whenever possible attended secular and religious musical performances. One Sunday early in their acquaintance, he took the Murrays to the Chiesa di Sant'Apollinare, where Augusta heard music by Giovanni Cavi. It was sung by castrati, whom some

Anglican visitors believed should not be permitted to sing in 'sacred edifices, especially in a country where emasculation prevails to an extent that requires discouragement of every kind'.[2]

On 27 February they all went to a concert when 'my dear Prince was very ill; & Augusta unhappy'. His condition had not improved the next day and the effect of his asthma made Augusta regard him fondly, but he became so unwell that she was distressed. For the first few days in March they abandoned the city centre for their excursions and took the air in the gardens of outlying villas. Soon Augustus was able to write a cheerful letter to his brother, the Prince of Wales, telling him that he was happy with his new gentleman, Baron Marschall, and that he hoped the war with France would not prevent his return to England.

Then he turned to the subject uppermost in his mind:

> My health is greatly restored which I owe not a little to the happy winter I have spent here. We have several very pleasant English families amongst them is that of Lady Dunmore which I frequent the most. Lady Augusta Murray often talks to me about you and she even flatters me so far as to find some resemblance between my dear George and me. Did she know that I was writing to you now I make no doubt she as well as her mother would join in their dutiful respects to you; sure from a pretty woman that must always be pleasing, and I shall tell her that I have done it. I love and respect Lady Dunmore exceedingly she has one of the most noble and honest hearts I ever saw. I never knew so good natured and pleasant a woman of her age.[3]

Indeed, Lady Dunmore loved Augustus as much as he did her but her attitude to his relationship with her daughter was short-sighted. She knew that Augusta made him happy and their outings were greatly enhanced by his presence. (It also meant that they did not need to hire a guide.) The Prince was a welcome diversion while they were in Rome and, conscious of the provisions of the Royal Marriages Act, she knew that marriage between Augusta and the Prince was impossible. It never occurred to her that either of them supposed otherwise and when Lady Templetown and others warned her that Augusta's relationship with the Prince was ill advised, she thought her friends were overreacting. Blind to the tragedy that was unfolding in her presence, she did nothing to prevent it.

On 1 March, while Virginia honoured invitations from Lady Corbet and the Princess Borghese, Lady Dunmore and Augusta received the Prince at home. They 'spent the evening very pleasantly' and 'he was so good, so charming, but so unwell that I was very unhappy'. Augusta wrote, 'I do dote on him' and, 'I wish his health was perfectly re-established.' She was beginning to feel 'the tenderest interest, the warmest affection' towards him, 'but can I talk of love, and him – no – I see the folly and wildness of the idea; *et je me tais*'.

By 3 March her resolve to keep silent was wilting. While her mother and Virginia were walking amongst the evergreen oaks, statues and fountains at the Villa Borghese, Augusta and Augustus 'went into the inner gardens, he & I sat together; I do love him & I believe that he does love me.' He showed her a letter he had written to Archibald Hamilton, stating his position. She was impressed by his honesty and admitted she loved the Prince 'for the confidence he places in me' and even more tellingly, 'I love him because he is unwell, & I love him more, because I see his heart is worthy of mine, & I do think mine is honest'.

On Monday, 4 March 1793, the day that George Washington took his oath of office in Philadelphia before his second term as President of the United States, Augusta took a momentous decision. After walking with the Prince in the grounds of the Villa Doria Pamphilj, she confessed to her journal with a note of desperation, 'dear Prince, you must be loved, you are too amiable not to be doted upon, my mother loves you as much as I love you, cries over your lungs and fever as often as I do.' His asthma had drawn declarations from Augusta that had been encouraged by her mother's naivety.

11

We Can Never Be Happy Together

Two days later the love affair deepened when the ducal owner of Villa Lante al Gianicolo invited Augusta to meet the Prince at a breakfast party. Gloriously situated high on the Janiculum Hill, the villa was the perfect setting for their tryst. Walking through its marble rooms, decorated with classical scenes and frescoes by Raphael, they entered a loggia to find Rome laid out below them with St Peter's to their left and the Tiber beyond.

Recollecting their conversation with a mixture of regret and pleasure, Augusta wrote, 'you may love me, my Prince but we never can be happy together'.[1] Despite her best efforts she had fallen in love with Augustus but knew that there was no future with him. Furthermore, she was unsettled to receive a letter in which he called her 'his, & his only' and she questioned whether 'any but a husband' should 'have that privilege?' After they had visited St Peter's and the Borghese Gardens, she noted, 'Oh my Treasure, I ought not to love you, you never can be mine … Alas do I dare love you my Prince?' Fraught with risk, the attachment was beginning to overwhelm her.

Their affair reached a climax in the gardens of the Villa Doria Pamphilj on 13 March 1793 when Augusta showed the Prince a devastating letter: Archibald Hamilton was to marry someone else. In her commonplace book Augusta wrote the following lines: 'I loved him till he loved me no more his [love] is gone by Caprice, or Satiety, – mine is gone by a sad necessity of not loving what has ceased to love me.'[2] Why had he rejected her after five years of devotion? It was not because they were first cousins. Such unions were common when the genetic risks were unknown. Augusta's paternal grandparents were first cousins and her parents were second cousins. The Prince of Wales would soon marry his first cousin, Princess Caroline, and in 1803 Archibald's sister, Susan, would marry Augusta's brother, George. There was however, one serious impediment to the relationship between Augusta and Archibald: she was nine years older than him. When Archibald's university friend, Lord Holland, married Elizabeth Webster, the new Lady Holland described the difference in their ages of two years and eight months, as 'a horrid disparity'.[3] In 1800 the Duke of Somerset's mother initially forbade him to marry Archibald's sister, Charlotte, because she was 'much older than the Duke'.[4] In fact, Charlotte was only three years his senior.

Offering Augusta comfort as she wept, the Prince assured her of his constant love and attachment. She had lost Archibald but now she was in love with a prince whose birth made him unattainable. Her life was at an impasse. Sobbing over her journal that night, she wrote, 'Oh fatal day, I blot you, I wish I could from the Book of Time.'

Augustus now saw his chance: Archibald's desertion was the catalyst for his proposal. On waking the following morning she received his letter, 'Oh auspicious morn how can I welcome you, plunged in the deepest regrets I rose to complain to record my sorrows, when a letter from my much loved Prince awakened me to joy. He talks of being mine forever talks of it by naming a happy marriage.' With resignation she concluded, 'Not that I imagine it can ever take place, but I love him more for it.'

There was, or should have been, an insurmountable obstacle to their permanent union: the Royal Marriages Act. Augustus needed his father's permission to marry but the King would only allow him to marry protestant princesses such as Augustus's mother, Charlotte of Mecklenburg-Strelitz, his grandmother Augusta of Saxe-Gotha, or his great-grandmother Caroline of Ansbach.

His new sister-in-law, Princess Frederica of Prussia, was everything that the King and Queen could have desired. Queen Charlotte happily informed Augustus that Prince Frederick's 'choice seems to be in every respect very proper, not only in rank, but the Princess's character and temper is such as to leave no doubt of his happiness. She is besides these essentials possessed of a variety of pleasing talents such as music, painting and in short all promises well.'[5] Lady Augusta Murray was no Princess Frederica. The King and Queen would never accept a British subject as a wife for their sixth son, despite the fact that she was the daughter of an earl with royal forebears. To this immutable fact Augustus was blind. The passion that he felt for Augusta was so strong that his mother's advice not to proceed without properly considering the consequences went unheeded.

Augusta has been denounced as contriving her union with a youthful Prince. The Queen's friend, Lady Harcourt, said, 'A thorough knowledge of the world gave Lady Augusta a great advantage over her artless lover, and she had the address to conceal, or gloss over, some of the earlier transactions of her life, and to persuade the young Prince to marry her.'[6] However, Augusta refused the Prince's first proposal and he himself later absolved her of coercing him. In a letter to his legal adviser five years later he stated, 'The candour and generosity my wife showed on this occasion, by refusing the proposal, and showing me the personal disadvantages I should draw upon myself, instead of checking my endeavours served only to add new fuel to a passion which already no earthly power could evermore have extinguished.'[7]

The strain of his passion for his 'Goosey' began to affect his health and the stress of her refusal exacerbated his asthma. While Virginia and the countess attended parties given by the Duchess of Devonshire and Lady Corbet, Augusta was also in a state of emotional turmoil and stayed at home while the Prince 'was ill, too ill to go out'. His asthma then became so severe that he was unable to leave his rooms for the next twenty-two days. His incapacity during those three volatile weeks means that every secret transaction, negotiation and disappointment is recorded in their love letters, carefully preserved by both parties. Attended by gentlemen whom the King employed to keep him informed of any misconduct, the Prince relied on his doctor to act as go-between.

With Augustus unwell, there was little incentive for Augusta to go out and she became increasingly introspective. Every morning she received long letters from the invalid. Gradually he wore down her determination to reject his offer of marriage and she fell further in love but the combination of her indecision and their enforced separation made them both deeply unhappy. Eventually the Prince overcame her qualms but it was a case of a sickbed swain desperate for love rather than an old bride capturing a young groom. As their son described it many years later, 'urgent importunity, and strong and often-repeated declarations of the most ardent affection, at length prevailed, and his proposal was accepted'.[8] Augusta had misgivings instantly, fearing that the Prince would repent of his decision.

When she eventually accepted Augustus, he was confined to his room with a high fever and no appetite so she was left to make arrangements for their clandestine wedding. Both parties took the religious part of their proposed marriage seriously. The Prince was devout and Augusta also attended church regularly when at home.

There was no Anglican church in Rome and British visitors attended private services, taken by itinerant clergymen, in their lodgings. Augusta asked an abbé for help finding someone to take the service but the first pastor he identified was suspicious. The pastor questioned the private marriage and 'required a certificate that attests, that no objection made secrecy necessary'. 'This discomposed me much,' wrote Augusta, 'but the dear Prince's letters console me, & perhaps the parson will not remain inexorable.' The cleric however, was adamant and Augusta instructed the abbé to enquire at the Armenian and other foreign seminaries.

Secrecy was essential. The Prince knew it was imperative that his father did not hear of the marriage until he himself 'should communicate the information in the manner which he should deem to be the most likely to assuage the King's anticipated displeasure'.[9] Once married, when he gained his majority in January 1794, he planned to tell his parents what he had done. Naively he believed that Augusta would charm the King and Queen and all would be well. Augustus had not witnessed the King's illness in 1788. He had been absent so long that he was out of touch with his father, especially his intractability, his need for loyalty and his strongly held views on royal marriage.

Prince Augustus forbade Augusta from telling her mother their secret. He believed that she would object because he had not asked his father's permission. He also refused to allow any witnesses at the wedding and told his bride that the strength of his and her emotions might embarrass outsiders. Furthermore, if the ceremony were to be kept secret the presence of witnesses would compromise the minister's anonymity. Therein lay a problem. Should it become necessary to prove that the wedding had taken place, the lack of witnesses would make such proof impossible.

When Augusta could not find a clergyman willing to marry them, the Prince took matters into his own hands although he was unwell. He betrothed himself to Augusta on 25 March and she recorded his troth with delight: 'Today my beloved Prince took a sacred, a solemn oath called on heaven to witness, swore before the Almighty on the Bible never to have any wife but me, & in future to look upon himself as sacredly promised to me; I accepted the religious promise that the Bible had witnessed, that had been addressed to the Almighty, & gave mine in exchange.' It was an oath that both parties kept for the rest of their lives.

On the next day, the Tuesday before Easter, he sent her a wedding ring 'which had witnessed his vows taken on the Bible; desiring me to wear it, until he could himself place one before the altar on my finger.' She accepted 'the auspicious omen' joyfully and in her turn promised 'to do all in my power to make him as happy as my endeavours, or wishes can effect'.

Frustrated both mentally and sexually, the Prince was desperate. He promised sacredly 'to be hers by an oath that never can be broken' and reminded her that: 'The sanction of the Church is only wanting to complete the business and give us the right of enjoying those privileges which, without it, are criminal; and this will come, must come, and shall come. The great and important point is done; we are betrothed.' Augusta had also sent him a ring, the one that Archibald Hamilton had returned to her. The Prince was plumper than Archibald and told her it was a snug fit, the ring 'being small will make that it never can come off again'.[10]

Augusta was engaged but could not celebrate her engagement with her mother and sister; she was also fearful that their suspicions might lead to discovery.

Terrified that if he saw her alone the strength of his physical desire might overpower him, Augustus cautioned against private meetings. He also thought that if they met for the first time on the day of their marriage, they would be happy in the belief that they had acted honourably and virtuously and that their restraint would be rewarded.

During Lent when opera was forbidden, oratorio took its place and on the day she received the Prince's wedding ring, Augusta heard a performance by Giovanni Pergolesi. His *Stabat Mater Dolorosa*, a meditation on the sufferings of the Virgin Mary at the cross, took place in Princess Santa Croce's rooms. Afterwards Augusta wrote despondently, 'my love was not there; still too unwell to go out'. On the Wednesday of Holy Week she swore on the Bible never to marry any man but Prince Augustus and wrote in her journal, 'I dare not yet thank my Almighty for giving me a husband who will ever love me, & whom my ardent wish is to make happy.' She added with cynicism, 'I dare not yet trust to his being mine according to the rights of our Church, & what are oaths unsanctioned there; they bind the honourable but they do not satisfy the world.'

Their search for a priest continued and Prince Augustus began to lose hope. Sometimes he was so ill that he could not go to bed and had to sleep upright in a special chair. He had looked forward to the lead up to Easter and its celebration by the Pope – the reason why many visitors came to Rome – but was forced to remain in his apartment surrounded by irritable attendants.

On 28 March 1793, Maundy Thursday morning, Augusta heard Mass celebrated in the Sistine Chapel by the Pope, who afterwards carried the Blessed Sacrament to the Altar of Repose (representing the Garden of Gethsemane) in the Pauline Chapel. From there she went to the Major Domo's windows to witness the papal benediction from the balcony of St Peter's. Then she 'returned to the Chapel where we saw him [the Pope] wash the pilgrims' feet & afterwards serve them at table in imitation of the last supper ... In the evening we went to see the princes of Rome perform the same ceremonies, & I at supper served also a pilgrim.' Meanwhile, Augustus fretted, writing to her noon and night in the fetid atmosphere of his room.

Plagued by visions of Augusta enjoying herself without him, he was scribbling in the candlelight when 'all at once a thought comes across my mind, and says, Is my little naughty wife a flirting with some Italian beau? – with a Mr. North? My own memory, my own conscience reproaches me, and says, How darest thou be suspicious?'[11] The object of his jealousy, Francis North, nephew of the former prime minister and elder son of the bishop of Winchester, was in love with Augusta and several members of their set had noticed. By 28 March Augustus had been apart from Augusta for more than two weeks and, with only her miniature to comfort him, his isolation made him mistrustful.

12

The Strong Desire of Doing Right

By Good Friday the Prince was in despair. Life without Augusta had become intolerable and he was on the brink of a nervous breakdown. More than anything he wanted to sleep with her but their religious principles prohibited a physical relationship outside wedlock, and they still had to find a minister to marry them.

He asked Augusta to stop searching because he no longer believed that the abbé's enquiries amongst the Greeks or Armenians would be successful and he doubted whether a wedding ceremony taken by one of them would be valid anyway. Previously he had been reluctant to compromise anyone he knew by asking them to perform a secret wedding but, with no alternative, he approached the Reverend William Gunn, whom he had met on an archaeological dig. No renegade rector in need of a quick fee, Gunn was a Cambridge-educated antiquarian, who spent his spare time researching in the Vatican library. Telling Augusta what he proposed, the Prince urged her the 'moment you tell me, treasure, my treasure, to speak to Mr Gunn, I will, and not before'[1] but Augusta regarded Gunn as 'the last extremity'.

In the evening, all alone, Augustus amused himself 'with thoughts of my Augusta, who is rambling about town, but much against her will, I am sure … I own I am rather out of humour with Lady Dunmore for running about town so, and yet she is not wrong, for to be at Rome, and not see the functions, is rather extraordinary.'[2] He guessed correctly: Augusta was in St Peter's to watch the Veneration of the Cross. Afterwards she listened to Gregorio Allegri's *Miserere*, set to the penitential Psalm 51 and commissioned for the papal choir to sing in the Sistine Chapel on Good Friday. The recital would have delighted Prince Augustus, who had now been incarcerated in his room for eighteen days.

When she returned that night, Augusta discovered that he was planning to speak to Gunn but not to disclose whom he wished to marry. At this she was aghast. She was determined that the Prince should protect her reputation when he approached the clergyman and she responded passionately. First she said that the rector must give his word never to mention the marriage. Second she insisted that Augustus tell Gunn her name, explaining, 'If you tell him your resolve, and do not tell him who the woman is you mean to marry, he may imagine it is some low person, some Italian, or, in short, any thing; and that the whim you dare not avow will soon pass, and he will most undoubtedly refuse having any thing to do with it.'

Becoming more and more vehement, she wrote:

> He will imagine I have been your mistress, and that humanity, commonly termed honour, now induces you to pity me, and so veil my follies by an honourable marriage. My own beloved Prince, forgive me if I am warm upon this subject. I wish you to feel you owe me nothing, and whatever I owe you I wish to owe to your love, and to your good opinion, but to no other principle. Tell Mr. Gunn, my own Augustus, that you love me; that you are resolved to marry me; that you have pledged a sacred word. Tell him, if you please, that upon the Bible you have sworn it; that I have done the same; and that nothing shall ever divide us; but don't let him imagine I have been vile. Do this, my only love; but pray take care of the character of your wife, of your Augusta.[3]

She ended on a brighter note, gently flirting with him, 'God bless my loved Augustus, my only treasure, my dearest husband. May I send him here a conjugal kiss; may I kiss him here before I go to undress?' She could not resist a taunt and recounted how Countess Chernysheva had whispered to her that somebody in Rome was passionately in love with her 'but when I expected to hear the loved name that gladdens my heart … she named – guess who, my treasure, – she named – Mr North. Alas how disappointed I was.' Lady Knight may have had Mr North in mind when she declared later that 'a man of fashion' had had 'serious intentions of espousing the lady, had not her conduct been faulty'.[4]

Red-eyed and wheezing, the Prince answered Augusta's protestations with a letter of more than twenty pages. While assuring her of the maturity and constancy of his emotions, he wanted her to know that he had always treated women with respect and implied that he was a virgin: 'I have been in all possible societies, owing to my youth and to my young head. I have been in very bad societies, but I never can reproach myself ever with having acted dishonourably.'[5] He accompanied his letter with his copy of Shakespeare's works, drawing her attention to one line:

> which is so consonant with my idea; I shall therefore put it here. It is in the Tempest, when Ferdinand, son of the King of Naples, speaks to Miranda, daughter of Prospero. He says, 'Oh! if a virgin, and your affection not gone forth, I'll make you the Queen of Naples.' These words, a little altered, my soul's delight, and they are mine. Of these two points I am convinced, and though not to be queen, yet to be wife, of thy Augustus, will make thee happy, will be my blessing.[6]

As night wore on, Augustus continued reminiscing, 'Little did I think,' he wrote, 'when first humbly employed as my Augusta's shoelatcher at the church of St. Jacomo, that I should aspire at so high a post as that of her lover and her husband, and yet that has come to pass.' He told her how he had had:

> a particular wish to make your acquaintance. I was very inquisitive when any body came from Naples, to know something about you. Ask Charles Greville if I did not question him most excessively and ask if Lady Augusta Murray then, but my Augusta now, was as merry and as lively as usual, and yet I had not seen you for many years, and was quite a child then. It was in eighty-five I saw you last, at a ball at the Queen's house. Little did I think then that that Augusta would become mine; would be my darling wife.[7]

When Augustus saw her in 1785, he was 12 and although she was then double his age her vivacity was memorable.

On Holy Saturday the Prince waited distractedly for the Reverend Mr Gunn's reply. Augusta went to the Basilica di San Giovanni in Laterano to watch a Jew being converted to Christianity, and on her return she learnt that the Prince hoped to hear from the rector the next day. Conscious that their marriage was now possible, it was her turn to be overcome with desire and she told the Prince, 'How I do adore you. How I do love you. Oh how I long, – did I say long? – I meant to say I die to kiss you; to be kissed by you; to be with you, at your knees; on your knees; prest to your heart; in short to be entirely yours; to be – oh dear I cannot tell.'[8]

After all the concerts, rites and rituals that she had witnessed in the build-up to Easter, Augusta missed the grandest Christian festival of the year. Unable to accompany her mother and sister to watch the ceremonies – high mass, papal benediction and illuminations at St Peter's – she wrote:

> Easter Day, you are come oh day! Great events have marked you memorably for man. For me too, you may be big with momentous events; Mr Gunn is to be asked to marry me to the dear, the amiable ... but I cannot write here, I must not. Oh fate what have you in reserve for me, alarmed & agitated I staid at home, alone, & anxious; everybody is gone to St Peters, to receive or to see the Pope's benediction, to see the functions, to talk of the ceremony, I stay at home to wait the decision of my destiny ... I cannot expect success, I do not deserve it, but yet, I would try to merit it, virtue, Religion, duty, aided by inclination, & the strong desire of doing right would I hope mark every day ... which I would supplicate from Heaven. I had a letter from the Prince he has not seen Mr G – & our fate is still undetermined.[9]

She spent Easter Monday with 'shadows and sorrows' clouding her mind but cheered up when Lady Templetown came for dinner. The next day, 2 April, was warm and Augusta took her first bath of the year. A lady would clean her face, hands and feet on a daily basis and her maid would sponge wash her from time to time, but immersion in a hip bath brought into the dressing room was an infrequent occurrence. Feeling refreshed and calmer, she sat down and wrote Augustus a selfless letter.

Despite their mutual promises on the Bible, if they were not married in Rome she told Augustus that he would be free of any commitment to her when he returned to England. Time, absence, and his family's opposition, 'for a father and a King may insist upon your breaking your promise' and 'new objects' might change his affections towards her. She reminded him that:

> Archibald had passionately loved me for five years, and for three of these with an ardour and assiduity I never saw surpassed, and yet I had not been six months out of England before I heard that he was going to be married to another woman. This may be your case. Younger and fairer women will court your regard, and you may detest the promise and the unfortunate receiver of it.

She reiterated her devotion to him but stated that his first duty was, after his Creator, to his father the King and to himself, and she loved him too much not to sacrifice herself. She concluded, 'I will not suffer you to feel tied to anything that may in future be disagreeable to you.'[10] This is not a letter from a grasping spinster, desperate for marriage on any terms. It is the communication of a woman in love with a young and handsome prince, concerned that he might regret his decision to marry her and not wishing to shackle him. Augustus did not listen; the only thing he wanted was to be married to his Augusta.

After a walk at the Villa Borghese later that day, Augusta learnt that the Prince had had a successful meeting with Mr Gunn. With no one to share her news, she wrote in her journal, 'what satisfaction awaited me! My beloved Treasure, I am then to call you really, my Husband, & my Lord.' Finally they had the result they wanted: somebody would marry them according to the rites of the Church of England. However, everything was not yet resolved.

While the couple wished to ensure that Mr Gunn would keep their marriage a secret, the rector, who understood the terms of the Royal Marriages Act, was equally concerned that they would never divulge his name and asked them to sign a paper to that effect. The Prince had assured him that 'nothing but the purest virtue' had passed between them and having obtained the clergyman's consent, he admitted to Augusta that 'if my conversation had not succeeded I should have had a desperate end; but every thing smiles now, my angel'.[11]

When Mr Gunn had attempted to dissuade him from his proposed marriage, Augustus nearly collapsed with emotion. The Prince vented his frustration and was so agitated that he did not remain five minutes in the same position, sometimes standing, sometimes walking about and often in tears. Although the King and Queen had treated him most graciously he said, he had not heard from the former for nearly three years and the latter for six months. All his brothers were settled in appointments while he was left without employment or purpose. The manner in which he was forced to live with overbearing gentlemen attendants, the uncertainty over the timing of his return to England and the question of his future destinations had a great effect on his spirits, which were correspondently low with his weak health. His mind was distracted and everything was made worse by his domestic ills. He confessed to William Gunn that he had several times been terrified that he might commit suicide.[12]

After this outburst, Augustus showed him their written vows of marriage and told him that he already considered Augusta as his wife. The Prince would have none other but her and could not live without her. It was quite clear to the rector that the wedding was at the Prince's instigation and that he had persuaded Augusta to comply with his wishes.[13]

The couple received a further setback. The next evening Augusta waited for the Prince as he had requested, but instead of him the rector arrived with an excuse. He gently explained to her the difficulties attending their proposed marriage and he noticed that she seemed entirely ignorant of any legal barrier. Then he told her that he neither could, nor should, marry them. After he had been shown out, worn out with worry, Augusta burst into tears and blamed the Prince for what had happened:

> All my hopes of happiness are fled; where can I fly, where can I go without misery being my constant companion; Mr Gunn will not, cannot marry us. I am lost & undone, & it is thee oh Prince, thy yielding, that drives me to despair, you would not press the man whom it was necessary to compel, you say generosity prevented you, I call it by another name; but it does not signify it equally works my misery.[14]

Unable to share the burden of secrecy with anyone else, she could not bear more disappointment and sent word to Augustus that their relationship was over. On the morning of Thursday, 4 April she was 'entirely wretched' and although a 'bright sunshine of hope' had blazed on her the day before, 'the darkest ray of despair' succeeded it. That night however, she could record that 'my lover, & my Prince came, then came a clergyman'.

13

Something Alarming Stops the Effusion of Joy

The bride and groom were denied their wedding night. Terrified of discovery, the Reverend Mr Gunn hustled away the Prince as soon as he could separate the newlyweds. Augusta, 'the happy wife of the most amiable the most honourable among men' hurried to her diary with a prayer, 'Teach me Oh Lord to deserve the favours you lavish upon me,' she wrote, '& Grant that I may ever have reason to bless this day.'[1] It was a pitiful supplication: her wedding was the start of trials from which only death would release her.

Waking the next morning, 'the first that ever shone on me as a wife', she lay in bed agonising. Alone and apprehensive, she was torn between passion for her husband and fear that their wedding was invalid. Although she and the Prince had overcome all apparent obstacles preventing them from becoming man and wife, she was aware that 'something alarming stops the effusion of joy'. What could be wrong with her? She had sworn not to disclose her marriage so all she could look back on was a rushed ceremony in her rooms when Mr Gunn was so flustered that he had omitted part of the service. She could not tell anyone that she was married and it was not in her nature to hide her emotions.

Their social circle in Rome could not fail to have noticed the relationship between Augusta and the Prince but the couple continued to meet by stealth and attended parties separately for the first few weeks after their wedding. Two days after they were married the Prince asked Augusta to go to Princess Santa Croce's party alone to avoid gossip. If they met by chance he took no notice of her, which made them both miserable. They could meet at the Hotel Sarmiento but complete privacy depended on the absence of Lady Dunmore and Virginia.

On 7 April Augusta recorded that, 'My mother dined at Mr Leighs, in the evening my Husband came to me, & staid till past ten … I need make no comments.' The next morning she wrote breathlessly, 'The Prince really became my husband.' They had waited so long and had behaved with such restraint that their longed for physical union left them both ecstatic. However, they could not enjoy the warm aftermath of conjugality. Augustus did not visit her that day 'to prevent suspicion'. A few nights later when he suggested visiting her, she regretfully begged him to stay away. It was the sad pattern of the weeks to come and the necessity of living apart, relying on clandestine meetings, was a strain. On Sunday, 14 April, having taken the sacrament in the morning, her mother and sister stayed at home so Augusta was 'dull' without a visit from her husband. 'May he ever come and may they ever go,' she admitted.

Baron Hanstein, one of the Prince's gentlemen, had become uneasy about his charge's new habits and there was a 'sad row' in his household 'about his coming to see his wife, to his Augusta, I suppose that they despise me, & call me his mistress, but time will justify me, & at present Heaven is my witness.' The baron wrote the Prince a letter full of 'remonstrances' but more significantly his suspicions trickled back to the King.

Although George III had not written to Augustus for nearly three years, his son continued to write to him fortnightly. Now married, the Prince sent his father a disingenuous communication on 13 April informing him that 'In a place like Rome one day follows another without much difference so that your Majesty can not expect from my pen, either news, or any thing entertaining'.[2] This apparently innocent missive was written on the day Augusta discovered that she was pregnant. She had conceived the first time they made love. Two days after they consummated their marriage she noted, 'I was not well, which is very odd.' Her pregnancy was difficult from the start and she suffered from prolonged bouts of sickness. While she was bound to keep her marriage and her pregnancy secret, she found it hard to join in the celebrations surrounding the marriage of Mr Dundas to Lady Jane Hope and the engagement of Lord Bruce to Miss Hill. Feeling nauseous and miserable about concealing her marriage, Augusta hoped that soon she could 'show the world I am not his mistress, & that the most holy ties have united us before we lived as man & wife'.

Now that Easter was over and the weather warmer, Lady Dunmore was planning to leave Rome but she wanted to fit in some last-minute sightseeing before their departure. Despite Augusta's indisposition, she participated in her mother's 'pergrinations', which were often lengthy and demanding.

On Thursday, 9 May they spent the whole day at St Peter's. They began by watching the Pope officiate at mass and give the benediction. They then passed through the Sala Regia 'which leads to the Sistine Chapel all painted by Michelangelo, to the Pauline Chapel' to the Sala Ducale and from thence to Raphael's three painted loggias. From there they went to the Stanze of Raphael, a suite of four apartments Raphael had decorated for Pope Julius II, on which she commented that, 'these are his most famous works, these are the paintings that have immortalised the Vatican, where all come to admire, or learn'. The one she liked most was the tripartite composition of 'St Peter being delivered out of the prison by an angel the different lights showed the great master'. The most splendid however, was the 'school of Athens, Plato & Aristotle are in the middle standing, Diogenes lying on one of the steps, Archimedes with a compass measuring, Zoroaster is there with a globe in his hand.' After touring the 'Church of St Peter' and the sacristy, she 'came home tired to dinner'. In her condition, she must have been exhausted.

Albrecht Dürer's water colour of a 'beautiful hare' enchanted her at the Palazzo Corsini and on another expedition Augusta spent an entire morning with her 'beloved Treasure' at the Palace of Titus, where the sculpture of Laocoön, sinuously wrestling with giant snakes, and the celebrated fresco, known as the Aldobrandini Marriage, had been discovered in 1506. She visited the Chiesa degli Apostoli and marvelled at the gigantic monument to Pope Clement XIV with three figures, the deceased and two mourners, by Antonio Canova, the most famous Italian sculptor since Michelangelo.

By mid-May 1793 the British Royal Family had learnt of the Prince's infatuation for Augusta and she noted sadly that, 'the Prince had letters from England which mentioned me. This made me unhappy alas it is long before I shall be talked of, & talked of honourably.' Her natural optimism returned the next day when she completed a volume of her journal by writing, 'a dear little girl, a Child of my Augustus's of my adored husband would complete my felicity … I end this book with a feeling of happiness which I have never known before at the closing of any of my journals.'

Towards the end of the month, Lady Dunmore and Virginia spent the night in Frascati, a popular retreat for wealthy Romans in the Alban Hills. The Prince and Augusta took advantage of their absence and luxuriated in a whole night of uninterrupted love. Augustus arrived soon after dinner and in their joint journal she wrote, 'Dearest Prince how happy this surprise, this early, welcome but unexpected visit made me.'[3] A few days later, Prince Augustus also went to Frascati, visiting 'the villas belonging to the Borghese family, Mondragone, Falconieri, etc', magnificent summer palaces with terraced gardens, cascades and fountains. One place not on the Prince's itinerary was the episcopal palace, the main residence of the bishop of Frascati, *soi-disant* King Henry IX of Great Britain. The bishop said later that he was sorry to have been unable to offer Prince Augustus 'civilities' because he had great respect for him.[4]

Augustus could not bear to be away from his wife for long. He returned the next day and she was ecstatic that:

> he rode from Frascati to Rome 12 miles in an hour & a quarter, but he was not fatigued, & my Antinous [Hadrian's beautiful, and significantly younger, lover] looked well; dearest soul of my soul how happy I was to see you, how I blest the welcome, the loved moment, that brought you to my arms, that pressed you to my heart. My darling Prince, my Augustus, you felt glad, you felt happy too, my Life; you kissed your wife my love as if a longer absence had divided us, and every dear kiss she returned with equal ardour, with as passionate a tenderness, with as fervent a love. At night my soul left me, but a night will come, when he need not leave me. Is it not so my treasure?

Concerned at her fragility, the Prince tried to persuade Augusta to rest. On 30 May despite her sickness, she enjoyed the Feast of Corpus Christi, the joyful festival proclaiming the Real Presence in the Eucharist of the Body of Christ. She and Augustus watched the triumphal procession of the Blessed Sacrament when the Host was paraded beneath an ornate canopy and displayed within a monstrance, or glass disc, set in a gilded cross. For the first time, she had the pleasure of walking arm in arm with her husband amongst the crowds and 'really enjoyed the satisfaction of feeling as if he liked me, when others were present.' It was a risk worth taking as it was their last day in Rome together.

That evening the Prince wrote in her journal:

> I wish thee a most happy journey … adieu dearest Augusta, adieu lovely room, adieu delicious bed all made supernatural by thy goodness to me … God bless thee my angel in a few days I shall follow thee but my heart thou takest with thee already, adieu dearest best of women the Lord be with you.

Now the Feast of Corpus Christi was concluded and the requisite sites visited, Lady Dunmore and her daughters could leave Rome en route for the Tuscan port of Leghorn, from where they would embark for England.

Augustus had hoped that his royal father would call him home before he left Rome. When no royal summons arrived, Doctor Domeier advised him to spend the summer on the shores of Lake Como, where he could await the King's instructions. Making his way north, the Prince knew that there was one more opportunity to see Augusta and he made plans to meet her in Florence.

14

My Darling was Leaving His Unhappy Wife

Despite being sick 'during the whole journey' Augusta enjoyed the drive through Tuscany, 'a most enchanting country, well cultivated & richly diversified' with olives and vines. She 'passed the Arno several times winding through beautiful hills, & seemingly a happier peasantry than those in the dominions of the Pope, where nothing, but poverty, dirt & famine met our eyes'.[1] They arrived in Florence on 4 June 1793 and rented rooms at the popular pensione run by Signora Vanini, an English widow. Lady Miller, the salon hostess, had stayed there in 1770 and described a typical apartment. It had:

> a large anti-chamber, an excellent bed-chamber within, and a room without a bed, which the French call *un cabinet de jour*, for the anti-chamber is a dining room; from the former we have a door that opens upon a terrace, with a balustrade round it, from whence is a fine view of the famous bridge [Ponte alla Carraia] with cycloid arches, the Arno, the town, etc. The apartment is hung with crimson damask, and ornamented with pictures.[2]

Normally the elegance of a well-appointed pensione in a good location would have pleased Augusta, but when she arrived at Vanini's she was disappointed 'to find that no courier had arrived to take apartments for my Prince'. Her hopes of seeing her husband were crushed and she was plagued by uncertainty and illness. William Gunn had advised the Prince not to tell Lady Dunmore about the wedding because of her 'open disposition' but the deterioration in Augusta's condition demanded a declaration.[3]

On 6 June she recorded:

> I was too unwell & my mother too anxious for me to keep longer a secret which the Prince had desired me to disclose to her, for which he had given me a letter to shew her. I gave her the letter last night. Today I hope to be more fortunate than yesterday, I hope to see my husband; alas I was born to marry my equal, to live happily with him, & not to dread each returning day.

The Prince had wanted to conceal their marriage until 'the minds of my Royal Parents as well as the public could have been prepared' but now he knew it was no longer safe to keep silent. He feared that Lady Dunmore's medicines, administered in ignorance of her daughter's condition, 'would occasion her to miscarry'.[4]

Although Augusta had been sick many times, her mother did not guess that she might be pregnant, let alone married. When asked at a later inquiry into the marriage if she had known about it beforehand, she answered with dignity and truth, 'I had not the most distant Idea of the possibility of it.'[5] Augusta's journal on her mother's response to the news of her illegal marriage and pregnancy is silent. Her husband had been uneasy on this subject and was relieved when he learnt of Lady Dunmore's reaction:

> I love her most sincerely because she has a good heart, that she is a good mother and above all that she is fond of my wife, her generous conduct on this occasion has filled me with gratitude she says … my angel that she will love me if I love you then let her love me for I love thee more than anything in the world.[6]

The Prince arrived in Florence with fond memories of the winter of 1789 when he had been a guest of the Grand Duke of Tuscany. When an invitation from Lord Hervey, George III's envoy at the Tuscan court, prevented Augustus from visiting his wife, her insecurity brought on an outpouring of self-pity:

> Oh Prince! if you yield to the impressments of a Lord Hervey when he wishes to keep you from your wife, what has she not to dread, from a

> Father, a King, a Brother, a whole family, & a whole train of allurements will beset you. The reflexion is too melancholy. I can write no more.

In the event Augustus did manage to see her that evening and the next two but by 10 June she was so unwell she thought that she might lose the baby. The doctor advised bed rest and she wrote peevishly, 'I wish I was well, I do not like Florence. I was sorry to spend my evening alone.' Usually an energetic tourist, she was confined to a stuffy apartment. The Prince's departure for Bologna on 14 June, en route for Lake Como, did not improve her mood. Her indisposition and apprehension for the future made her jealous and grudgingly she wished her husband happiness 'except what is found in the society of women'.

Feeling stronger a few days later, she visited Piazza della Santissima Annunziata, where she saw Andrea della Robbia's sky blue enamels, each featuring a swaddled baby, in the arcades. That evening she was surprised by a visit from her uncle, Lord Archibald Hamilton, and her cousin, Alexander, who called at Vanini's bringing her a letter from the Prince. It contained news of a royal command that both astonished and frightened her: the King had ordered his son to return home 'by water' immediately. All her petty concerns were cast aside. What could the letter mean? Was it good or bad news and, most importantly, how much did the King know?

While Augusta was subsumed by myriad questions, Augustus was overjoyed. After eight years on the Continent, he was going home. The letters he had dutifully sent to his father had borne fruit and now he had proof that he not been forgotten. He responded gladly, 'Never, never was I more agreeably surprised than with the arrival of Count Munster who brought me the long wished for order of returning home accompanied with one of the most gracious letters from your Majesty which I ever received.'[7] Retracing his steps, Augustus hurried back to Florence to finalise his travel arrangements.

On 20 June Augusta 'spent a very happy day with the Treasure of my soul, he seemed glad to go to England', which consoled her for 'this unexpected event'. Although nervous, she acknowledged that, 'if he is pleased, & he has no regrets I can have none'. The next day she was much happier and could write, 'My days flow happily, & evenly I see my Prince constantly,' but on 23 June the Prince 'received a letter from the King which changed his plans, which lowered his spirits'.

Augustus spent several hours with her before he departed at eight o'clock in the morning on 28 June. Pretence was no longer necessary with Lady Dunmore and as the Prince and Augusta lay in bed together, they prayed that the King or Parliament would grant them an independent establishment. As the sun rose above the hills surrounding Florence, it glinted on the River Arno below and Augustus bid his Augusta a sad farewell. They thought that they would not meet again until they were reunited in England. How would the King acknowledge his son's adored wife, and how would he take the news that his son had married one of his subjects and that she was already with child? What would the future hold for his yet unrecognised spouse?

When the Prince left, Augusta was still laid up. The Tuscan summer was increasingly oppressive and she was so overcome with the heat that Lady Dunmore was obliged to change their apartment. While the countess and Virginia dined with William Beckford, who was also staying in Florence, and attended a ball given by Lord Hervey, Augusta was too ill to attend either occasion. On the first day of July she wrote unhappily that she was 'sick all morning & very unwell killed with heat, & ennue, I detest Florence now that my Prince has left it'. There was nothing to detain her in the city of Michelangelo, the birthplace of Dante and the home of the Medici. She left on 6 July 'without any regrets, as soon as the heat was sufficiently allayed to travel, which was about 8 o'clock in the evening'.

Lady Dunmore's carriage, transported from England, was unsuitable for midsummer journeys in Italy. Generously upholstered with leather and silk to withstand the chills and damps of England, its lack of ventilation would have made it unbearable in Tuscany, where temperatures reached 100°F. Darkness was the only feasible time to travel; even then the carriage was stifling because the Murrays subscribed to the belief that a 'through air should never be suffered; if on one side the coach glass should be down, the other should be up'.[8] Augusta was also suffering from 'costiveness' (constipation), which she thought was caused by the acidity of Italian wines, and 'in some measure from the agitation of the body in travelling', rather than her pregnancy and the lack of exercise.[9] After spending two nights on the road, they arrived in Leghorn, where Lord Archibald and Alexander Hamilton joined them. Augusta was returning to England as she had set out, in the company of Uncle Archibald.

In 1793 the population of Leghorn was 40,000, including a Jewish community of 18,000 and the families of forty British mercantile agents. One of the Mediterranean's chief ports, Leghorn was originally built as a profitable source of income for the Grand Dukes of Tuscany and its defences were critical to the protection of Pisa. On the landside the Fortezza Nuova protected the town, while on the seaside, the Fortezza Vecchia, a picturesque tower rising above the massive brick walls of the harbour, safeguarded the quays and warehouses. Like an avuncular arm, the great mole, or breakwater, defended the waterfront and a few days after their arrival, Lord Archibald took them 'a rowing round the Mola'. They might have been surprised to learn that Sir Robert Dudley, the son of Queen Elizabeth's favourite, was credited with designing it while he was in exile in Florence at the beginning of the seventeenth century.[10]

The busy port intrigued Augusta. European and Levantine merchants thronged the quays, where shipping from many nations jostled for a berth. She watched slaves loading Tuscan wines, olive oil and anchovies onto ships destined for faraway peoples and she admired the Duke's galleys lying nearby in a smaller haven. Inland there was a fine piazza and a small canal district called *Venezia*. The exteriors of the best houses, built on marble thoroughfares, were painted with scenes from the Grand Duke's marine victories over the Turks. Leghorn was an agreeable place, which was just as well because the length of time that Augusta had to spend there nearly drove her mad.

On 14 July she was 'wakened early by the report of the guns belonging to the nasty French frigate commemorating the annual revolution of their Republic'. When Augusta arrived in Leghorn, France had been at war with Britain for five months, which necessitated a naval convoy for their journey. The wait for a convoy would be lengthy but they made what plans they could by going 'on board several ships, & and fixed upon the *Constantine*', a 289-ton merchant ship, to take them home.

A 16-mile canal, dug for the convenient passage of merchandise, connected Leghorn with Pisa, where Prince Augustus awaited his ship. When not detained by Lord Hervey, he managed to visit his 'dearest Goosy'. In the middle of July he was troubled to receive a letter from his father dated 20 May, entirely different in tone from the first friendly one he had received. Infuriated, Augustus believed that one of his gentlemen had informed the King about his relationship with Lady Augusta. He was however, sure that when his father wrote the letter, nobody except the two protagonists and Mr Gunn knew that he was married.

The Prince's reply to his royal father, signed 'Your Majesty's most dutiful affect though afflicted son, Augustus Frederick', is one of the most poignant letters he ever wrote:

> What can be the cause of this God knows, who can have dared to ruin a son in the opinion of his father, a father who has constantly been so kind and good to me? ... Your Majesty has been pleased to signify your intention for me to enter the Church, but alas I [am] no more fit for this career, neither my health, nor the present style of life I have observed, permits of it. This confession I fear will do me harm but rather would I starve than enter a career which I could not maintain with dignity. There was a time when I most fervently wished for it, two years ago even I wrote to your Majesty on the subject, circumstances no doubt prevented me from getting then an answer, neither had I a right to expect one, I could only propose, but after a silence of more than two years all hopes seemed to me to have disappeared. As much as it was my wish then to enter into it, and as fit as I then felt myself, as little do I now. Your Majesty could not wish me to adopt any measure that might bring discredit, as this certainly would, not being able to act up to strictness of character, which is at all times requisite in so sacred a profession and particularly so at this moment.[11]

The circumstances of the Prince's marriage altered his previous choice of ecclesiastical employment but he could not enlighten the King. If George III had allowed his son to come home two years earlier to pursue a career in the Church, Augusta Murray's place in history might have been limited to a single line in the Dunmore family tree. As she does not mention the King's letter in her journal, it appears that Augustus did not alarm her with its contents.

Joseph Farington, the gossipy diarist and painter, on hearing the rumour that Augusta was pregnant, stated that the Countess of Dunmore chased the Prince to different places in Italy and when the danger and impropriety were pointed out, she seemed insensible. However, we now know that Augustus had intended to spend the summer on Lake Como when his father's command altered his itinerary. The Murray ladies had always planned to embark at Leghorn. They did not go out of their way to pursue the Prince but encountered him in Florence and Leghorn, two places through which both parties had to pass on their way back to England.

At the same time as uneasy relations were ensuing between the Prince and his father, Augusta had a disagreement with Lady Dunmore. On 21 July she wrote, 'I was very wretched all day owing to a conversation I had with my mother.' Augusta's relationship with the countess was generally excellent but the words they exchanged that day made her miserable. Charlotte Dunmore was warm and light-spirited but the news of her daughter's illegal wedding must have shocked her. She fretted about Augusta's unremitting sickness and as the pregnancy became more visible, Lady Dunmore was anxious to set sail at the earliest opportunity. While she remained apparently single, Augusta's condition – soon to become obvious – would compromise her reputation irrevocably. Every day they were detained in Leghorn waiting for the convoy increased the strain between mother and daughter. No wonder that Lady Dunmore was at best harassed and, at worst, thoroughly bad-tempered.

The relationship with her mother might have been tense but while Augusta was in Leghorn, the Prince fell more deeply in love with her. Enchanted by her presence, he spent as much time as possible with her the week before he left for England. He savoured his unfamiliar intimacy with a woman and took delight in watching his wife at her dressing table, writing in her journal on 30 July: 'I came to my dearest Goosy who was just got out of bed and dressing her hair.'

Augusta saw the Prince for the last time on 2 August when he breakfasted by her bedside before boarding his ship, HMS *Aquilon*. The next day she wrote sorrowfully:

> At five I rose to see whether a wind was risen that would carry my soul's delight from me … alas a breeze which they called favourable, swelled the sails of the *Aquilon*, & my darling was leaving his unhappy wife: at ten yesterday he bid me adieu; at ten today I saw, bordering the horizon the vessel that conveyed him on whom my hopes of future happiness rest.

When Augusta heard the gunfire celebrating the birth of the Grand Duchess's daughter, she bitterly contrasted her own situation with that of the new mother. The ducal birth prompted her to write, 'My Treasure I have wished your child to be a girl, but as a boy might more resemble you my wishes are divided, my husband told me that we were to have sailed today but alas it is again put off.' Her hopes were raised when

Captain Vashon, the commander of their convoy of sixty-seven ships, offered them his barge and requested them to board the *Constantine*. As Augusta noted dolefully, the convoy would 'terribly retard' their voyage, but it was the lack of wind that initially prevented them from setting sail and a 'calm, a sad calm' kept them within sight of Leghorn. Augusta's boredom was offset by visits from Captain Vashon himself, who had taken part in the American War of Independence, and Captain Troubridge of HMS *Castor*.

Two days later they had made little progress and she wrote, 'No change in our situation, scarcely opposite to the Island of Gorgona, & quite unwell. – I am very sorry to be here but I trust that an end will be found to these ennuis.' Apart from the lack of wind, some merchant shipping from Leghorn, due to join them, was slow to join the convoy. On Saturday, 10 August, after five weeks' frustration and delay in Legorn, a 'wind perfectly good brought us before Genoa'. The fair wind had not come a moment too soon but they were obliged to anchor outside Genoa while Captain Troubridge went into port to bring out more merchantmen.

The four-month journey to Falmouth was tortuous; Augusta was becoming larger every day and, like everyone else on board, she was frustrated by the delays. She was perpetually sick, possibly caused by hyperemesis gravidarum, and her condition was cruelly exacerbated when she was at sea. Overriding every practical consideration was fear and her apprehension increased as she drew closer to England, where she would arrive visibly pregnant and apparently single.

15

I Hope Never Again to Set My Foot in a Ship

Detained outside Genoa waiting for the second merchant fleet, the convoy could not take advantage of the friendly breeze and once more Augusta's desire to proceed was thwarted. The *Constantine*, bobbing about on the Ligurian Sea, stayed firmly at anchor; by the evening the wind had dropped, it was 'perfectly still' and Augusta 'had no other resource than submitting patiently to inevitable destiny'. Marooned at sea, she recalled the hot days the family had spent on the York River, where they had taken refuge from the Virginian rebels in the summer of 1775. Now in 1793, becalmed beneath a similarly blazing sun, Augusta was four months pregnant and she sweltered in her cabin, loosening her stays. Worse than the heat and the discomfort, however, was her fear of the future.

Every evening she exercised by walking up and down the deck but the view of Genoa soon lost its charm. After three days, Captain Troubridge returned with a merchant fleet that swelled the convoy to more than 100 ships. Everybody on board the *Constantine* welcomed the strong wind that blew up on 15 August and allowed the ship to continue. There were constant reminders that Britain was at war with France. Approaching the French coast later that day, Augusta heard continuous firing at some distance before they passed two English frigates and came up to four men-of-war – Admiral Cosby's squadron going to refill its water supply at Genoa – and about six in the evening they came within sight of Lord Hood's 'grand fleet' off the Isle of Marguerite.[1] At the outbreak of war, Samuel Hood, Rear Admiral and friend of Horatio Nelson, had been appointed commander-in-chief in the Mediterranean and was charged with maintaining British supremacy there while keeping the French naval base at Toulon under observation.[2] Sailing along the enemy shore, Augusta was not soothed by the knowledge that they were in more danger then than they would be at any other point on their journey.

With Lord Hood heading their convoy and aided by favourable winds, they made some progress. Passing Nice, Antibes and several other French towns, they noticed the Tree of Liberty, festooned with tricolour rosettes, erected on the fortresses. Approaching Toulon in some trepidation, they had an unexpected and most welcome encounter. At about one o'clock the convoy came up with three ships of the line: *Romney*, *Colossus* and *Robust*. Each captain 'came on board to see us' Augusta noted cheerfully and she rejoiced to see that one of them was her kinsman, George Elphinstone. Lady Anne Keith, the first wife of Lady Dunmore's father, and George's grandmother had been sisters. The merry gathering aboard the *Constantine* and Captain Paget's reassuring news that Prince Augustus was near Barcelona, safe off the shores of Spain, was a tonic. Moreover, there was a possibility of seeing him in Gibraltar.

All three ladies were seasick in 'the terrible Gulf of Lyons' but the passage along the Spanish coast was aided by 'a very fair, but very strong wind' and they sped along with views of the hills of Granada to their right. On 2 September they reached Gibraltar. Captured during the War of the Spanish Succession in 1704, it was Britain's only naval base in the Mediterranean and thus of great significance. Terminating the flat promontory ahead, the precipitous rock was a spectacular sight, shooting up to a height of nearly 1,400ft. As they entered the Bay of Algeciras and sailed past the mole into the harbour, the sight of union flags flying over the town was comforting. Augusta looked up at the garrison clustered at the base of the natural fortress: everything there was under British rule, presided over by a British governor, and she knew that she was safe. Waiting to disembark, she watched British warships taking on water, beef and barrels of rum and hoped that Augustus would still be there.

He had departed but had left 'a dear long packet, the history of his days since the one on which he left his lonely Augusta' to console her. She had no time to brood because the moment they were settled in their hotel, they received a succession of visitors. First, General Sir Robert Boyd, the elderly Governor, then the Lieutenant Governor, General O'Hara, paid their respects. Once engaged to Horace Walpole's friend, Mary Berry, who was young enough to be O'Hara's daughter, he had remained a bachelor and now kept two mistresses on the Rock. He had been second in command at the surrender of Yorktown and was delighted to meet the family of the last royal governor of Virginia.

Despite her disappointment at missing her spouse, Augusta enjoyed her stay in Gibraltar. The company of women was at a premium in the garrison and the Murrays were warmly welcomed. On two evenings the Countess of Dunmore gave a *Thé* at their hotel when 'officers, Generals, & Colonels came'. Sir Robert Boyd had recently lost his wife and invited Lady Dunmore and her daughters to dine on two consecutive nights at the Convent, the governor's residence on Main Street. Augusta liked her host but her enjoyment at the first of his dinners on 3 September was spoilt by news from Paris.

She learnt 'with infinite horror, that the unfortunate Queen of France ... had been put to death the 10th of last August'. Utterly appalled, she wondered what might British subjects, when provoked, do to their monarch and his family? She also heard 'with regret that Charlotte Corder her that had killed Marat was guillotined' but was heartened to hear 'that the aristocrats of Toulon had opened the gates of that port to Ld Hood'. In the name of Louis XVII of France, Hood had replaced the hated tricolour with the ancient white flag of the French monarchy. Soon afterwards Marseilles followed Toulon's example. There was further good news when Lord Archibald Hamilton arrived in Gibraltar on 6 September and took up residence with them. He had travelled on a different ship from Leghorn and to everybody's relief agreed to accompany them on board the *Constantine* thereafter.

On 12 September Augusta recorded that 'my little thing begins to move a great deal' and that she was frequently unwell. When Sir Robert Boyd held a handsome ball in their honour she regretted that at five months pregnant she was too big to dance. Visits to the Convent were not only for social purposes: the King's Chapel next door was the garrison church and for the first time since she left England Augusta attended divine service in an Anglican place of worship.

Their stay coincided with the anniversary of a spectacular incident in Gibraltar's recent history. During the American War of Independence, the Spanish joined the campaign against the British and besieged Gibraltar, menacing the Rock by land and sea. In an enemy offensive on 13 September

1782 the British succeeded in destroying a line of specially constructed floating batteries, blowing up two of them and setting fire to the rest. On 'the day annually kept' Augusta watched a firework display, which seemed a wholly appropriate commemoration of the events eleven years earlier.

General O'Hara also arranged a 'charming ball' in the Murrays' honour but Augusta was again unwell. However, she attended another engagement the kindly soldier put on for them: a picnic on the mainland. Rowing across the bay, they landed at Algeciras and drove to San Roque, a typical Andalusian village of whitewashed houses with clay-tiled roofs. They dined in a sweet-smelling and 'angelic orange grove' nearby, where Augusta saw spiny aloe succulents, cork trees, prickly pears and 'many other productions of these hotter climates, which care can hardly preserve in England'. They 'returned late at night by water, a beautiful moon, & an unclouded heaven rendered the scene enchanting'. On 18 September the easterly wind, the *Viento de Levante*, began to blow and Captain Vashon asked them to prepare to embark if it persisted the next day. It did not persist. The wind became westerly and their stay in Gibraltar continued.

Augusta wrote up her diary while she waited: 'we walked, we lounged about, we regretted the being detained at Gibraltar, & I wrote to my loved Prince'. They visited the parade ground and took a carriage ride around the Rock, where she 'was extremely charmed with the wildness & grandeur of the various scenes'. One evening they went to Europa Point, Gibraltar's southerly tip. A week after the Levante had teased them with hopes of departure, Captain Vashon sent instructions to prepare to embark immediately as the wind was fair. Relieved to be on the move, Augusta made a final note in her journal, 'Just as we were setting off arrived, the *Egmont* & the *Terrible* line of battle ships, & the *Isis* frigate from Toulon to carry away the different regiments ordered from Gibraltar; they carried news of a great army of republicans marching from Marseilles.' Subdued by the news of the mustering of the French Army, they left the Rock after a three-week stay 'with some degree of regret'.

The Levante swept the *Constantine* through the Straits of Gibraltar into the Atlantic Ocean and after a rough passage, during which they were 'most extremely ill', the Murrays sailed into the Bay of Cadiz on 27 September. The town itself was situated on a low rocky peninsula that projected 5 miles into the sea and caught the cooling breezes. Watchtowers on top of the merchants' houses vied with the domed cathedral and numerous churches on the skyline. The citizens of Cadiz took the evening air on the roofs of their tall limestone houses, designed around inner courtyards, which were paved with marble. There were two theatres, one for French comedy and one for the Spanish classics, as well as an Italian opera house. It had a population of 80,000 and at first Augusta was happy there. She was 'much pleased with the cleanliness of the streets, the situation of the town & the dress of the common people', although she was 'too ill to go about in the morning'. Augusta noted that following the custom of southern Spain, ladies were veiled when they went out.

New faces and acquaintances were always welcome in Cadiz and its small expatriate community was pleased to receive Lady Dunmore and her daughters. On their first day they went to a play and visited the *Alameda*, the principal avenue and place of public promenade. Arthur Gordon, a hospitable and wealthy old man, who liked to entertain visiting Scots, invited them to supper, a light meal, which often included a warming drink and soup, taken late in the evening around 10.30 p.m. Gordon was an exile from the battle of Culloden and ran a successful sherry business. That evening, desiring to please his three guests, he arranged several displays of a new Spanish dance, the bolero, which was performed in national costume. Augusta was fascinated by this relatively slow dance accompanied by guitars and castanets, but did not admire it as much as the south Italian tarantella. The next night they 'went to the opera where the famous Count O'Reilly came to be presented to us; il est disgracié de [sorte] que son pouvoir n'est plus grand, mais il inspire encore de la curiosité.' An Irishman in the service of Spain, Alexander O'Reilly had had a colourful army career including an unsuccessful invasion of Algiers for which he was disgraced but he was soon to be appointed commander of the base at Toulon to assist the monarchists.[3] He was a former governor of Cadiz and had initiated a number of projects, like the rubbish collection, that made the town so pleasant. Augusta was not well enough to accompany her mother and Virginia to Jerez to see the sherry bodegas; instead she dined with O'Reilly's wife, the patrician Spaniard, Rosa de las Casas. They promenaded in the *Alameda* and went 'from thence to a concert attended by Mr Duff', the British Consul, and the captains of her convoy. She came home 'much tired & glad to go to bed'.

To her annoyance, a 'perfectly unfair wind' detained her in Cadiz. On 1 October the wind had not changed but a visit from 'all the Spanish Admirals and Commanders' relieved the waiting, although they brought disquieting news that the French had taken one of their frigates. Augusta was too sick to visit the island 'where they keep their dock yards' but when her mother returned that evening they 'all went to a Thé, & supper at Mr Gordon's; in short to what the Spanish call a _Tourtoulia_ & the Italians a *conversazione'*.

The day after, having spent a week in Cadiz, she left 'with infinite pleasure'. The convoy now comprised 130 ships but on 6 October Augusta wrote laconically that the *Constantine* 'parted with our fleet determined to run it at all risks & reach England as soon as possible'. Their captain's decision to cut loose and proceed without protection as they approached the French coast appears inexplicable. The Bay of Biscay however, is notoriously stormy and perhaps he reckoned that a scattered convoy was worse than useless and that they had nothing to lose.

Initially their journey continued without incident. 'Days are not worth recording,' Augusta wrote, 'that are past in expectation of fair winds which do not arrive, suffice it to say that we past the Bay of Biscay.' It seemed that they were over the worst but on 11 October as they neared 'the chops of the Channel', an easterly wind rose up and swept them off course to the Scilly Isles. Eventually a light wind blew them into the Channel on 20 October, an 'angelic day', and Augusta was overjoyed to be near England. Boats from the island of St Mary's sold them provisions but after the boats left they 'were becalmed & our Capt was apprehensive that a lugger in sight, & which seemed to be chasing us, was a Frenchman'. On the morrow, 'a most terrible day of alarms', the *Constantine* was chased by a French frigate and 'a dreadful calm prevented our flying'. To everyone's relief, the vessel 'altered her course & seemed to steer for the French coast ... heaven protected us & [we] were not taken'. It had been a close call.

Augusta could now see the shores of England, 'that land where I have known every sentiment that the heart can feel; which I left with such reluctance, & to which I return within this hated ship.' Lying off Falmouth waiting for their bill of health, they learnt that the French had also had the temerity to menace HMS *Blonde* close to Falmouth. Captain Markham had been chased by three French ships and only escaped 'after heaving over board her anchors, provisions, & every weighty thing'.

Augusta's trials were not yet over. The weather was terrible, she was still being sick and the bill of health had not appeared. In the newspapers brought to her on board she read that Augustus was with the King and

Queen. She grew impatient and wretched, hoping that he would do her justice and 'not let an ignorant world condemn her'.

On Monday, 28 October 1793 after frustrations of every kind, ill winds and unremitting sickness, Augusta disembarked at Falmouth. She had waited outside port for a week but at last the boat 'arrived with our bill of health, a more welcome leave, we never received, we left the *Constantine* with infinite pleasure, & I hope never again to set my foot in a ship'.

In the late eighteenth century the status of an unmarried mother was unenviable and, as so often at pivotal moments in her life, she turned to heaven for comfort. Stepping onto the wet quay, she begged her God, 'Oh my maker let me on my landing raise my voice in prayer … now that I am arrived in England, let me not find myself an object of scorn & contempt; let the Prince do me justice; & Oh my Saviour bless me and my baby.' Her request however, went unheeded.

Part II

16

Dear London

Augusta had been uneasy ever since she left Rome but now that she was in England she was panic-stricken. She was right to be apprehensive. To her consternation, a chance encounter with Lady Anne Fitzroy in Falmouth made it clear that Augusta and the Prince had been the subject of London gossip. If the King accepted her as his daughter-in-law and their child as legitimate, the future for Princess Augustus Frederick as a respected member of the Royal Family was full of promise. If not, she faced lasting dishonour and disgrace.

The journey from Falmouth to London took them eleven days. Leaving Truro on 30 October, a 'melancholy day', they drove through 'dreary country' to Bodmin.[1] From there they continued to Launceston, which Augusta considered 'an ancient ugly town where a ruined castle stands on a proud eminence & commands a fine prospect, through a wild & beautiful country partly in Cornwall & partly in Devonshire'. At Okehampton they slept 'in a nasty town & a more nasty inn; the weather making both still appear more nasty'. Happily, Exeter was an improvement: she was 'charmed with every varied scene' and she dined and slept well. She admired Glastonbury Abbey ruins, was struck by Wells Cathedral and on 4 November arrived in Bath, 'much increased' in size since her last visit. After Devizes, Marlborough, and Newbury, they reached Maidenhead, where Susan awaited them. Augusta was overjoyed to see her sister, who was also expecting a baby.

Views of Windsor Castle provoked mixed emotions; Augusta longed for her 'dear Prince, felt happy though unwell' and at the same time 'extremely anxious'. After a change of horses in Hounslow, their coach finally drew up at 16 Lower Berkeley Street. The journey from Italy had been exasperating, lengthy and enervating; Augusta had embarked at Leghorn in the August heat and three months later she reached 'dear London'. While her future was uncertain, at last she was home.

That autumn all talk in the capital had been of the war with the French Republic. Although Toulon was still in British hands, the campaign to wrest Dunkirk from French privateers menacing British ships in the Channel was going badly. At the same time French Royalists in exile in England were offended by the refusal of Prime Minister William Pitt to recognise the son of Louis XVI as the rightful King of France, and a month before Augusta's arrival, King George III had called the French to rally behind the standard of a hereditary monarchy.

When Prince Augustus arrived on 22 September at Spithead, the eastern entrance to Portsmouth harbour, he was the only one of the King's sons to be unemployed in the services. A thoughtless letter from his brother, William, had informed him that the Prince of Wales commanded his own Regiment of Light Dragoons and Frederick, Duke of York, was leading the British troops on the Continent, where Ernest and Adolphus were also engaged. Edward was on his way to the West Indies with troops from America, and William himself, the only one in the Royal Navy, was soon to serve with Lord Howe in the home fleet.[2]

Meanwhile, his sisters were compelled to be dutiful daughters, shuttling back and forth with their parents between Windsor and London, and it was with them that Augustus spent most of his time. Waiting for an appropriate moment, he longed to disclose his marriage and imminent fatherhood to the King, but he knew that the timing of his revelation was critical. Augustus felt superfluous and with time on his hands he ensured that a packet of love letters awaited Augusta on her return.

Until he could disclose his marriage, his strategy for his wife over the coming weeks relied on Lady Dunmore's cooperation:

> Were I to tell you, my amiable Augusta, that your arrival in England had made me happy, would not be saying enough; it is something more than that. It is a superlative blessing ... My mind is not accustomed to deception; but if we wish to work for futurity we must carry on the deception for some months longer ... You must desire Lady Dunmore, if she loves me, to conceal her arrival as much as possible; to see very few people in

> London, and you none at all, for fear of a discovery; and then, while she goes into the country, I will contrive your coming here; but my dearest Augusta, you must not expect to see much of me, except in the afternoon; for in the first place my mornings are entirely taken up with my sisters, and, secondly, if I were to come to thee during the day, you might be found out.[3]

The Royal Family's residence at Windsor prevented him from paying her an immediate visit, and he had to wait for 'a favourable opportunity' before he could see her. Greatly relieved to receive his 'very charming' letter – she needed constant reassurance – Augusta sent their Roman servant, Monticelli, to Windsor with her reply, resigned herself to further delay and settled down to a quiet life in Mayfair.

Susan was living with them and relayed all the family news. Jack had recently been made Master and Commander of the fourteen-gun HMS *Weazel* and was going to Lisbon. Leveson had entered the Madras Civil Service and George was looking after the family's Scottish affairs. Her father would not return from the Bahamas for another two years, but it appears that Augusta had told him about her marriage and he had responded sympathetically because a letter from 'dear Father', awaiting her return, greatly pleased her. Aunt Euphemia was also let into the secret; otherwise her door was 'shut to everyone'.

After a week at home, she began to feel lonely. She had been away for more than a year and longed to see her friends but, as instructed by Augustus, she 'saw nobody'. She admitted to herself that she liked 'society however I do this to obey my Prince, *et cela me console*'. She was obliged to stay at home to conceal her 'situation from a curious world, & an angry King'. Susan and Euphemia were welcome companions, two windows onto the outside world from which she was barred. She had received a letter from Aunt Susanna but when she came to call, Augusta stayed upstairs.

The Prince's letter of 14 November described family discord at Windsor. He had confided in his favourite sister, Princess Elizabeth, and told her of his plan to go abroad, which would benefit his health and allow him to live with Augusta and their child. He reported to his wife:

> There has been of late much ill-blood in the family here, which quite kills me. I see that matters are coming to a crisis, which makes me desire to

> get away, but nothing relative to my departure is as yet settled … Lisbon seems to me most favourable, as it is so much nearer for you … I have never openly spoken to any one on the subject. The only person I have talked to at times about it, and without mentioning any thing particular, is my sister Elizabeth, who told me, that whatever might happen she would not forsake me … If I can keep Elizabeth and Sophia my friends that is all I can desire or do desire; for they are the only ones who are sincerely attached to me … the others change according to the wind … Your arrival, you know, stood in the newspapers, so that the Queen was informed … and I understand she said to Elizabeth, 'I see it is not over, by the agitation Augustus is in' and there she was right, because I was excessively miserable at the moment, not knowing where you were.[4]

Tuesday, 19 November was a dull day. Augusta settled some bills, 'aired, & longed to do something more'. Her sickness was persisting and although in the eighth month of her pregnancy, she was still unwell. The next day, for the first time since they had parted nearly four months before, she was united with Augustus and wrote happily, 'I record the morning & evening of this day, both were spent with my loved Prince … I hope he loves me, I am sure I love him.' She had much to tell him of delays, ill winds, Gibraltar, Cadiz and being chased by the French. He spent the next night with her and left for Windsor in the morning.

On 30 November Augustus was unable to come to her so she went to Windsor and at eight months pregnant it was an uncomfortable journey. To avoid detection, she hired a hackney chaise under the assumed name of Mrs Maxwell. Travelling out of London on the Bath Road, she dined alone at Cranford Bridge near Staines 'but the solitude of the dinner was well made up to me, by the agreeable tête à tête' in the evening with her husband. Augustus was forced to admit that he had not made any progress with informing his father about their marriage.

On the first day of December Augusta:

> rose, & remembered with surprise that I was a Mrs Maxwell at Windsor, that I was separated from my family, & not owned by any other; not that I repine at my situation, as long as my Prince is good to me, & does not repent the having made me his wife … My morning was spent alone; my husband is the son of a King, & I must submit to the absences his

> situation may require, in the evening he drank tea with me, & at night paid his Augusta another visit.

She spent a solitary morning reading 'a stupid novel', *Memoirs of Mary*, in which the author, Susannah Gunning, attempted to clear the names of her daughter and herself from accusations of attempting to entrap the Marquess of Blandford into marriage. It was however, Augusta's cousin, Lady Susan Stewart, who eventually married Blandford and Augusta rejoiced at her cousin's luck. Putting aside her book that evening, she was delighted to see the Prince, who 'stayed with her till the too near approach of the morning might have made it dangerous for him to have been seen returning to the Castle'. The next day she left for London, where she trusted that 'a fortunate event will take place that must quiet all the fears & anxieties of my family'. The fortunate event she referred to was her second marriage.

Lady Dunmore had become as agitated as her daughter during the *Constantine*'s passage to Falmouth, but she hoped to secure both the reputation of her daughter and the legitimacy of her unborn grandchild by persuading Augusta to be remarried in London. The countess was rightly concerned that the wedding in Rome, with neither certificate nor witnesses, would not be recognised. Augusta was happy to comply with her mother's wishes, although she regarded the Roman ceremony as binding and could not believe that any earthly power, however elevated, could divide what God had joined together. Indeed, her innocent faith in the validity of both of her weddings was to cause her unhappiness for the rest of her life and the wellspring of her resentment never ran dry.

Lady Dunmore persuaded Augusta to start making arrangements for the second wedding the moment she arrived in England. The countess knew that organising a secret ceremony in London with a Prince of the Blood would be difficult and with Augusta's baby due in the New Year, time was short. Augusta chose to be remarried at St George's, Hanover Square, which was situated in the neighbouring parish across Oxford Street. However, if she and the Prince rented the lodgings in South Molton Street kept by Mr and Mrs Jones, both loyal servants of the family, the bride and groom could be said to be 'of this parish'.

Therefore, on her first night in England Augusta had written to Mary Jones, her dressmaker, telling her that she would like to take the rooms for herself and a Mr Frederick, a private gentleman from Devonshire. Augusta was pleased with the pseudonym because there was a Sir John Frederick living in the parish, who, as far as the church authorities were concerned, might have a relation named Augustus. In the same letter, Augusta had asked Mrs Jones to find her sister, Susan, and come with her to meet them in Maidenhead where she could impart further instructions, unsuitable for communication by post.[5]

When they met in Maidenhead, Mrs Jones was astonished to see that Lady Augusta was pregnant and was even more surprised when Augusta asked her to deliver a notice of marriage to the clerk at St George's, and impressed on her that no time should be lost before the banns were read on the next three Sundays.[6] Back in London, Mrs Jones called at the house of the church clerk, Mr Caleb Greville, but he was out. Impressed by Lady Augusta's need for urgency, Mrs Jones asked the girl to whom she delivered the notice whether renting her South Molton Street lodgings would make the bride and groom parishioners. Receiving an affirmative answer, she hurried back to Lower Berkeley Street.

Two days after visiting the clerk's house, Mrs Jones heard the first reading of the banns of 'Mr Augustus Frederick' and 'Miss Augusta Murray' at St George's. Mary Jones attended the church on the next two Sundays and on 24 November Augusta could tell Augustus, 'the banns of our marriage were published today for the third and last time, dear Prince, I hope it will please you as much as it does me to find that we are safe; & may be properly married in England.' Everything was settled before Augusta's final visit to the Prince in Windsor before the wedding; it had all been done in record time with Augusta's customary efficiency.

The second marriage ceremony on Thursday, 5 December 1793, like the first, was a shoddy affair. Mrs Jones left South Molton Street before dawn. No one fashionable was out so early and it was still dark when she crossed Oxford Street and headed north towards Manchester Square. When she turned into Lower Berkeley Street there was a Hackney carriage waiting outside number 16.

Going through the mews, she entered the house. Lady Dunmore was upstairs helping Augusta to dress and when the bride appeared at the top of the stairs Mrs Jones had difficulty hiding her disappointment. Lady Augusta should have dazzled on her wedding day but she came down dressed in a plain linen gown with a white veil.[7] Mary Jones recalled the gorgeous gowns she had stitched for Augusta over the years: overskirts of silk and taffeta, petticoats of satin and brocade, fine lace fichus, dresses for court, cloaks she had lined with fur against the winter cold and wide-brimmed hats, topped with ostrich feathers and festooned with ribbons. Finally she remembered the wardrobe she had made for Lady Augusta's visit to Paris in 1787. It was a dismal comparison with what Mrs Jones now saw: an unadorned and heavily pregnant bride descending the stairs slowly and carefully. A footman was ready with Augusta's black cloak and just before eight o'clock she turned back, bade her mother farewell, and Mary Jones followed her onto the street.

17

I Was Again Married

Dawn was breaking as they arrived at Hanover Square. Augusta and Mrs Jones walked up the church steps and through the portico into the vestibule, where a veiled figure wearing a white gown was waiting in the darkness. Aunt Euphemia had come to support her niece at the most important assignation of her life. It was a typically selfless act because, by attending Augusta's wedding, her aunt was breaking the law.

The bride was wracked with nerves: if the Prince were detained, their secret might be discovered and the wedding called off. Even worse, she feared that he might have second thoughts and stay away, but Augustus kept his word. He was dressed as plainly as possible in a brown great coat, 'like a Common Shopkeeper',[1] and the officiating curate later commented that the Prince and Augusta 'were not all distinguished by their Dress from the appearance of persons in Trade'. Thus disguised, the son of the King and the daughter of an earl were united once more, this time on a winter's day at the altar of a fashionable London church. Their marriage, number 819 at St George's that year, was a double ceremony: two couples were married at the same time. In the vestry the Prince signed the register as 'Augustus Frederick' and Augusta signed beneath as 'Augusta Murray'. Finally Mr and Mrs Jones signed as witnesses and the ceremony was concluded. As she made her promises for a second time Augusta knew that her love for her husband was as deep as it had been on 4 April when Mr Gunn married them in Rome. She was now Mrs Augustus Frederick but was she also Princess Augustus Frederick? Her future lay with the will of the King, the law of the land and the imminent birth of her child.

At home she recorded the event:

> Dear Thursday, always propitious, always fortunate to me, this morning I was again married in St George's Church, Hanover Square to the loved Prince Augustus, my marriage at Rome would have satisfied me, sanctioned in Heaven, approved of by the almighty, according to the forms of our Church & perfectly conducted, how could any alarms arrive in my mind? But my mother wished it, my Prince liked it because of his child, & I most willingly consented, the banns had been published & all proper forms attended to, the legitimacy of my baby was no more doubtful, & though I could trust my beloved husband it was right that no change presided over the birth of an infant whom the Court will wish to bastardise. Ly Euphemia Stewart, & Mr & Mrs Jones were the witnesses, & secrecy will I flatter myself preserve my own amiable Prince from the resentment of his parents.[2]

Augusta was mistaken. No one could have foreseen the intervention of a certain earl with whom she had once had a connection.

The day after the wedding, the Prince returned to Windsor, where he became unwell. Augusta joined him as Mrs Maxwell on 13 December. Nearing the end of her pregnancy, she did not enjoy the 23-mile journey from Mayfair to Windsor. She spent most of the day being jolted in a carriage, dined at Colnbrook and in the evening arrived at her 'little lodgings'. Despite varying her occupations – she read, she wrote, she did some embroidery and she drew – Augusta was forlorn, admitting that 'habit has made a large family, or Society, pleasanter to me than solitude'.[3]

The Prince had been home for nearly two months and the English winter, so long avoided on the Continent, had brought on his asthma. The strain of the second wedding made his condition worse and the King informed his son that he should go abroad for a cure. On 18 December when the Prince visited Augusta in London he told her that he hoped to go to Rome and was secretly planning for her and their child to join him after the accouchement. On 20 December the King wrote to the First Lord of the Admiralty asking how soon a ship would be available to take the Prince to Leghorn 'as I find my son Augustus very desirous of removing to a warmer climate and much inclined to return to Italy.'[4] The King added that Augustus should not leave for Portsmouth until there was either a northerly or easterly wind, as he did not wish his son to be detained unnecessarily.

That day the Prince left for Windsor and on Christmas Eve Augusta met him there. Her first Christmas as a married woman was not what she would have chosen; rather than being in the company of her family, she was alone in lodgings. She felt guilty that she had failed in her Christian duty: 'I never spent a Christmas Day in England without going to Church, this one was spent in solitude, and at home; I like society, & I like my own little husband, I wish he could spend more of his time with me.' She ate in her room, spending what should have been the merriest of days without friends or family until the Prince arrived in the evening. He spent the night with her but became so unwell that she was frightened.

Unable to bear the thought of her daughter alone in Windsor, Charlotte Dunmore left London and joined her on 26 December. Overcome by her kindness, Augusta wrote, 'To my great consolation my mother arrived, I was extremely happy to see her, and we past the day very comfortably. I was very sorry however to pass the whole of it without either seeing, or hearing from my own little spouse, but he expected the Prince of Wales, & all the royal family were to be together.' The next day Augustus managed a visit but they were both unwell, she was still being sick and he was asthmatic, although they 'spent the night, as a good married couple ought'.

The Prince of Wales arrived at Windsor Castle on 29 December to wish Augustus farewell so he could not visit Augusta. She lamented that the day was:

> uncommonly fine, but what is a fine day to me who am not allowed to walk, or stir out of the house; I am not permitted to show myself because I am the wife of a Prince who still does not own me; my character in the world is doubtful I cannot tell what my existence in it, is, I am low, & not happy. Had I been married to my equal, I might have enjoyed life, I might have enjoyed the comforts of the married state, I might have been the solace of his family, & the example of my own.

She was still being sick on 30 December but her mother was with her and the Prince made a late night visit after he had had supper with the Prince of Wales. New Year's Day 1794 was equally unsatisfactory. Augusta described it as a 'day, & a year not begun under favourable auspices. I felt wretched the whole of it … still I am but an unacknowledged wife, & I have lost the esteem which virtue claims.'

She left Windsor with her mother on 2 January and arrived in London to find Jack at home. Augusta was pleased to see her brother 'but sorry to find his great reluctance to my present situation, it is right he should feel this, & I love him for it; honour is necessary to the well being of every person in society.'[5] At the start of a career in the Royal Navy, Jack was afraid that his sister's situation might compromise his progress in an era when patronage was crucial.

Meanwhile, at Windsor Castle as the birth of his child approached, the strain caused a decline in the Prince's physical and mental health. Thanking the Prince of Wales warmly for his recent kindness, Augustus described his unresolved marital state as 'one of the most unpleasant in the World from reasons which [I] cannot mention. Many many times has my mind been so overcome with despair that I have been nearly almost distracted.'[6] Augustus was naturally of an open disposition and the burden of silence preyed on him as he made plans to depart. He was distraught at the thought of his ship being ready before Augusta had given birth and having to depart before he could see his child.

On 4 January, a chilly winter's day, the Royal Family went to see *The Duenna*, Richard Brinsley Sheridan's play with songs, but Prince Augustus did not join them 'on account of a Cold'.[7] He missed dinner at Frogmore the next day and Mr Farquhar, the Scottish physician favoured by the Prince of Wales, was summoned from London. Although Augustus's health improved, he missed the ball at Windsor Castle on the night of 6 January when the King and Queen danced until 3 a.m. On Friday, 10 January the Queen rejoiced that Augustus could dine with them 'after a confinement with the Asthma for a week'.[8]

Monday, 13 January was so frosty that the King was unable to take his daily ride and instead he walked out with Colonel Greville and Count Munster. That day the Prince received the news that HMS *Aquilon* was ready to receive him in Portsmouth and after dinner at four o'clock, Prince Augustus saw the Queen in her rooms for the last time alone. In the evening the Royal Family went to Hannah Cowley's play, *The Belle's Stratagem*. They returned to the castle by 11.30 p.m. but the Queen noted in her diary that, 'The Prince Augustus did not supp with Us.'[9] Augustus had received news of such significance that by then he was already on his way to London.

Augusta's pregnancy, throughout which she had barely known two consecutive days without sickness, had drawn to its conclusion. Following the recent fashion for employing 'man-midwives' as accoucheurs, she had engaged Dr Andrew Thynne, a respected lecturer in midwifery, to assist her and on that frosty Monday, early in 1794, he had safely delivered a baby boy.

The timing could not have been tighter. In order to see his wife and meet his son before departing for Portsmouth the next day, the new father raced up to London the moment the play had ended in Windsor. Arriving in Lower Berkeley Street, the Prince sped upstairs to find Augusta barely conscious. She was so poorly that he could not bear to tell her that he was leaving for Italy later that day and did not say goodbye. He had to be back at Windsor Castle for an early departure and, fighting back his emotions, the Prince tore himself away from his wife and child at four o'clock in the morning. He would see neither Augusta nor his son for more than six years.

18

This Unpleasant Business

Prince Augustus left Windsor Castle at 8.30 a.m. accompanied by Count Munster, Monsieur Tatter and Doctor Domeier. The moment he reached Portsmouth he wrote and explained to his wife why he had not said good-bye. He also outlined his plans for their reunion and reminded her to use their secret code:

> In any other situation, my dearest Augusta, it would have been impossible for me to have parted without taking leave of you; but as such a circumstance might have endangered your life it was not to be thought of. The very night that I got the information of your being brought to bed was the last I was to spend in England. Nothing in the world could or should have prevented my seeing you, and I was as good as my word. At leaving the little infant, I kissed and blessed my boy, – our boy; I prayed for my wife, – for thee, my angel.

He then turned to practical matters and the arrangements he had made for her to join him in Italy:

> Gunn is to call once a week to know if you have any orders, and is to bring you … three hundred pounds, which is all I can afford till you come to Bologna … My friend Dornford will send you an account of the road as far as Augsburgh … and from Gibraltar I will send you your route as far as Rome. Gunn is to attend you always, and to be your servant. A courier you must have, and find out yourself, for else you will be cheated beyond

> description. Dornford is to get you your passport also, under the name of Mrs. Stuart, for two servant maids, two servants, and our little child; Your first letters to me directed at Leghorn … As for you, if you are well, the last week of February or first week in March, you might set off … Do not forget when you begin to write, if it is anything of consequence, to make use of the cipher.[1]

While a fair wind carried away Augustus, it was feared that Augusta's life was 'given over'.[2] After the birth she succumbed to puerperal fever – infection of the uterus – a disease that could be fatal. Thus weakened, her 'alarms' began. On 16 January she 'heard that Lord Radnor had seen the Prince's marriage and mine in the Register of St George's Church, & that he had informed the Privy Council of it'. While his conduct appears incomprehensible, one explanation for it may lie with his former connection with Augusta's family.

The Earl of Radnor's brother, Edward Bouverie, had been married to Augusta's sister, Catherine. When she died leaving a baby boy, perhaps the Murrays and Bouveries quarrelled over the custody of the motherless child? The little boy's death the next year might have made a delicate situation worse, when the Murrays' last connection with their beloved Catherine was severed.

A second reason for Lord Radnor informing the Privy Council about the wedding at St George's may have been a desire to ingratiate himself with his friend, the Prince of Wales, who had visited Longford in 1785. There is an unusual painting at Wimpole Hall dated about 1787, entitled 'Allegorical Scene with the Prince of Wales … and Friends in a Boat', and Radnor is one of the few on board. Whatever his purpose in divulging Augusta's second wedding, if the earl wanted vengeance on her and her family, his success was complete. The question remains: why was he inspecting the St George's marriage register in the first place?

For the sake of secrecy, Augusta's wedding, the first of seven marriages registered at St George's that day, took place early in the morning of 5 December. Later that day the wedding of John Davinier and Dido Belle took place. Dido, memorably depicted with her cousin in a charming double portrait once attributed to Zoffany, was the black ward of Lord Mansfield. Her husband, Davinier, was a Frenchman, who may have worked as a steward at Kenwood, the Mansfields' London home. It is possible that

Radnor attended Davinier's wedding in his role as governor of *La Providence*, the establishment in Finsbury that cared for Huguenots.

Before his elevation to the House of Lords, Radnor's longest speech in the Commons had been against the royal marriage bill, which he resisted at every phase. His former opposition did not however, prevent him from hurrying to Lord Loughborough, the Lord Chancellor, to disclose the illegal marriage of 'Augustus Frederick' and 'Augusta Murray'. At the same time, he contacted *The Times*, which printed a paragraph describing a wedding:

> very lately performed which is likely to furnish the tea-tables at the west end of the town with a topic of conversation for the winter. One of the parties is a young gentleman of very high rank, who has just gone abroad. The other is the daughter of a northern Peer, who it is whispered, has already given an *unequivocal proof* of her attachment to the gentleman alluded to, but as it is yet *nameless*, we are under the necessity of leaving our fair readers to *guess* the nature of it.[3]

Powerless, ill and without her husband's support, Augusta found herself at the centre of a maelstrom. On 19 January the Government commanded her to appear before the Privy Council but she was too ill to receive the order.

It has previously been accepted that the King did not know about the second wedding until the Lord Chancellor told him about it on 24 January. It is debatable however, whether Lord Loughborough's unwelcome intelligence was in fact news to George III or whether Augustus himself had informed him before leaving for Portsmouth. On 9 January the Prince told Augusta that he had prepared a letter informing the King that he was married.[4] Princess Elizabeth had become so agitated when she saw it that Augustus was dissuaded from giving his letter to the King. Fearing that her younger brother was oblivious to the punitive terms of the Marriages Act, the Princess proceeded to spell them out to him. As he listened to her, it was his turn to become agitated: he heard that anyone convicted of contravening the provisions of the Act could be transported and their property confiscated.

He told Augusta that Princess Elizabeth was:

> afraid that the King, in his anger, would resent my behaviour; and avenge himself, not only upon me, but you also, which would be the ruin of us both. That I had much better not say a word till when you are gone

> abroad, and of course out of danger … Should you still wish, my Augusta, I will present the letter tomorrow to the King … I trust in some days to be better; but I am as yet most dreadfully weak. In six nights I have only slept once … though all my baggage is on board a ship, yet, should [you] want me to stay, Augusta, I will.

He was trapped: on one hand he wanted to keep his marriage secret until he was came of age, when the time would be more propitious, and on the other he was anxious to admit the truth to his father straightaway and clear Augusta's name. It was tragic that he failed to realise that there never would be a good time to tell the King.

The contentious letter was not delivered on either 9 or 10 January. However, it appears that the Prince did give it to his father before he departed because he fled from Windsor without taking leave of the King, a crime of lese-majesty, which in normal circumstances he never would have risked. On arrival in Portsmouth he explained to his father that it had been impossible 'to take leave of your Majesty. I fear'd the agitation it might occasion you knowing myself that it was more than I could bear. This engaged me to escape as I did and hope [it] will therefore meet with your Majesty's approbation.'[5] His optimism was unfounded.

Although the Prince had been absent during the King's illness of 1788, like the rest of his family, he was wary of provoking further malady. Despite Princess Elizabeth's advice, it was in Augustus's trusting nature to inform his father that he was married. Had he not left the explanatory letter, Augustus's leave-taking would not have occasioned George III agitation, and while saying goodbye to his father would doubtless have been sad, it would not have been unbearable.

The Prince wrote to Augusta with affectionate concern aboard the *Aquilon*:

> Today is a week my soul that our dear little child was born, so that I may trust you are in a fair way of recovering. One of my principal griefs at present is my being totally destitute of information relative to you. My warmest prayers are daily offered up for thee my Angel … You have given me so many indubitable proofs of your disinterested affection for me, you have suffered so much for my sake My Dearest Augusta that [I] never can be grateful enough.[6]

While Augusta's troubles were just beginning, Queen Charlotte was missing Augustus. She had felt his long absence abroad keenly and treasured the few months that her sixth son had been home. The Queen knew how much he loved Lady Augusta Murray and on 25 January 1794 made a melancholy note in her diary. The King had ordered 'the Chancellor the Archbishop of Canterbury & the other Ministers to proceed in this Unpleasant business as the Law directs, Augustus having Married under Age being against The Marriages Act'.[7] The Queen was right to be melancholy. She, more than anyone else, knew the terrible effect Augustus's transgression would have on her husband's fragile equilibrium.

19

Big With the Greatest Mischiefs

The Royal Marriages Act had arisen from the King's horror at the inappropriate marriage of his brother, Henry, Duke of Cumberland to the commoner, Mrs Horton. According to Horace Walpole, she was a 'coquette beyond measure, artful as Cleopatra, and completely mistress of all her passions and projects', moreover she had 'the most amorous eyes in the world'. Her family was contentious because her brother had taken the parliamentary seat for Middlesex despite being beaten to it by John Wilkes in the by-election of 1769. The House of Commons had been outraged and the prime minister compelled to resign. Aware that Anne Horton would be an unpopular choice with the monarch, the Duke declined to ask the King's permission before secretly marrying her in 1771. When the infatuated Duke confessed to his brother, King George was gravely affected. As paterfamilias, he expected to be consulted on the subject of his brothers' marriages and Henry's lack of fraternal care and dereliction of duty wounded him. Hurt and angry, George made a resolution: he would prevent the repetition of similar offences with the force of law.

The King's resolve was sharpened by personal experience and there were deep-seated reasons for feeling let down. As Prince of Wales, he had fallen in love with Lady Sarah Lennox but had sacrificed personal pleasure and had dutifully given her up. Sarah had been everything that the diffident young Prince admired. She was vivacious, attractive and confident, and he admitted guiltily that the sight of her made his emotions 'boil'. However, she was the sister-in-law of Henry Fox, a politician he loathed. Fox's powerful Whig faction threatened Lord Bute, a Tory and George's mentor. Bute counselled firmly against the Prince entangling himself with Sarah Lennox and pointed out the pitfalls of an alliance between monarch and subject, especially one from an ambitious political family. The young Prince was chastened and obediently suppressed his own wishes, promising never to marry a British bride or his own 'countrywoman'. With difficulty he subsumed his passion and asked his advisors to find a European princess, who would not be a focus of political or dynastic ambition. Having pondered the list of candidates, he finally chose Princess Charlotte of Mecklenburg-Strelitz.

On the afternoon of 7 September 1761 the 17-year-old Princess disembarked at the port of Harwich. She had endured a long and stormy passage and she spent the first night on English soil at Lord Abercorn's house in Witham. The following day she arrived in Romford at midday and proceeded to St James's Palace, where to her astonishment she was informed that she would be married that evening. With no time to recuperate, the exhausted girl entered the Chapel Royal soon after ten o'clock wearing an ill-fitting wedding dress, which swamped her small figure.[1] Lady Sarah Lennox, radiant and smiling, attended her, and King George, waiting at the altar, fixed his gaze firmly on his wife-to-be and did his duty. Moments later the little Princess from Mecklenburg-Strelitz was Queen of England.

Ten years later, when discussing the Cumberlands' unfortunate marriage with his other brother, William, Duke of Gloucester, the King recalled Lord Bute's advice. Such connections were 'big with the greatest mischiefs' and fraught with danger to the Crown. He referred to the Wars of the Roses when York and Lancastrian kings often married members of the nobility.[2] The King told his brother that the Crown should command respect at all times and, warming to his theme, reminded him of the time that it had forfeited the people's respect and Parliament had initiated the downfall of Charles I. (In 1757 George II, fearful of the power of the 'noisy populace', had permitted the execution of Admiral Byng for failing to prevent the French taking Port Mahon in Minorca. The King withheld his clemency despite the wishes of many, including a number of MPs, Horace Walpole and Voltaire.)[3] George III reminded his brother that his predecessors had withstood two Jacobite rebellions and although the threat from that quarter had diminished, the young pretender was still alive on the Continent. He ended his lecture by telling William that it was the Royal Family's duty to help him uphold his role as King of Great Britain.

If the Duke of Gloucester did not blench at this discourse, he should have done. Like his brother, the Duke had not asked the King before getting married. Not only was his bride, Maria Waldegrave, a British subject, she also was illegitimate. Particularly shocking was the fact that the fine-looking widow was eight years older than her husband. As the King talked, the Duke of Gloucester squirmed but he did not confess because he knew his brother's capacity for bearing a grudge; if a member of the Royal Family defied his authority, neither forgiveness nor sympathy was forthcoming. The King had excluded the Cumberlands from court and he did not acknowledge the Duchess of Cumberland. Unwilling to face social isolation, the Duke of Gloucester retired from the royal presence, unsettled and embarrassed.

In order to avoid another unpleasant shock like the Cumberland wedding, the King began to discuss legal measures with Lord North, the Prime Minister, and Lord Mansfield, the Lord Chief Justice. They formulated a bill to prevent descendants of George II from marrying without the previous consent of the monarch, his heirs and successors. Every marriage contracted without such consent would be null and void. However well-born the chosen bride might be, were she a British subject and the King had not given his permission, the result would be ruin and rejection for both parties; importantly, any offspring from such a union would be illegitimate. The bill stated that if a royal petitioner, being over the age of 25, did not receive the consent of the monarch, he could give notice to the Privy Council and if within a year neither House of Parliament had objected, he would be free to marry. Finally, anyone knowingly or wilfully solemnizing, assisting or attending such a marriage would be liable for prosecution.

The nascent bill was presented to the House of Commons on 4 March 1772. It came with a royal message giving His Majesty's reasons for the proposed law: paternal affection for his own family, anxious concern for the welfare of his people and the honour and dignity of his crown. Both message and bill caused uproar. MPs regarded it as a piece of personal legislation coming from the monarch and opposed what they saw as an attempt to extend the royal prerogative. The King however, made it clear that he expected the support of everyone in his service and that he would remember those who failed to support him. Every politician knew that George III never forgot a perceived slight and after a difficult passage the bill was passed nearly three weeks later. On 1 April the 'Act for the better regulating the future Marriages of the Royal Family' received royal assent and soon after Queen Charlotte became pregnant again. Of all her children, Augustus Frederick was to be the most affected by the well-meaning, if punitive, piece of legislation, which had entered the statute books just before his conception.

A few months later, the Duke of Gloucester's wife was also pregnant and, as her husband feared, the event forced him to inform the King that he had married in secret six years before. Deceived a second time, George ordered an investigation into both the Gloucester and Cumberland marriages. Both were declared valid and although neither witnesses nor certificates were produced for the Gloucester union, the legitimacy of their first child, Princess Sophia, was confirmed. Like the Duchess of Cumberland, the Duchess of Gloucester was never received at court and, for the time being, she and her husband were ostracised. Both royal dukes learnt to their cost that, when crossed, the King made a formidable adversary to those who fell short of his high ideals. His concept of kingship encompassed every member of a dutiful Royal Family acting with propriety at all times and those who compromised this dearly held vision could not expect clemency.

Writing sadly in her diary on 25 January 1794, the Queen knew that this was the treatment that Prince Augustus and Lady Augusta could now expect from the King. She added that 'orders are given to stop Ldy Dunmore and Her Daughter joining Him [Augustus] or leaving England'.[4] Not only had Lord Radnor revealed their secret wedding, he had also foiled the Prince's plans for a reunion with his wife and child in Italy.

20

Anxieties and Miseries

The judicial process examining the legality of their marriage started with a Privy Council inquiry on Monday, 27 January 1794, by coincidence the day that Prince Augustus came of age.[1] If all had gone to plan, it was the day on which he might have received his own establishment. Augusta's diary entry for the first day of the inquiry is pitiful. It was written after a 'great lapse of time' because she had been too ill to record her sorrows and 'too wretched to value life'. It described a 'week of anxieties & miseries' when her mother, Aunt Euphemia and others appeared in the Council Chamber, located at the back of Whitehall on the edge of St James's Park. The whole weight of the establishment was assembled to inquire 'into the Circumstances attending a supposed Celebration of a marriage' between His Royal Highness Prince Augustus and Lady Augusta Murray.[2]

A panel of eleven of the most powerful men in the land led the inquisition: senior office-holders in the Church, the Law and the Government of Britain. Two secretaries taking minutes sat at the side and a beadle stood to attention by the door. The first person to appear before this formidable array was the rector of St George's church. He was required to produce the incriminating marriage register but had not been present at the wedding and was unable to answer any of their questions, so the deputy clerk of the parish, Mr Caleb Greville, was called and sworn in. He did not know who had originally brought the notice of the marriage and assured the panel that he neither knew the witnesses nor noticed the protagonists because he had been preparing the register in the vestry. On being probed about the possibility of bribery, he responded, 'I have received no extraordinary Fee for some time past.'[3] The Reverend John Downes, who performed the ceremony, was then sworn in and requested to look at the register. He did not know either of the parties and also declared that, 'The Fee given was nothing more than the ordinary demand.'[4] On the crucial question, 'How do you know that the persons presenting themselves to be married, are the persons named in the Banns,' he answered, 'We take no other means but to Examine the Entry, and find, whether the names agree. We trust to the assertions of the parties, and to their signatures in the Books.' On the question of previous residence in the parish, Downes informed the panel that it was all taken on trust; the clerk has 'at least the assurance of the parties that they are of the parish, of which they state themselves to be'.[5] The church functionaries had been no help and now the Countess of Dunmore was called.

Her mother had brought her up with a highly developed sense of her royal lineage and the dignified manner in which she entered the chamber confirmed her ancestry. It was a fortnight since the birth of Augusta's child and the countess had left her hovering between life and death; she was determined to protect her daughter's reputation. Her Ladyship, still a beautiful woman, was in her 54th year; her feistiness did not desert her and if any member of the panel thought that they could cow her, they had underestimated the Countess of Dunmore.

Inside the Privy Council chamber she was introduced, sworn and offered a chair. She sat down with dignity and glancing up, scanned her interrogators, most of whom she was more accustomed to meet in the drawing rooms of fashionable London than in a court of law. She recognised the Lord Chancellor. Lord Loughborough was a fellow Scot; he was a contemporary of her husband and also a member of the Select Society in Edinburgh. She then spotted Lord Amherst, the Commander in Chief of the Army, and like Lord Dunmore a former governor of Virginia; she glimpsed Henry Dundas, the Home Secretary, also from the higher ranks of Scottish society. She picked out Lord Hawkesbury, the Chancellor of the Duchy of Lancaster; there was William Pitt, the Prime Minister, and his cousin, Lord Grenville, the Foreign Secretary. Facing the council, Charlotte Dunmore was under pressure. While her position was unenviable, she had a nimble mind and, refusing to compromise herself or her absent daughter, she gave the performance of her life.

She denied any knowledge of Prince Augustus's plan to marry her daughter in Rome and when asked if she knew who had solemnized the wedding, she responded, 'I have not an Idea. – The Prince made a point with my Daughter that she would not tell, and I never asked her, as she was under this promise.'[6] The point was pursued. Did she know any clergymen of the Church of England then in Rome or its neighbourhood in April 1793? Lady Dunmore was vague. She appeared to think hard and after a few moments responded, 'There was I believe, a Mr Wheeler, and a Mr Gun, but I hardly recollect.'[7] In fact, she knew exactly who had solemnized her daughter's wedding because she had recently been blackmailed.[8]

Monticelli, the Italian servant who had admitted Mr Gunn to her lodgings in Rome, had eavesdropped on the first wedding ceremony and on their return to London threatened to tell the King if the countess did not comply with his pecuniary demands. (After consultation with Prince Augustus, Lady Dunmore had submitted to the venal domestic.) She next faced a question concerning Augusta's age, and incensed by their impertinence, she prevaricated, 'She is past Thirty one, but I do not just at this moment precisely recollect how much.'[9] That day, that unhappy Monday, not to be celebrated in any way, was Augusta's 33rd birthday. Of course, the countess knew her daughter's age but she would give them only a partial truth and no more. She was not going to inform the world that Augusta was twelve years older than Prince Augustus.

They then enquired about the whereabouts of Lady Augusta's child and whether he had been privately baptised. When they asked, 'Does your Ladyship know the reason for Solemnising the Marriage a Second time in England?' she answered without thinking. Initially flustered, she replied, 'Nothing but to make the Child not a Bastard,' but she recovered quickly and continued, 'I speak incorrectly, for I could not look upon the Child as a Bastard, after the marriage at Rome.'[10]

Having confirmed that a letter from the Prince had informed her of the first wedding, she was told, 'Your Ladyship's prudence will not have suffered you to destroy it – it must not now be destroyed, and it must be produced. It is very material in every point of view that it should be produced.'

Lady Dunmore was unimpressed. 'It is a private Letter,' she countered, 'written to excuse my Child for her Reserve towards me, and surely it will be very hard to oblige me to produce it.' Her personal feelings were of no concern to the panel and they proceeded to threaten her, telling her that:

> There can be no reason why your Ladyship should make any difficulty in producing it, to His Majesty's Privy Council. In fact it is better for you that it should be produced here than in any other place, where it may be called for, and where the production of it will be compelled.

Undaunted, Lady Dunmore announced that she considered it 'a private Correspondence, and it is from delicacy to the Prince I wish not to produce it'. With a flourish she concluded, 'I have it not now about me.' The Privy Counsellors were weary. As the winter afternoon wore on they realised that they would glean little more from the countess and adjourned the inquiry until the next day.

When the proceedings opened the next afternoon at two o'clock, Lady Dunmore was relieved to see that Lord Amherst and William Pitt were absent.[11] She was immediately called on to produce Prince Augustus's letter. Her answer astonished them: she could not give it to them because she had burnt it. When she had told Augusta the previous evening that the council wished to see the Prince's letter, her daughter had been so affected and had given her so many reasons why the document should not be produced that the countess had thrown it in the fire and she said that no copy had been taken.

Asked to relate the contents of the letter, Lady Dunmore said it contained nothing more than a disclosure that a wedding had taken place in Rome between her daughter and the Prince by an English clergyman in full orders, as well as the excuse for her daughter for having kept the secret from her mother. It was the possibility of this last point being publicised that had caused Augusta such anguish. The panel was so surprised by Her Ladyship's account that she was asked to withdraw while they agreed an appropriate way to proceed.

On her return, they revisited the subject of Lady Augusta's age and asked, 'Have you enabled yourself by any further recollection to state more correctly than yesterday the age of your Daughter Lady Augusta?' Such insolence was beneath Lady Dunmore and she dismissed their enquiry with brevity, 'I have never thought of it since, and can add nothing to what I said yesterday on that subject.'[12] When asked about her motive for the celebration of the marriage in St George's church, Lady Dunmore explained that, like Augusta, she regarded the Roman marriage as valid in the sight of God but because of the lack of witnesses and certificate, she wished her daughter to be married again by the Canon Law of the Church of England. The countess was then requested to withdraw.

She had done a superb job in safeguarding her daughter's character, although she had been forced to acknowledge that, 'I may have said that a Marriage with a Prince of the Royal Family was illegal, and I may,' and here she paused, 'perhaps have told my Daughter so, upon her telling me of her marriage.'[13] She had answered their questions clearly and briefly, aware that concision would help her keep a clear mind. Outside the chamber she sat down, fatigued. The effort of retaining her dignity, checking her emotions, and answering coherently while not giving anything away, meant that she was near to collapse. Collecting herself once more, the countess heard her sister called in.

Lady Euphemia admitted to the panel that she was the only person who knew the identity of the groom at the ceremony at St George's. She told them that she had not signed the register as a witness because there was no room on the document. When Mrs Jones was called in, she confirmed to the panel that neither she nor her husband had any idea that the bridegroom was the son of the King; she had been told 'that he was a relation of Sir something Frederick, and that I need not be afraid of any thing I had done'.[14] Mrs Jones did admit that curiosity overcame her later. When Lady Augusta revealed the groom's identity, Mary Jones had been to the theatre to have a better look at him. She also told the panel that after the London wedding the bride and groom and Lady Dunmore were 'pleased it was over'.[15] Mr and Mrs Jones were the last witnesses to be called and the inquiry came to an end. Now Augusta had to wait for the lawsuit instituted by the King.

The Gentleman's Magazine was quick to state that the crux of the suit rested not on the non-performance of the wedding ceremony but on the legal incapacity of the Prince to contract a marriage before the age of 25 without the King's consent.[16] The Royal Marriages Act, the journal informed its readers, declares that any union transacted without compliance to this condition is absolutely null and void. The *Magazine* then showed its colours:

> It is not pretended that the King's consent was given or asked; but, on the other hand, it appears that a marriage has been celebrated in the face of the Church, with all the forms prescribed by law for every man and

> woman in England not descended from George II and that issue has been born of that marriage, such as it is. But as the case is to come *sub judice*, we shall say no more upon it at present, leaving it, as we are bound to do, to the tribunal competent to decide a question, which involves no less important a matter than the eventual inheritance of the crown.

It is true that Augustus married Augusta Murray against the provisions of the Marriages Act but, as noted some years later, it was 'no new event, in such a family [as hers], to become connected with Royalty in marriage'[17] and *The Gentleman's Magazine* published its opinion in forceful terms:

> Lady Augusta is daughter to the Earl of Dunmore, at present governor of the Bahama islands, and a younger branch of the Duke of Athol's family. Her fortune is certainly slender; but, if *birth* might give pretensions to great alliances, there is no Prince in Europe who could say a match with Lady Augusta would disgrace his rank. She is sprung from everything that is noble, everything that is royal, in England … and also from the most illustrious houses on the continent.

Indeed, her father's forebears included members of the Plantagenet, Tudor, Orange and Bourbon dynasties and her maternal grandfather, the Earl of Galloway, was descended from the royal House of Stewart.

When Augusta was born, her parents did not name her after one of their distinguished forebears or close family members. Charlotte Dunmore's sister, Lady Susanna, had recently become a lady of the bedchamber to the King's eldest sister, Princess Augusta. Unwilling to forgo the opportunity for future patronage, the Dunmores took advantage of the royal connection and christened their second daughter in honour of the Princess.

Susanna, now Marchioness of Stafford and an intimate of the King and Queen, believed that she had much to lose from her relationship with her dishonoured niece and swiftly distanced herself from the unhappy young woman. Her husband, the marquess, sat in the cabinet as Lord Privy Seal and Susanna was adept at using his position for the dispensation of patronage on behalf of her family. She had been instrumental in obtaining positions for Lord Dunmore in America and the Bahamas.

The marchioness was deeply disappointed; she had held Augusta dear. With the public revelation of the marriage, Lady Stafford was furious. One of her daughters had married the heir to the Duke of Beaufort and she feared that her niece's lamentable behaviour would compromise the eligibility of her other two girls. The marchioness did not dither. To protect her family and herself from being tainted by association, she disowned her niece with alacrity.

A chance encounter between Augusta and her aunt in early 1794 acted as the catalyst for one of the most self-serving letters Lady Stafford ever composed. In an attempt at damage limitation she disassociated herself from Augusta in a letter to George III that revealed more about her own aspirations than the failings of her niece. She told the King on 7 February:

> I am not the most ungrateful, nor the most unworthy of beings, which I certainly should be, had I in any way had any part, or any knowledge of this lamentable affair. I declare upon my honour that I was totally ignorant of every part of it when I came to London, & without the smallest suspicion that there was any foundation for the reports which I hear'd in the country – but Lady Augusta not appearing twice that I was let into the house made me suspect that there must be another cause than cough & fever to keep her out of sight – but till the end of the week before last, I had not the misery of knowing that so near a relation had caused so mortifying a sorrow to your Majest[y]. I will not endeavour to express the deep concern it gives me. I only wish to convince your Majesty that I am not the abominable creature I should be if I had been even privy to it. No Sir – I am perfectly blameless in every way, and I think I am incapable of forgetting the goodness, the kindness & protection with which your Majesty had honor'd me for so many years. I think I am incapable of having any knowledge or share in any transaction that must give you uneasiness & disturb the peace of your mind. I think it necessary to add that I had not seen Lady Augusta since her return to England till yesterday, when I unfortunately hear'd that Lady Dunmore was very unwell, & they shew'd me into Lady Dunmore's room where Lady Augusta was. I was exceedingly surpriz'd & much hurt, in this unforeseen manner, to have done what I determined against … I enter'd into no conversation with her; she cried, & I said nothing to her. Nor do I mean ever to see her again if that is what your Majesty chuses. I wish to pay my duty to the Queen and your Majesty, but at present my health and spirits are so bad that I dare not attempt it – and I fear too, that ignorant as I have been of

> the whole of it, yet it may be very disagreeable to your Majesties to see a near relation of those who have caused you so much disquiet and uneasiness. I am sorrier than I can express.[18]

Despite Lady Stafford's protestations, although Augusta did not tell her own mother about the wedding until later, she herself had written to inform her aunt about her marriage in Rome on 30 April 1793. That evening when everybody had gone out, she had stayed at home to receive Augustus and, having asked his permission, wrote and told Lady Stafford that they were married.[19] She took great care that her aunt should receive her letter and entrusted it to her cousin, Alexander Hamilton, who was going to meet his father at Leghorn before departing for England. Alexander did not return to England in the company of his father, who came back in the *Constantine* with Augusta herself. We will never know if Augusta's letter ever reached Lady Stafford, or if Susanna was, as she protested to the King, 'totally ignorant' of the wedding. It seems unlikely.

The marchioness's conduct was indicative of the consequences of incurring the rage of King George. It was a shocking example of the treatment to which Augusta could look forward, reserved for those who were banished by the King and excluded from court. By contrast, Augusta's other aunt, Euphemia, had supported her. By bravely attending her niece's second wedding, she had knowingly contravened the provisions of the Royal Marriages Act.

21

The Effects of a Fatal Marriage

After the Privy Council inquiry, the King asked three lawyers for advice on the best way to proceed relative to his son's marriage. They were a close-knit trio, comprising two brothers, Sir William Scott, and his younger brother, the attorney general, John Scott,[1] as well as John's university friend, Sir John Mitford, the solicitor general. Sir William was a judge of the consistory court of the diocese of London, the most important matrimonial court in England with the power to determine the validity of a supposed marriage.[2]

They began their report for the King by declaring that 'in order to obtain a declaratory sentence of nullity of marriage' the suit should be prosecuted between the King and Lady Augusta in the Court of Arches, the appeal court for ecclesiastical matters within the province of Canterbury.[3] In considering the participants in the wedding other than the Prince and Augusta, the report stated that although the Royal Marriages Act states that anyone could be convicted, who knowingly and wilfully solemnises, assists or is present at a marriage under the circumstances mentioned within the Act, the clergyman, clerk and witnesses at St George's Church were not culpable because they were ignorant of the Prince's rank. To support a prosecution, evidence must be given that the person married under the name of Mr Augustus Frederick was indeed the Prince, but neither of the witnesses, Mr and Mrs Jones, could provide such evidence, as they did not know him.

While Lady Euphemia Stewart had confessed to being present at the ceremony, making her the only person who might incur the penalties of the Act, it was difficult to charge her without ascertaining that she knew the Prince 'previous to the marriage'. If such evidence could be procured, she could be prosecuted but only 'if your Majesty, in your royal wisdom shall see fit'. The lawyers acknowledged that Lady Dunmore was absent from the wedding itself, although she had previous knowledge of it and had facilitated it, so she too could be proceeded against 'for a contempt at the Common Law', but again only if His Majesty thought 'such a proceeding expedient'. It appears that the three lawyers were merely doing their job by indicating such possibilities to the King and did not necessarily recommend them. They advanced no other legal proceeding concerning the wedding at St George's, and they found no grounds for prosecuting anyone who had participated in the first wedding in Rome.

As a result of the report, Augusta was served with notice to appear at the ecclesiastical Court of Arches, subsequent to a case started by His Majesty King George III: the Cause of Nullity of Marriage. Faced with the possibility of the King annulling her marriage and bastardising her child, Augusta had only her mother to support her. Her father was in the Bahamas and her husband was in Italy. The Prince corresponded with her every day except when he was travelling. The letter he sent on their first wedding anniversary, 4 April 1794, when he had held a dinner to honour the date, was one of his most passionate. He wanted her to defy his father's command not to leave England and urged her to:

> hasten to my arms, my charmer, and I will acknowledge you in spite of Parliaments ... I will fight for you, my Augusta ... I will die thy husband ... Should the annulling of our marriage take place, which I doubt, my Augusta, it will make no difference in my sentiments, my charmer ... My life is very monotonous, and till yesterday I have been very melancholy.

He wanted her to join him as soon as she could after the inoculation of their son with the smallpox virus. Having been at home when similar immunisations had caused the deaths of his youngest brothers, Alfred and Octavius, Augustus knew how dangerous the procedure could be.

Two weeks later the Prince was sympathising with her over her forthcoming court appearance: 'You tell me, my soul, that this month your trial is to come on. I tremble for it, because my best half is to endure the whole attack which pride, envy, and malice can invent, whilst the other is at Rome incapable of rendering any service ... Darling of my heart, how I adore you; how I long for you; how I wish for you and our little boy.'[4] On 12 May he told her how desperate he was for news of her trial 'though some people have learned to hint that it would not be successful'. Again he implored her to join him, although 'this circumstance must be arranged as clandestinely as possible else if our enemies might get wind of it that might provide themselves with an order from the Chancellor which might prevent you leaving the country'. She should ask Jack, her brother in the Navy, and 'consign your effects in England to some safe person and come out with as little luggage as possible ... Do not take Gunn with you I will order him to follow afterwards'.[5] For the sake of speed, he suggested that Augusta should leave their son with Lady Dunmore.

The thought of the trial had caused Augusta and her mother weeks of distress and it was not until 25 June that their coachman was instructed to convey them to Great Knightrider Street, near St Paul's Cathedral. Their destination was Doctors' Commons, a complex of small quadrangles where judges, proctors (solicitors) and advocates (barristers) lived and worked, administering law in the ecclesiastical and admiralty courts, their names displayed on boards in the manner of an Oxbridge college.[6]

The strain she had undergone since the birth of her child had weakened Augusta, nevertheless she was determined to retain her dignity and fight her cause. She kept her answers brief, and like her mother at the January inquiry, was quick-witted and brave.[7] Asked whether she was 31 years of age or over when she became acquainted with the Prince, she denied it. Unwilling to admit her age, and seeing where the question was leading, she gave an equivocal answer. While she was indeed 31 when she had encountered the Prince in Rome, as he had reminded her, she had first met him some years before at a ball at the Queen's House. She rejected the unflattering suggestion that 'she did prevail or endeavour to prevail on His said Royal Highness to consent to be married to her'. She told them that when he first proposed to her she refused him as it was likely to be 'injurious' to him and would 'give offence to their Majesties'. Under duress, she had at last consented to his desire for marriage on condition that it should be private and kept a secret. She did confess that she had heard of the Royal Marriages Act 'but she was not acquainted with the purport or tenor of the said Act of Parliament, neither had she any means at that time of ascertaining the same' and she believed that the Prince was not acquainted with its contents either.

The principal of the Court of Arches, Sir William Wynne, was uncompromising in his judgement. In the dining room, off the Common Hall where the courts were held, the portly lawyer declared that at the beginning of the case Prince Augustus was a minor under the age of 21 years, and as he had not yet attained the age 25 years, he 'was not nor is capable of contracting matrimony without the consent of his Majesty'. In contrast to the Attorney-General's report, the wording of Wynne's decree, particularly in respect to Augusta herself, was savage. Concerning the 'pretended' wedding in Rome, he announced that there was insufficient proof by witnesses that any such ceremony had taken place between Augustus and 'Lady Augusta Murray, spinster, falsely calling herself the wife of his said Royal Highness Prince Augustus Frederick' and 'the said pretended marriage was and is absolutely null and void to all intents and purposes in the Law whatsoever'.

The judge also pronounced that the London wedding 'or shew or effigy of a marriage was in fact had and solemnized, or rather prophaned', a description that wounded Augusta, and is likewise 'null and void to all intents and purposes in the Law'. His destruction of her character and reputation not yet complete, the judge went on 'to pronounce, decree and declare, that his said Royal Highness Prince Augustus Frederick, was, and is, free from all bond of marriage with the said Right Honourable Lady Augusta Murray'.[8] The force of law was enacted against Augusta, who was blamed for a marriage that in fact had been instigated by Prince Augustus. This document was laid before George III and his ministers at the Court of St James's on 23 July.

His Majesty's work was complete. He had upheld the dignity of the monarchy and, moreover, set an example to Augustus's siblings. It had taken six months to legislate against the transgressors of the Royal Marriages Act. His sixth son had been parted from the woman he adored and the mother of his child. He was no longer legally bound to Lady Augusta Murray and she was forbidden to join him in Italy. She quickly began to feel 'the effects of a fatal marriage', of which one of the cruellest was the discovery that she was liable for the legal expenses.[9]

Lady Knight, amongst others, enjoyed Augusta's fall from grace. She had written to a friend in March, 'I heartily hope that the law will do all that the King can wish, that some little pension will be granted, and that she will be sent into civil banishment.'[10] Lady Knight partly attained her wish. While Augusta's pension was a contentious subject for many years, polite society, taking its lead from the King, lost no time in ostracising her. Once the darling of the ballrooms of London and Paris, Lady Augusta Murray was banished from court, shunned and disgraced. The Prince, however, did not desert her or lose hope that she might join him.

His letter of 28 June, addressed to Her Royal Highness Princess Augustus Frederick, expressed his 'content' at the result of their child's inoculation and his relief that their son was 'perfectly recovered'. Now that the medical precaution was overcome, Augustus hoped that their son could 'travel without the least inconvenience' and requested his wife to join him as soon as possible:

> Though your letter of yesterday forebodes me no good, by informing me of the unfortunate sentence that will, for the moment condemn our cause … I must most particularly intreat thy departure from England … you may rest assured of my receiving you at my house, acknowledging you to be my wife … I trust now my dear Goosy, permit me to refresh your memory once more, and to entreat you to make as much speed as possible to join your own husband, and believe me ever, till death us do part, your ever affectionate and soley devoted husband and friend.[11]

In the last entry of her journal – too wretched to continue a habit 'contracted in happier times' – Augusta recorded her response to the King's wrath and his vengeance. Until the day she died, she regarded both of her weddings as binding in the eyes of God and in her view the King had placed the law of the land above the laws of the deity. In a stream of consciousness undisturbed by punctuation, she reacted bitterly to the hypocritical and unlawful decision:

> They annulled my marriage, they went beyond the power of law, their measures were illegal for it was never known before to annul a marriage of which there were no proofs, & to subject the one contracted at Rome to the arbitration of a tyrannical Court of a King who governed himself very little according to the precepts of the Gospel though he seemed with holy zeal to pray, & attend its public worship but when any of its ordinances mitigated against his inclinations, passions, or humours, he soon forgot the maxims of the Bible, & made use of that power vested in his hands for more virtuous purpose to oppress the weak, & wreak his vengeance upon those who have never injured him. A time may come, when

> he will have less despotic sway, [and] if heaven hears my prayers that time will soon arrive.

Her outburst took no account of the terms of the Royal Marriages Act, which she and Augustus had never fully comprehended. She prayed that the Prince would honour his commitment to her, for, 'What God hath joined let not man put asunder is a holy axiom, the King sees no use to attend to that precept, though I believe he thinks that "honour the King", another maxim of the same Book should be regarded with reverence.'

She signed the entry, which she dedicated to her husband, 'your devoted wife Augusta or Princess Augustus Frederick', and closed her journal forever.[12]

22

My Unfortunate Companions of Woe

In the absence of Augusta's journal, the Prince's letters from Italy become an essential source of information. Initially he corresponded, dutifully if not willingly, with the King. He reported on his journey to Leghorn, where he disembarked on 1 March 1794, but then stopped writing to his father. In early April he told Augusta that, 'I have received no letters from any one of the family; and considering this as a silent order not to write, I shall certainly accede to it.'[1] He was never mentioned at home and his sisters were forbidden to write to him or receive his letters. However, when his son stopped corresponding, the King expressed his displeasure and Augustus was forced to explain himself to the Prince of Wales, his sole conduit to the Royal Family.

He informed the Prince of Wales that:

> my heart never for a moment bore the least rancour whatsoever, against any of the family, though my feelings have been hurt by the violence of the measures adopted. When a letter might have settled everything amicably, I do not see why so much force should be employed. The moment a law suit was to determine a misunderstanding of this nature it was no longer a private consideration between a father and son, but a public prosecution between his Majesty and Prince Augustus Frederick.[2]

While the King was unforgiving, the Queen bore Augustus's exclusion with characteristic stoicism, but her wifely loyalty prevented her from writing to her son.

After seven years abroad Augustus had been at home for less than four months and he was now back in Italy in disgrace. He took a house at Grottaferrata, 12 miles south-east of Rome, set amongst the vineyards near Frascati. It was a picturesque place dominated by the lofty campanile of the church of Santa Maria and an impressively fortified eleventh-century abbey, which contained a library with rich manuscripts. When Augustus died, his book collection numbered over 50,000 volumes, including a thousand editions of the Bible and other important codices.[3] Perhaps the Grottaferrata library became a sanctuary at a time of profound unhappiness and inspired his love of ancient books.

The King intended that his son's separation from Augusta should be permanent, but Augustus's devotion to his wife showed no sign of dissipating. Missing his 'lovely Gussy' and their son, he told her on 6 September, 'I cannot describe to my own charming wife the strong desire I have of seeing our dear little boy.'[4] At home the baby's christening was proving to be a problem.

It could not take place until the manner of recording his parents on the baptism register had been resolved. Consulted by the Bishop of London, the Lord Chancellor said that he believed that 'the entry should be in the usual manner of those cases where the child to be christened has no father whom the law acknowledges in that character; that is described only by the name of the mother'.[5] Augusta was indignant; she would never accede to such a preposterous suggestion, so the ceremony did not take place.

Later, careworn and demeaned, she recalled her frustration at hearing that the Chancellor had deprived her son of one of the 'common rights of all men, the privilege of Christianity, [and] has refused him baptism'. She concluded, with a lightly veiled reference to the King, 'this I write, that I may remember my wrongs, that I may remember how inimical I ought to be to usurped authority; & how ill I have been treated by those I had never wished to injure, by those for whose prosperity I have prayed'.[6]

While Prince Augustus's marriage had infuriated his father, the King warmly endorsed the Prince of Wales's choice of wife. Obliged to produce a legitimate heir to the throne and in the hope that Parliament would relieve him of his debts, by 1794 George knew that marriage was now an unwelcome necessity. Caroline of Brunswick appeared to be ideal: as well as being a European protestant princess, she was George III's niece. The marital history of her bridegroom was however, complicated.

A decade earlier the Prince of Wales had undergone a form of marriage that had not been sanctioned by the King and was thus against the provisions of the Royal Marriages Act. His wife, Maria Fitzherbert, was Roman Catholic, and the Act of Settlement disqualified from the succession anyone married to a Catholic. Choosing to ignore his first marriage, the Prince settled down to do his duty and arrangements were made for the royal wedding. Meanwhile Augustus, smarting under paternal censure, congratulated his brother generously, heartily wishing the Prince 'every felicity this world can give'. The union between George and Caroline was a calamity from the start so it was fateful that Augustus addressed his letter of congratulation on a sheet of mourning paper, a circumstance that he admitted was 'truly ridiculous'.[7]

Prince Augustus spent Christmas 1794 with the King and Queen of Naples at Caserta, their palace outside Naples, similar to Versailles in scale and grandeur and surrounded by a park complete with an 'English Garden' filled with follies. Although his host and hostess were 'kindness itself', he admitted to the Prince of Wales that his 'heart and head are both broke'.[8] On his son's first birthday in January 1795 Augustus told his brother that:

> I flattered myself that after Government had broke my marriage in so cruel and unprecedented a manner as they did, everything would have ended there. My own private peace of mind and honour, which are the only two blessings I possess, have been totally ruined ... My only desire now was to busy myself in some remote corner of the Continent and then to occupy myself about the happiness of her whose misfortunes I am solely the cause of and the education of my boy ... I understand a most arbitrary and unconstitutional promise has been exacted from Lady Augusta never to join me, and in such a manner that when produced to the public eye must shock every man ... I am no Jacobin, but certainly will not keep a rank in society which tends only to ruin my peace, and tranquillity, and serves merely for to give others the faculty of trampling me down ... you will certainly know that disappointed love is capable of every rashness of every folly this world can create.[9]

In February 1795 Augustus received news of a military crisis: the French had taken Amsterdam. He was so anxious that he wrote to the King offering his 'services in what way your majesty may think most expedient'.[10] He cannot have honestly expected to receive an answer and he did not. Six weeks later he hired a courier to carry an important letter to his father. Augustus explained that:

> the very critical situation in which I now stand forces me to enter upon a subject I have as studiously avoided ever touching, as your Majesty has cautiously evaded it. Nothing but the most violent anxiety bordering upon despair could ever engage me to converse upon a circumstance I have had so little encouragement to open my mind upon. Here my duty requires me to speak and painful as the task is, your Majesty must be acquainted with my sentiments … Lady Dunmore's daughter, Lady Augusta who is certainly attached to me by such ties, that if even my country does not acknowledge them, are not the less dear to me, lies most dangerously ill.

He emphasised that the 'physicians do not even hesitate to declare it a Decline'. Informing his father that as her doctors recommend a change of climate 'you will not refuse her such a remedy but on the contrary give the necessary directions. In an object that so intimately concerns the whole future happiness of my life your Majesty will I trust excuse my freedom. On her my thoughts are fixed, and with her my life must end.'[11] The King remained implacable and refused to issue the instructions that might have resulted in the Prince being united with his wife.

In 1794 Augusta appears to have visited Hastings for recuperation, taking her baby to live by the sea at East Hill House. A plaque on its façade states that 'HRH The Duke of Sussex with Lady Augusta Murray and Colonel D'Este resided here in the summer of 1794'. As we know, Prince Augustus was in Italy at the time and their son became known as Colonel D'Este many years later. By the autumn of 1795 Augusta's health and spirits were so poor that she moved to the West Country in search of a remedy. She decided to try the picturesque town of Teignmouth on the Devon coast. Two bathing machines had joined the fishing boats on the red sands by 1762, when the small resort began to capitalise on the fashion for sea bathing. The novelist Fanny Burney had visited as a young girl and two years before Augusta's arrival a local banker proudly told one of his clients that the Dukes of Somerset and Beaufort had stayed recently.

According to the *Royal Magazine*, the medicinal benefits of a sojourn in Teignmouth knew no bounds: 'people from all parts resorted to the town to drink the sea water, with the result that cripples recovered the use of their limbs, hysterical ladies their spirits, and even lepers were cleansed'. However, Augusta led a retired life in the town and *The Times* reported that 'to the regret of all who know her appears very unhappy'. Enforced separation from a dearly loved spouse, social ostracism and a court case have never been the ingredients for health and happiness. Occasionally she could be seen on horseback but was 'too ill to ride by herself'.[12] Even the donkey races held on the Den, a fragrant greensward covered with thyme, failed to dispel her misery.

While Augusta was in Teignmouth, the Prince of Wales married Caroline of Brunswick in April 1795. The Princess of Wales found herself immediately with child and Princess Charlotte was born at the beginning of 1796. It was little consolation for Augusta to compare the lot of her son, declared illegitimate, with that of the little Princess. Augustus had now moved to Rome and, cut off from his family, learnt of his niece's birth from an announcement in the public press.

In November 1795 he had written to the King entreating him 'to consider the very dreadful situation I am in. On the one hand the fear and anxiety of offending your Majesty, on the other my duty to protect those who have suffer'd on my account, whom I love, and to whom I am doubly linked by an unfortunate Child, who was doomed to misfortune from the very hour he was conceived ... Can a man of feeling who through an involuntary error has become a father forsake his child because the Law is ignorant of his birth?'[13] The Prince did not receive an answer.

In May 1796 he was still unsure of His Majesty's intentions towards him and tried to tell the King that his heart wished to combine his 'duty to you and my affection towards my unfortunate companions of woe for ever the union of misfortunes'.[14] He requested a meeting with the King for a few hours in which some remedy might be found and he asked the Archbishop of Canterbury to help him find a country that could acknowledge Augusta as his wife and his child as legitimate. Optimistically he suggested Hanover, where the law might allow a morganatic union between a Prince of Hanover and Lady Augusta, a descendant of the

House of Orange. However, the archbishop reminded him that 'you are the Son of the King of Great Britain, & that wherever you go, or wherever you reside, you can never divest yourself of the Character of a British Prince'.[15] A conciliatory letter from the King in June offered to set his mind at ease and make an allowance for Augusta and the child, on the condition that the Prince acknowledged 'that the Law of this country has decidedly prevented the possibility of a marriage and that the farther continuance of any connection must cease'.[16] The King's proposal was abhorrent to Augustus; he would never abandon the wife whom he adored.

On the third anniversary of the consummation of their marriage the Prince sent another passionate letter. He was in Civitavecchia, the port of Rome, where he was reviewing the Swiss Army troops, financed by King George III. Missing Augusta dreadfully, he reminded her:

> To this day My Treasure do we owe the origin of our dear little boy – to this day am I indebted my love for having consummated our marriage – the grace of God sanctioned our union four days before – but this day three years ago was the first full pleasure I enjoyed of my wife. Yes my love with transport do I recollect it and with infinite satisfaction do I mark to thee my best half … the pleasure you acquired in giving me satisfaction are anecdotes that never can be forgot in my good book … how happy how blessed did I feel on the occasion and how much would I give now to find myself at this very moment in the same dear arms and pressed against that unfortunate but faithful and honest breast. Dear Precious woman how I do adore thee at this moment and how warmly I feel the wrong done us. You can not conceive My soul … ye gods how much I do sigh for thee could I but have thee for an hour … I am really so very passionate at this moment that I will for once follow my Goosy's example for fear of betraying myself. I think when my wife gets to this passage she will get angry and therefore I will put here a kiss for to make my peace with her O here it is my angel and accept it as warmly as one of those I gave thee on the dear [?] day. God bless and preserve thee … convey my blessing to our dear little boy whose picture I trust you will get done for me soon, are the last words of thy most truly affectionate and faithful husband and friend, Augustus Frederick.[17]

Towards the end of his stay in Civitavecchia he told the Prince of Wales that anyone who 'thinks I will give up the partner of my misfortunes and my child insult my feelings and I have no other hopes for remedy but in myself'.[18] That Augustus would sever all connection with his wife in return for an allowance was unconscionable. However, as Prince Augustus was her only means of support, Augusta's financial situation soon became critical.

ady Augusta Murray, reproduction of a photograph of a portrait by Robert Fagan, 1793/94.
Royal Collection Trust/© Her Majesty Queen Elizabeth II 2019)

Prince Augustus Frederick, Duke of Sussex (1773–1843), sixth son of King George III and Queen Charlotte, by Guy Head, oil on canvas, 1798, NPG 648. (© National Portrait Gallery, London)

The Pineapple in the walled garden at Dunmore; the keystones beneath are dated 1761, the year of Augusta's birth.

Augusta's Jacobite grandfather, William Murray, 3rd Earl of Dunmore (1696–1756), who married his first cousin, Catherine, daughter of Lord Nairne. (Private collection)

Augusta's father, John Murray, 4th Earl of Dunmore (1732–1809), wearing Highland Dress of the 3rd Regiment of Foot Guards, by Joshua Reynolds, 1765. (incamera/Alamy Stock Photo)

Augusta's mother, Charlotte, Countess of Dunmore, possibly by James Lonsdale. (Private collection)

The Governor's Palace at Williamsburg, Virginia: Augusta's home from 1774 to 1775.

The Gower Family, *c.*1776–77 (oil on canvas), George Romney (1734–1802). The four younger children were Augusta's first cousins. (Abbot Hall Art Gallery, Kendal, Cumbria, UK/Bridgeman Images)

Augusta's brother, George Murray, Viscount Fincastle, 5th Earl of Dunmore (1762–1836), by James Lonsdale.

Lord Archibald Hamilton (1770–1827) by Thomas Gainsborough, 1786, oil on canvas, Waddesdon (National Trust) Bequest of James de Rothschild, 1957, acc no: 2558. (Photo: Waddesdon Image Library)

Lady Augusta Murray with her son, Augustus. (By kind permission of DACOR Bacon House, Washington)

Augusta's children, Augusta Emma and Augustus D'Este *c.*1804, possibly by Thomas Phillips.

Augustus Frederick, Duke of Sussex, by James Lonsdale, 1817. (By kind permission of the Master and Fellows of Trinity College, Cambridge)

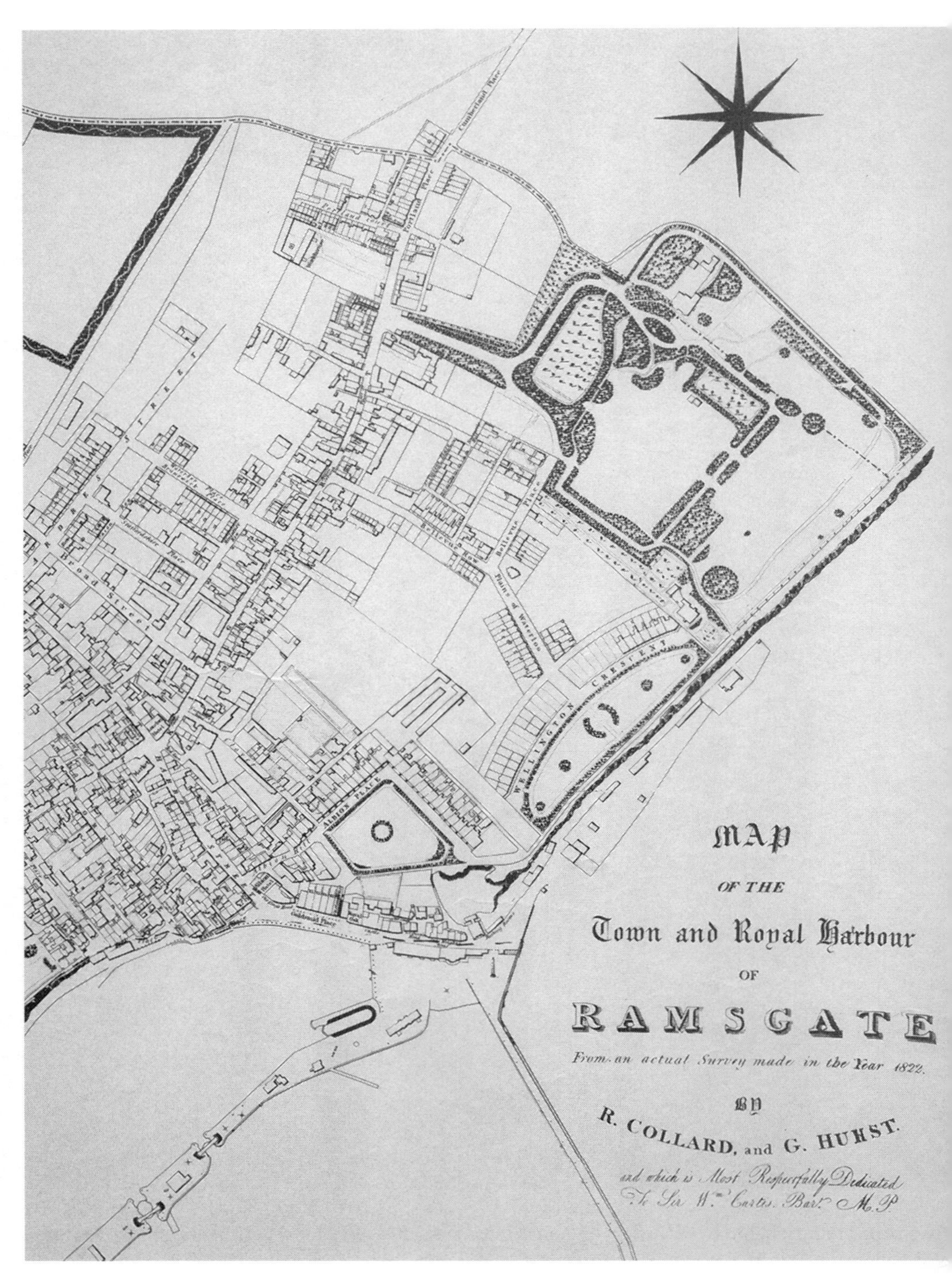

Map of the Town and Royal Harbour of Ramsgate, 1822, showing the Mount Albion estate beneath the compass. (Photograph: Jaron James)

/ount Albion, Augusta's home in Ramsgate, *c.*1850 when her estate was being developed. Holy
'rinity Church behind the house was built on a site donated by her daughter, Emma D'Este.
Kent County Council Libraries Registration & Archives)

Augusta's last resting place: the D'Este Mausoleum at St Lawrence, Ramsgate. (Photograph: Jaron James)

23

Beggars of Us All

On their way back from Teignmouth, Augusta and her mother broke their journey at Clifton and at the end of February 1796, to Augusta's infinite gratitude, the Reverend James Taylor baptised her son in his hillside church. His name was registered as 'Augustus Frederick son of Augustus Frederick and Augusta Augustus Frederick'.[1] The child had celebrated his second birthday before Augusta had been able to find a cleric willing to christen him and the long-delayed ceremony salved her religious conscience and assisted her recovery. She continued her recuperation by taking the sweet-tasting waters, rich in calcium and sulphates, at Hotwells, a fashionable spa on the banks of the River Avon between Clifton and Bristol. While suffering from a 'stink, occasioned by the vast quantity of mud and slime which the river leaves at low ebb under the windows of the Pump-room', it was nevertheless a 'charming romantic place' where the pure air, wildflowers, and hillsides grazed by sheep, made the scenery delightful.[2]

By 1797 Augusta urgently needed assistance with managing her finances. Penury compounded her problems to such an extent that her family approached William Adam, son of John, one of the famous architect brothers, for help. William recalled many years afterwards that his 'long connection & intimacy with the late Earl of Dunmore and his family, led them to apply to me, to represent the pecuniary difficulties of Lady Augusta'.[3] Choosing to train as a barrister rather than an architect, he later became a Whig MP and gained a reputation for sound financial management and the handling of debt. He advised amongst others Charles James Fox, the Duke of York and the Prince of Wales.[4]

When Adam began assisting Augusta with her financial affairs, she had recently moved out of her sister Susan's house and her siblings were lending her money in order to pay the rent of 73 Baker Street. She was however, desperate to buy a home and told Adam that she had seen a suitable one with 'two good rooms in it, (this my little Treasure's lungs require) it is unfurnished but I who see nobody, want no furniture, & it is to be sold for £3,500 … if it could be bought for me in Prince Augustus's name, it would save me all further rent & taxes & then my case would not be so desperate as it now is … my child cannot breathe & we are suffocated with smoke; & yet I pay eight guineas a week.'[5] In order to escape London's injurious atmosphere, Augusta spent the summer of 1797 at Bognor Rocks, an exclusive seaside resort lately developed near Chichester.

Charlotte Dunmore's finances were also in a parlous state and James Heseltine, the proctor at Doctors' Commons, was chasing her for payment of Augusta's legal bills. Lady Dunmore could no longer afford to keep a carriage, a shaming and inconvenient drop in status. Sending her best wishes to Mrs Adam from her address in Great Quebec Street, she regretted that 'not having a carriage I cannot do it in person for this said marriage has made beggars of us all'.[6] Soon she was informing William Adam that, 'I am at this moment without one single half crown in the house.'[7] The countess had once been the highest-ranking lady in America and the contrast between her life in the governor's palace in Williamsburg and her current existence – being forced to rent a London house without a carriage – was pitiful.

Augusta herself was trapped in a vicious circle. Her family was impecunious and she depended on Prince Augustus for her income. He had to rely on his father for a pension and was kept short of money. Meanwhile, the King refused a grant to Augusta as long as the Prince insisted upon regarding her as his legal wife, an attachment that Augustus regarded as sacred.

He was now living in a seaside house at Portici, near Naples and, as always, the King and Queen of Naples received him kindly and he also enjoyed the hospitality and support of Sir William and Lady Hamilton. While his link with Augusta remained robust, it was strained when Giuseppina Grassini, the most famous Italian singer of her day, attracted his attention. When she sang at the wedding of the daughter of the King of Naples, the Prince was bewitched. He first saw her at the height of her powers – both vocal and sexual – and he was smitten; the contrast between her dark hair and pale face entranced him as much as the power of her contralto voice.

Augustus celebrated his 25th birthday in 1798 and although temporarily enmeshed with the diva, his permanent plans still centred on Augusta. Writing a lengthy letter to Thomas Erskine, his legal adviser, he gave details of his courtship and marriages. The Prince reminded Erskine that now he had reached the age of 25, English law allowed him to step forward and claim his wife. He asked the lawyer to help him see that justice was done and explained that Lady Augusta had been prosecuted 'the second day after she was brought to bed, and perfectly defenceless, for her husband was absent. The laws themselves, if not the nobler feelings of humanity, ought to have actuated her prosecutors to delay for a time their violent plans, which at the moment certainly did great harm to her health.'

Laying on the emotion, Augustus declared that the 'heart of every man of feeling, and more especially of every husband, ought to bleed at such a tale of woe'. Concluding this unfortunate history, he questioned, 'whether I can prosecute the perpetrators of this barbarity, and get that despotic and dreadful sentence revoked by which my wife was prostituted and my own child bastardised'.[8]

He wrote to Augusta on 6 February:

> My intention is to come home the instant I feel myself the least strong … I have been very ill with my old complaint … the French will be at Rome in a few days … My father's attentions to me have been such that he has either entirely forgot me or wishes me to believe as much … I received a letter the other day from my brother Ernest who writes to me very kindly indeed. He is the only one of my brothers except the Duke of Clarence also, who keep up any correspondence with me. Augusta my truly and deservedly loved wife soon shall all this be at an end for shortly you shall be with your husband and friend P.S. 1,000 kisses to our little boy.[9]

Although Grassini was merely a diversion, there was concern at home for his moral welfare and at the beginning of March a most unwelcome visitor appeared at the Prince's house in Naples.

Unknown to Augustus, the King had despatched Colonel Edward Livingston, an efficient, sanctimonious and dull Scot, to settle the Prince's affairs and remove him from Neapolitan temptation. On his arrival at Portici, Livingston found disorder on an Augean scale, riotous parties, debt and impropriety: the Prince had even borrowed money from Pope Pius VI and was cohabiting with an Italian. He told the King that Augustus, who was 'of an indolent and easy temper, not nice in his society and an easy prey to designing men' had for some time been 'directed by a set of very improper society whose interest it was to keep up a division betwixt the Prince and his attendants'.[10] This unsavoury group was 'entirely master of all his actions' and had been 'the cause of him acting in public and private in a very improper manner'. Livingston blamed Italy's depraved morals for the Prince's way of life and, no doubt referring to that impudent siren Giuseppina Grassini, told the King that 'such was the power that woman had over the prince she made him carry her in his galla coach, with the royal liverys on great festivals and public processions, where all the court and nobility were [which] gave great scandal and offence, even to this corrupted people'.[11] Livingston put a stop to the parties but could not prevent the Prince from inviting Grassini to dine in his apartment. The Scot – thoroughly shocked – began making preparations to remove the Prince from Naples as quickly as possible.

It was not only that Augustus's morals were at risk; his person was also in jeopardy. Livingston told William Pitt 'that a prince of the Blood Royal of England cannot leave this country without satisfying his creditors; some of them demand ready money and threaten to arrest the prince if not paid directly,' but Sir William Hamilton stepped in and paid the debts, thereby preserving 'the safety of the prince and the honor of the country'.[12] French troops had occupied Rome, deposing and taking the Pope prisoner. It would not be long before they overran Naples and Livingston feared that they might abduct Augustus and force the British Government to ransom him. He would now carry off Augustus to safety, 'Napoleon having been at Genoa and ... the French fleet with all the plunder of Venice ... being at Corfu.'[13] On 4 April Livingston begged William Hamilton to see General Sir John Acton, who was in charge of the Neapolitan navy, 'and entreat him to give positive orders for the speedy sailing' of the frigate, which would remove the Prince from all danger.[14]

With the arrangements in place, Livingston paid off the Prince's two black coachmen and on 8 May Augustus departed from Naples with a reduced entourage. Count Münster and Monsieur Tatter had been relieved of their duties and the Prince's party now consisted of five servants, Doctor Domeier, Livingston and William Hillary, the equerry. William Hamilton had always considered the Prince's comfort and happiness and when Hillary, a convivial young man of similar age, arrived in Naples in 1796, he introduced him to Augustus. The Prince invited his new friend to take lodgings in his hotel, and soon afterwards appointed him equerry. Hillary would remain the Prince's friend for many years and in 1824 he founded the Royal National Institution for the Preservation of Life from Shipwreck, later renamed RNLI.

The royal party crossed Italy and at the port of Manfredonia boarded His Neapolitan Majesty's ship of the line, the *Archimedes*. After four days in hostile waters the vessel arrived at the port of Trieste accompanied by two frigates. With his charge safely disembarked, Edward Livingston could breathe easily. At the end of May, Augustus arrived in Vienna. Livingston told King George that 'the prince has met with a very friendly reception from the [Holy Roman] Emperor, the Empress and every branch of the royal family' and assured the King that he had not had it in his 'power to find fault with any part of the princes conduct since we left Naples and I now flatter myself he may continue to behave in the same desirable manner'.[15] Augustus spent the summer recovering from a dangerous asthma attack.

Before he left Vienna in September the Prince met Captain Thomas Capel, on his way to London with Nelson's dispatches from Egypt. When Capel informed him that Admiral Nelson had defeated the French at the mouth of the Nile on 1 August, the Prince became one of the first Englishmen to hear of the victory. While taking leave of their Imperial Majesties, Augustus proudly announced the glorious news that Nelson had burnt the French Admiral's ship, *L'Orient*, and had taken nine other enemy ships. The British had not lost one vessel and only 100 men had been killed or injured, including 'the brave admiral Nelson [who] was wounded in the head with a splinter but not dangerously'.[16] Buoyed up by these tidings, the Prince departed. He spent a short time in Dresden and reached Berlin on 22 October 1798.

He arrived worn out, discouraged and unwell. Although welcomed by the King of Prussia, Frederick William III, and offered rooms in his palace, Augustus was low. The journey had induced further bouts of asthma, which necessitated him sitting upright at night, and he had been unable to sleep in a bed since leaving Vienna. Like many who attended the Prince and witnessed the fortitude with which he bore his ailments, Livingston told the King, 'I never saw any person suffer worse or bear his suffering with more patience.'[17] Doctor Domeier advised the Prince to spend the winter in a warm climate and with Italy and France out of bounds, suggested Lisbon, Gibraltar or Devonshire. The King, however, said that England was not an option, 'this island must not be thought of, and indeed our damps would render it probably the more fatal than any other were there not weighty reasons to render the idea otherwise highly improper'.[18] The Prince and Lady Augusta must be kept apart. The Prince himself would not consider going to Gibraltar without a military rank, which the King was unwilling to grant.

In the end Augustus remained in Berlin. He spent six months living at the palace, where he recovered slowly although his mood dipped when he heard that two of his brothers, Edward and Ernest, had been granted establishments. In April 1799 Livingston could report to George III that Augustus was much better and he suggested that His Majesty might employ his son in one of his armies. If Augustus were placed with a steady general, who could slowly build up his responsibilities, Livingston believed that the Prince would find a purpose in life and his health would improve. Unfortunately His Majesty did not act on the sensible proposal.

Augustus spent much of the summer confiding in William Hillary, who noted that the Prince spoke 'without reserve on all his Family … particularly in regard to Lady Augusta Murray'. The equerry was sad to see that Augustus was 'unwell in his bodily health and suffered much distress and anxiety of mind from the proceedings which had been instituted in England under the Royal Marriages Act'. Augustus told Hillary that in all his correspondence with the King, the Archbishop of Canterbury and the Lord Chancellor, he 'maintained the legality of his marriage and the legitimacy of his son … and his wife being a descendant of a sovereign house of high standing was eligible by the laws of the German Empire to form such a connexion and that their son, the Prince … was a lawful and legitimate Prince of Hanover'.

One Saturday in August 1799, the two men were spending the morning quietly at the Prince's hotel in Berlin when a servant brought in a letter containing astonishing news. Augustus looked at it attentively and exclaimed, 'Why Hillary this is from my wife.'[19] Augusta was in Berlin. Summoning his carriage, Augustus went straight to her hotel and brought her back to his house, where she was installed in the apartment recently vacated by Beau

Brummell's brother. The Prince dutifully told his father of Augusta's arrival and gave the letter to his valet de chambre to take to England.

After a separation of five and a half years, why had she waited until the summer of 1799 to visit her husband? The Prince told his father that:

> My Augusta having been violently alarmed by the reports she got relative to my health ... determined to verify the truth of them herself ... The motive which engaged her to this step, as also the proof of her affection towards me, are a cordial to my drooping heart, and I confess the moment I saw her was the first happy instant I have experienced since my departure from England.[20]

Augusta's estranged aunt, the Marchioness of Stafford, had been the origin of the incorrect report that the Prince was in mortal danger. Believing that her husband was dying, Augusta had hastened to Berlin.

She needed all the courage she could muster to undertake the lonely expedition to Prussia. She entrusted her 5-year-old son to Lady Dunmore and, travelling as 'Mrs Ford', disobeyed royal orders and left London for Berlin. The usual route was via the port of Harwich, across the North Sea to Cuxhaven, and down the River Elbe to Hamburg before continuing for 180 miles overland to Berlin. German inns were notoriously dirty and the food they served was often excrable. Augusta's journey was arduous at the best of times but with only her maid as company, it was a brave undertaking.

When she arrived, Augustus informed the King of Prussia about his unexpected visitor and asked him to protect her. Ever truthful, he said that he had received Augusta according to the dictates of his conscience, which meant treating her as his wife. He was in no doubt in what manner this should be and, as William Hillary described, 'he sent for the principal persons of his household who were called in to whom he said in the most marked manner "This Lady is the Princess my wife and as such you will consider her."' Hillary noticed 'that they lived in great harmony together at that time as man and wife'.[21] Finally accorded the status that she felt was her due, the five weeks Augusta spent in Berlin were closer to happiness than any other time she experienced with her husband.

Once Augusta had recovered from the fatigue of her journey, she and Augustus went sightseeing in Berlin, where the Brandenburg Gate had recently been built. They made an excursion to the citadel at Spandau and they visited Potsdam to see Sans Souci, Frederick the Great's summer palace, situated above an ornamental terraced vineyard. Hillary attended them on these trips and remembered that 'conversation frequently turned upon their marriage, the cruelty of the attempt to invalidate it'. He recalled that 'they both frequently expressed their conviction that the marriage at Rome could not be overturned however the Royal Marriages Act might affect that Marriage which had taken place in England'.[22]

Augusta's sudden appearance in Berlin sent Mr Arbuthnot, Edward Livingston's replacement, into a spin. His flurry of letters to the King, who was in Weymouth, and to Edward Livingston, who was taking the waters in Bath, provoked consternation in England, where everyone was on holiday. Arbuthnot complained that because the Prince was already several hundred pounds in debt, not only was Augusta's visit thoroughly imprudent, it was also expensive. He told Livingston that although she had been granted a pension of £1,200 in July 1796, she 'complained much of some debts she has contracted in England not having been paid as she had been taught to expect'.[23] Arbuthnot refused to acknowledge however, that Augusta made the Prince happy and that his asthma attacks had ceased.

Along with the one he took to the King soon after Augusta's arrival, the valet carried letters from Augustus to the Prince of Wales and to Lord Thurlow, nominating him as executor and guardian of his son. The servant was also instructed to return with a precious consignment: the child himself. A couple of weeks before Augusta's arrival in Berlin, the Prince had entrusted his eldest brother with the protection of his child. Augustus told the Prince of Wales that he intended to teach his son 'to look up entirely to you and to know that from you alone in some future day he is to expect that justice from which [he] is now maliciously deprived'.[24] However, the Prince of Wales was unsupportive. George knew that the King might overlook Augustus living with Augusta as his mistress, as he had done with the Duke of Clarence and Mrs Jordan, but that he would never accept Augusta as his brother's legal wife.

Therein lay the stumbling block: Augustus refused to consider Augusta as anything other than the wife he had married in the eyes of God in Rome and London. It was six and a half years since their wedding in Hanover Square and the Prince of Wales, who knew the King better, now regarded Augustus as both idealistic and foolish in keeping up the pretence of a legal marriage. Having lost patience, the Prince of Wales began to work behind the scenes to undermine the relations between his brother and Lady Augusta. Indeed Lord Loughborough, the Lord Chancellor, told the King on 27 August that the Prince of Wales showed 'an earnest desire to extricate the Prince his brother from so improper & so dangerous a connection,' and that the Prince believed if Augustus were at home 'it would not be difficult to make him perfectly sensible of his real situation, & to remove from his mind that species of attachment which he now seemed disposed to uphold, by showing him how unfit it was in every point of view to form an object of serious concern to him'.[25]

On receiving the news of the reunion in Berlin, the King left affairs to his eldest son and his ministers. He told the Lord Chancellor that he was happy that the Prince of Wales felt 'so properly on this very strange and improper meeting', that he saw no advantage, only inconvenience, in allowing Augustus to come back to England and that he would wait for the chancellor's opinion before he replied to Arbuthnot.[26] The Chancellor agreed that the Prince should not come home as it might encourage Lady Augusta to think she could join him.

The couple's child, left in Lady Dunmore's care, became a bargaining chip. The King and his ministers agreed that they must make plans quickly to prevent him from being taken to Berlin, but how were they to ensure that he stayed in England? William Pitt, in his role as Lord Warden of the Cinque Ports, had invited the Lord Chancellor to stay at his official residence, Walmer Castle near Deal, and on 29 August Loughborough was happy to inform the King that he would hurry over to Canterbury to see the Prince of Wales, who was currently on holiday there. He would ask him to advise Prince Augustus that his child must not leave England.

The next day, in order to keep Loughborough fully informed, the King sent him the letters he had received from Arbuthnot, Livingston and Henry Dundas, the war secretary, as he himself did not choose 'to employ too many engines, in a business which I am convinced requires great discretion rather than expedition; the public talk is occasioned by Lady Augusta Murray's arrival at Berlin, not the number of days or weeks she remains there'.[27]

The strategy for keeping Augusta's child in England continued to vex the Lord Chancellor and he consulted the King on 1 September. Should the Prince of Wales remove the child from Lady Dunmore before telling Augustus? It might be more expedient to inform his brother first 'that he would take charge of the child and place him where he would be properly brought up'.[28] Although there was a risk that the child would be conveyed to Berlin in the meantime, Lord Loughborough favoured the latter plan, which would neither provoke an outcry nor irritate Augustus. Helpfully, he went on to suggest that should Lady Augusta Murray oppose such a scheme, the Prince should be convinced that she regarded her own happiness more than that of her child or him.

The Lord Chancellor was no friend of Augusta or her family; he had destroyed the reputation of her cousin by marriage, William Beckford, after Beckford's misguided affair with Loughborough's nephew. Loughborough went on to assure the King that he agreed with him, as did Mr Pitt and Mr Dundas, that 'the number of days the business may continue in its present state at Berlin is of no consequence, & it is far from being impossible that these days may soon seem abundantly long to Prince Augustus, especially if during that time he is secluded from the usual intercourse & amusements he has found in that place'.[29] It was quite beyond Lord Loughborough to imagine that, with Augusta at his side, the Prince required no other amusement or that their household in Berlin might be a model of domestic happiness where husband and wife savoured every moment of being together. Loughborough finished his letter to the King by suggesting that the foreign secretary should be informed of the unlikely possibility that Lady Augusta might be received at the Prussian Court. On 4 September King George gave his approval to every proposal, although the 'only difference I could have wished in the plan would have been the securing of the child, but if others are of another opinion I am far from pressing it'.[30]

That day the Prince of Wales took matters in hand and ordered the valet de chambre not to leave London without his permission. He then settled down to write an emollient and practical letter to his brother in Berlin:

> Reason & calm reflection, My dearest A, must tell you how vain & useless it is to cherish illusions which no inward wish or desire, however reasonable or fair can either gratify or accomplish, and be assured that nothing can be more insurmountable than the attainment of that object, namely the establishing L. A. Murray as your wife, which you profess to regard as the summit of the system you have laid down for your future happiness in life, for believe me that the obstacles to its completion are <u>insuperable</u> & <u>invincible</u>. It is not only the King's determination on this point, & which I am persuaded can never be softened that is to be got over, but the

very Law of the Land must be repeal'd before you can have the power to confer on Lady Augusta the title you wish. This law you may consider & protest against as severe & unjust but all opposition to it will be in vain & fruitless, and all remonstrance consequently futile & unavailing, for our lot of birth & station, my dearest brother, makes us all amenable to it ... As this favourite wish of establishing your marriage with Lady Augusta therefore cannot take place, let me conjure you & her in the name of God to summon your fortitude and good sense on this occasion & with true greatness of mind at once give this idea up ... The immediate sacrifice which L.A. may make will do her infinite honour, for it will not only be rescuing you, but preserving her own family from the King's displeasure which otherwise I fear is inevitable. As to your son, my dear Augustus, I will protect him with a father's care therefore banish every anxiety about him, I pray, & abandon all idea if such has been your intention of bringing him to you, for I am positive that will never be allowed. Altho' I am confident that neither the King, or the World, would ever have interfered, nor questioned you as to any female friend who might privately live with you, had not you, pardon me for saying, attempted to give Lady A. a rank that was inadmissible & she unfortunately persisting in that error you both set out with, it could not fail to excite His Majesty' nature and naturally invite his displeasure ... It is my earnest advice & request that L.A.M. should return to England when I shall always feel pleasure in paying her every civility in my power. Again I must beseech you to consider what I have so strenuously recommended, & strictly to recollect that the sentiments I have given you are dictated by undisguised friendship & affection. An acquiescence in my judgement in them will be your surest road to happiness, but all opposition, my dear A. will be fruitless or perhaps fatal to the interests of you both.[31]

Convinced that Augustus would agree to his request to remove the child into his care, the Prince of Wales proceeded to write a letter, entirely different in tone, to his brother, the Duke of Cumberland. He instructed Ernest to:

find out whether Lady Dunmore is in London or at Brighton, or where she is, & that you will lose no time in waiting upon her & expressly stating to her that I have authority to desire that Augustus's child may be

> forthcoming ... However painful, I cannot mince the matter in a business of this nature, and therefore I must instruct you to unequivocally assure Lady Dunmore that I have reason to know that any opposition to this demand will be attended with very unpleasant consequences to both Lord Dunmore and Lady Augusta Murray.[32]

With magnificent disregard for the Prince of Wales's threats or any orders other than those of Prince Augustus, the countess despatched her grandson with his father's servant. Therefore when young Augustus arrived in Berlin on 17 September, it was to the inexpressible joy of his doting parents but contrary to the wishes of the Prince of Wales, the King and the Lord Chancellor.

The little boy's experience of the Prussian capital was short and confusing. He was introduced to his father for the first time and treated like a prince, yet two days later he and his mother were preparing to leave. William Hillary recalled that when it was 'known that this visit to HRH of his wife and son had caused serious displeasure to the King ... it was decided that the Princess and the young prince ... should return to England' and the day before his son's arrival, Prince Augustus had regretfully informed the Prince of Wales that his wife would soon be leaving.[33] He also conveyed the hope that his eldest brother would protect the three of them and added that he could not write a long letter, as he was so unwell. The departure of his wife and son did nothing to improve either Augustus's health or happiness and he 'expressed great regret at parting' with them.[34] Hillary accompanied them to Hamburg and part of the way down the Elbe, and from there they sailed to an uncertain reception in England.

After Augusta's stay in Berlin, the Prince hoped that she might be pregnant again. She was aged 38 and it is clear from recipes for draughts to be taken at bed time 'for pains at a certain time' and a recommendation for a warm bath 'pour les règles' dated 20 June 1799 in her 'Book of Cures' that she was still suffering from painful periods.[35] However, another undated heading in the same notebook, *Miscarriage*, implies that if she were pregnant when she left Berlin, the baby may have been lost. After only five weeks together, the Prince's hopes for a second child were unfulfilled.

His wife's visit changed the Prince's winter plans. Before Augusta's arrival he had been corresponding with Grassini, whom he had promised to take into his household when he returned to Italy, but the Berlin visit swept away all thoughts of the grasping diva. Writing to the Archbishop of Canterbury on 28 August, Edward Livingston doubted 'whether or not Lady Augusta may not be a less dangerous and less expensive companion than La Grassini, who certainly was intended to meet his Royal Highness in Italy, where the Prince says he is to pass the winter … she is a most corrupted and dangerous woman'.[36] Even Arbuthnot sympathised with Augusta in Berlin, saying:

> If she keeps her word & goes quickly away from hence I really think she is entitled to some merit, which may perhaps induce his Majesty graciously to excuse the fault she has committed & not take away her pension, of which she is much afraid. She looks upon her return as a great sacrifice, as Prince Augustus has told her that if she remains she will be acknowledged as his wife & received with the honours due to that rank.[37]

His Majesty did not excuse the fault but neither did he remove her pension on her return to London, an event the newspapers noticed on 24 October.

As soon as she and their son had gone, the Prince regretted his decision to allow them to leave. He felt sure that they could have withstood the King's fury more effectively if they had stayed as a united family. Having heard nothing from his wife since her departure, he wrote Augusta a stricken letter on 1 November, the 'sixteenth day since you sailed from Cuxhaven and as yet I have no news of my soul's dearest delight … though I am perfectly ignorant of all the plans that our enemies will have formed in England yet I cannot help feeling that we should have done both much better to have remained together … my whole soul is with thee my whole body longs for thee.'[38] Six and a half years after the wedding in Rome, the Prince's passion for Augusta was undiminished.

24

I Am to be No Further Troubled on that Subject

Augustus was nursing his grievances when he received the Prince of Wales's letter of 4 September. Its unpalatable, though realistic, contents caused a permanent cooling in the brothers' relationship. George's proposition that Augusta should live privately with Augustus, as a mistress rather than a wife, revealed a 'wide difference of opinion' from his former suggestion advising Augustus not to consider a morganatic marriage in Germany because his son might inherit the Electoral States of Hanover. Augustus was at 'a loss how to account' for his brother's change of mind and in a fit of misery he poured out a list of injustices.

The treatment he had received at the hands of the King convinced Augustus of his dislike for his sixth son. It rankled with him that their father had broken his word by promising him an establishment at the same time as Ernest. Unreasonably, Augustus blamed the King for his asthma by forcing him to Göttingen, where the climate 'was the cause of my first indisposition thirteen years ago'. The question of their father being able to harm Augusta or any of her family on Augustus's account was 'almost too indelicate' for him to touch on but if such an event took place, he would return to England knowing that he would not be received at court.

If the King refused to make appropriate provision for Augusta and pay the 'debts, which she had contracted from having had no allowance made her the three first years of our separation', as Lord Loughborough had promised, Augustus would be forced to publish all the correspondence relating to these sad occurrences. He wished to see his wife put 'in that way of respectability as to allow for the education of our child, for her keeping her carriage, and having those comforts which she can enjoy at a distance from me'.

Augustus informed the Prince of Wales that the only reason he had allowed his wife to return to England from Berlin was to please the King and now he asked his brother to have her 'properly established as ought to be the case, if not you know the consequence, for if a single hair of her head is touched I shall consider it as an order for my immediate return to England'. In the heat of the moment he finished his letter by refusing the Prince's 'generous offer' of taking charge of the education of his son, as it was 'incompatible with my feelings of honour and duty to have him either educated or treated otherwise than what I conceive is his due. The loss is entirely mine but I trust a moment's reflection will make you see the impossibility of my entering into those views of yours.'[1]

Augustus had begun his letter by telling the Prince that 'during the short stay that I made in England we met so very seldom that our acquaintance even then could barely be called intimacy' but however aggrieved he felt, maintaining good relations with the Prince of Wales was essential. His eldest brother remained Augustus's only channel to the King, on whom Augustus relied for revenue. Therefore on 2 October he wrote to the Prince of Wales more calmly. He asked George to be guided by Lord Thurlow in the care and education of young Augustus and 'in case of any accident happening to me I have reckoned on your friendship and steadiness to accept of the guardianship of my son jointly with Lord Thurlow and his mother'.[2] By this time the Prince of Wales had lost interest in trying to help his brother or his nephew and it was left to Augusta to negotiate with him in London.

The relationship between Lady Augusta and the Prince of Wales was already strained and the matter of his unopened letters did not help her cause. Prince George had often disappointed her in the summer when she had expected him to call. At the end of November she tried again and asked him to visit her at her house in Hertford Street to discuss the protection of her child. He replied that 'indispensable business' meant that he was unable to meet 'Lady Augusta Murray' and proposed two other days.[3]

Mr Thomas Tyrwhitt, one of the Prince's officials, forwarded him her response, a 'foolish note of Lady Augusta Murray's which I am confident would give great uneasiness to Prince Augustus, and be in no way supported by him'.[4] Mr Tyrwhitt however, was wrong: she was merely following the

Prince's instructions to receive letters directed only to 'Princess Augustus Frederick'. The Prince of Wales was incensed but Augusta's action was vindicated by the letter she received that week from her husband telling his 'dearest Goosy' that, 'I can assure you my life and soul my affection and love for you is unbounded and will never alter but with my existence.'

On one hand Augusta wanted to respect her husband's directions and honour the position of her son, but on the other she did not want to offend the Prince of Wales. She tried to explain her dilemma by writing two letters on 13 December. The first was to the Prince of Wales's friend and neighbour, Rear Admiral John Willett Payne, in which she wrote, 'If I renounce Prince Augustus's name when I have his positive orders to the contrary – I seem in my own eyes to wish to dispense the tie by which we are united – he may accuse me, & so may my boy in future, of being the first author of the child's blasted hopes.'[5]

The second letter to the Prince of Wales was a brave but hopeless attempt at clarification and reconciliation:

> I cannot bring myself to sign my own infamy, & the death warrant of my boy. – I cannot mean any disrespect to your Royal Highness nor can I presume to disregard your advice, – but while I have Prince Augustus's positive orders to the contrary, I cannot renounce his name … – as long as he does justice to me, & his son, I cannot act injuriously to either; – hitherto he has considered me as his lawful wife, & his boy as his legitimate child; How can I then be the first, to abjure this time for myself, & abrogate this claim for my boy?[6]

The Prince of Wales was unconvinced.

By the end of March 1800 Augustus could no longer bear being separated from his family and asked his eldest brother to inform the King that he was coming home. Boarding the *King George* packet at Cuxhaven, he arrived on 5 May and immediately went to Hertford Street. Two days later Augustus spent the evening with the Prince of Wales, who told the Lord Chancellor that his brother had arrived and the next night Augustus requested an audience with the King. George III was deeply offended that his son had returned without his permission and told Lord Loughborough that Augustus 'does not give any explanation that I can think sufficiently explicit of his giving up the absurd ideas he has as yet adopted, to give me reason for admitting him into my presence'.[7] As long as Augustus continued to cling to his so-called marriage, he was not welcome.

The Prince decided that his best strategy, in order to obtain a reasonable pension for both himself and Augusta, was to give in to the King's wishes at the same time as staying with his wife and child in Hertford Street. Consequently, the next day the Lord Chancellor was able to tell the King that Prince Augustus 'was perfectly convinced that his former ideas were without foundation and that he must ever respect the uneasiness which his actions had occasioned to you His Majesty'.[8] Augustus had obtained legal advice from Thomas Erskine informing him that any marriage contracted 'in any country upon earth' which was not in accordance with the Royal Marriages Act 'must ever remain absolutely and indefensibly void'. The Prince then asked for advice on what 'conduct he ought to pursue' and Erskine declined to respond other than in the presence of Lady Augusta Murray and Lord Fincastle. Once all three were assembled, Erskine bravely informed them that keeping up the appearance of a condition that was 'so very opposite to the truth' was neither consistent with plain reason nor a sense of honour.[9]

Augustus was determined to dissemble and the King told the Prince of Wales on 12 May 1800 that he was pleased to learn that Augustus 'is at length convinced of the invalidity of the unwise step he took some years past, and that I am to be no further troubled on that subject', whereupon he granted Prince Augustus an audience the following day.[10] At the end of the month the King received a letter from the Lord Chancellor stating that it was not 'the intention of Prince Augustus to retain either Mr Livingston or Mr Arbuthnot in his family' and the detested gentleman attendants were finally despatched.[11]

Whatever the Prince may have intimated to the King and his ministers for financial reasons, he did not give up Augusta. In July the couple vacated the house in Hertford Street and the Prince established himself with Augusta, their son, and Lady Virginia Murray at one of the best addresses in Mayfair: the house at the corner of Grosvenor Square with its front door on Lower Grosvenor Street. In November 1800 they received a visit from an old friend, the connoisseur John Rushout, who had received Augusta at his villa south of Naples in the autumn of 1792. He noticed that in their home, Augusta was styled as Princess Augustus Frederick and the Prince treated her as his legal consort. Her title, however, did not extend beyond the fiefdom of Lower Grosvenor Street. Augusta's acknowledgement by the King and Queen and the rest of the Royal Family was out of the question, although members of less regular circles accepted her. When Sir William and Lady Hamilton returned from Italy in 1800 they stayed at William Beckford's house in Grosvenor Square. That winter Cornelia Knight attended a curious party there and was surprised to find both Emma Hamilton's former and current lovers, Charles Greville and Lord Nelson, in attendance as well as Nelson's long-suffering wife and Prince Augustus and Lady Augusta Murray.[12]

By December Augustus's health could no longer sustain the English winter and as the French had overrun Italy, he chose Lisbon as his winter refuge. In order to avoid any gossip, the King commanded that the chief minister at Lisbon should be clear that the Prince's residence there was for the benefit of his health and he would live there incognito as Count Diepholz, one of George III's Hanoverian courtiers. On 18 December, the night before he left, Augustus 'prepared a statement reaffirming his two marriage ceremonies, accompanied by a paper signed by Dr Thynne, testifying that he had delivered' young Augustus.[13]

Augustus left his family in Lower Grosvenor Street and, having been delayed by contrary winds, set sail from Portsmouth on HMS *Endymion* on 28 December. Jane Austen's brother, Charles, was one of the naval officers on board and when he wrote to the novelist at the beginning of 1801, she relayed some of his news to their sister, Cassandra. The officers, Jane said, 'were very well satisfied with their royal passenger, whom they found jolly and affable, who talks of Lady Augusta as his wife, and seems much attached to her'.[14]

One night during the journey to Lisbon, conversation at the captain's table turned to the conduct of women and the duty of a friend to warn another if his wife were unfaithful. Passionate as ever, Augustus informed his fellow diners that he would fight the messenger first and then enquire into the truth of the information. He told Augusta:

> Such are my sentiments relative to you, my soul that I never could for a moment harbour a suspicion on your head; and I tell it you in order that you may know my manner of thinking. Indeed, I firmly believe there is not a better woman in the world than you are. I am convinced I have not such another friend in the world, and am certain no woman can nor ever

will make me so happy as you do. I feel it; and often with ecstasy dwell on this subject; saying to myself that for to leave you I must not only be the most infamous wretch in the universe, but also the greatest fool existing. I may, and I have, wronged you, certainly at times; but my repentance ought to merit your forgiveness, when my determination is never to do so again. Oh, my Augusta, I love you; indeed, I adore you; and I am sure I never shall be happy till we meet again.[15]

The tone of this letter implies that their six months together in London had not perhaps been unalloyed bliss.

The entries in Augusta's commonplace books can be confusing because she rarely indicated whom she was addressing. There is however, one item that may help explain the reason for the Prince's departure to Lisbon:

I foresaw yr absence would deprive me of the solace I had derived from yr love,' she wrote, '& yet it was I who urged yr departure, & caused our seperation – but what stubborn conflicts did I go thro' with my dearest wishes, ere I could obey the voice of Reason & the reward of my victory is regret & sorrow. I could not but perceive you were formed to be happier, than I could make you & I won from you the consent to our seperating which divorced me from happiness & left me to misery & myself.

On the next page she adds, 'several tedious torturing months had dragged their slow lengths along'.[16]

In London Augustus had been in an unenviable position. He was unwelcome in polite circles and reliant on his unacknowledged wife for diversion and comfort. Young Augustus was 6 years old when the Prince returned to London and other than spending one day in Berlin with him, his father was a stranger. Augusta had indulged their son, and the little boy, who was accustomed to having his mother to himself, may not have welcomed the unknown interloper. Life in Lower Grosvenor Street for the Prince must have been both restricted and frustrating.

Before that the only extended period that Augusta and the Prince had spent living together was in Berlin, but the time with her husband in London opened her eyes. 'His perfections had taught me to discover their opposites,' she acknowledged, and 'as I lived with him I became discriminating. – what might once have charmed me pleased me no more, the observing his noble, sensible manly character had quickened my perception of moral distinctions; – I was no longer to be imposed upon by appearances.'[17]

With the departure of her husband, Augusta was left in London to maintain their house and child without a regular source of income. She was unhappy and alone. Two days after he sailed she wrote, 'Life without you, is to me a desert.'[18] Lady Virginia moved out of Lower Grosvenor Street in January: living in the company of a miserable sister without the Prince quickly lost its lustre. Although Virginia's presence alleviated Augusta's loneliness, the Prince was right when he told her that, 'in some manner she puts you out of your way, and therefore you are better without her'.[19]

On 14 January 1801, the seventh anniversary of his departure from England after the birth of their son, Augustus recollected 'perfectly the scene of agony' he underwent before leaving at four o'clock in the morning.[20] However, any bickering in London now forgotten, he was optimistic for their future together and believed that by May his affairs would be settled and they would never have to be separated again. He asked her opinion about Brownsea Island in Poole Harbour, which was 'to be let for two hundred and fifty pounds a year for seven years' and told her:

> I think by all accounts the place would do for me and is only a hundred miles from London which would be just one day's journey. Will you inform yourself about everything my own little loved Goosy and let me know about it. I think we could be so happy there and that it would do my health a great deal of good ... it would be quite like a little kingdom there. We might live forgotten by all the world and forgetting everything but ourselves and our own boy.[21]

It is debatable whether Augusta, cosmopolitan, sophisticated and well-travelled, would have been happy on an island on the south coast with a colony of red squirrels as her neighbours but the Prince's pipe dream confirms that he had no plans to desert her when he departed for Portugal. It also appears that neither of them knew that Augusta was pregnant again.

The Atlantic breeze blowing up the wide River Tagus to the hillside city of Lisbon made it a popular destination for Englishmen like Augustus, who suffered from respiratory and other illnesses. On arrival in the Portuguese capital he took lodgings at the Necessidades Palace, a long, low, baroque confection with pink walls and white stonework, used to house visiting dignitaries. Situated in one of Lisbon's public squares, it was the only royal residence to survive the city's catastrophic earthquake, tsunami and five-day fire of 1755. The earthquake had taken place on 1 November, All Saints Day, when most people were in church and the results were so horrifying that Enlightenment philosophers, including Voltaire, seriously questioned the Leibnizian concept of optimism that 'All is for the best in the best of all possible worlds.'

At first the Prince did not like Portugal. He acknowledged that its temperate climate was pleasant but told the Prince of Wales that this 'place to me is the most horrid of any I ever was at' and for a man who enjoyed association with other nationalities, he was frustrated that 'strangers are never admitted into any Portuguese society'.[22] His allowance left him little opportunity to enjoy Lisbon. It was administered by James Trail, a gentleman whom he loathed and had been foisted on him at the suggestion of the equally hated Robert Arbuthnot. The Prince of Wales instructed Trail to give his brother £8,500 per annum, to be made up of £5,200 for his household and travelling expenses, £2,000 pocket money (clothes, masters, charities and presents), Doctor Domeier's salary was to be £300 and Trail himself would receive £1,000. Augustus could employ no more than six servants; a maximum of twenty guests were permitted at his table in any one week and he could keep only six horses or mules.[23]

In London Augusta was as miserable as her husband. She was continually harassed for payment of bills incurred while Augustus was with her in London. Setting up a home fit for a prince had been expensive and they had not stinted themselves. They spent £330 with Rundell & Bridge, jewellers and goldsmiths to the Crown; Augusta's sedan chair, costing £34, came from Griffin & Co., the firm patronised by Queen Charlotte; there were bills from booksellers, a laceman, cutlers and confectioners and their black footman, Mr Lemon, was owed £30. These expenses were surely the responsibility of the Prince rather than Augusta and she was so short of money that she resorted to the King for help.

In order to ensure that her letter reached him, it was written on his birthday, 4 June. Knowing that 'nobody would even venture to present this letter as coming from me, – if it ever reaches your Majesty I shall owe my success to artifice; I have endeavoured as well as I could, without absolutely asserting a falsehood, to make it be believed' that it came from Prince Augustus.

She told King George that she had been 'abandoned, & shunned by the World, for ever excluded from all my former enjoyments, believed to be the object of your Majesty's particular detestation'. Writing directly to the King was a desperate measure but she was in despair.

The grant of £1,200 per annum that she received from the civil list for the maintenance of herself and her child, when all the deductions were taken, now amounted to £800 and was 'paid with cruel irregularity while the price of everything is centupled'. Moreover, having received no income for three years before she was granted the pension, she had incurred debts on which she was compelled to pay £600 interest. She requested that if anything more could be done for her, the money might not be granted from the civil list, which incurred deductions and long arrears. The long letter was written with passion and conviction and drawing to a close, she declared, 'How to finish this letter I know not, I have no person to tell me, & I dread your Majesty's displeasure; – do pray Sir forgive me, pity me, & do not crush the wretch you can save.'[24] When she wrote to the King, Augusta was seven months pregnant. She did not know if he would receive her letter or if he would answer her plea but she had nothing to lose. On 9 (not 11 as often stated) August 1801 she gave birth to a daughter, Augusta Emma, who would always be known as Emma.

25

This Sad Reverse

In November 1801 the King conferred peerages on two of his younger sons. In Lisbon Augustus did not hear the news until the beginning of the new year when Adolphus, the new Duke of Cambridge, told him that he had become the Duke of Sussex in England, Earl of Inverness in Scotland and Baron Arklow in Ireland. He was therefore unaware of his elevation to the peerage when he wrote to the King and the Prince of Wales on 7 December 1801 informing them that he had decided to separate from Augusta. What drove him to cut his ties after his tenacious, but ultimately fruitless, battle? We can never be sure why he finally gave her up but after eight years of attempting to have her acknowledged as his lawful wife, his decision to detach himself does not appear to be have been influenced by the possibility of a peerage.

In Augustus's letter to the Prince of Wales informing him of his wish to part with Augusta, he enclosed another one to her, to prove to his brother that 'what has been so long wished for is at last come to pass. We are to meet no more. My whole wish now is to make her comfortable.'[1] When he left for Lisbon in December 1800 he and Augusta still loved each other and eleven days after his departure she acknowledged in her commonplace book that, 'I cannot silence the claims of an heart demanding you as its right.'[2] The unexpected news, sent via the Prince of Wales, was a terrible shock to her.

Augustus explained to his father that circumstances had forced him to alter the relationship he had maintained for so long: 'The imprudent conduct my Augusta has adopted and to which from the most scrupulous point of honour I would not listen till in possession of ocular demonstration I am now obliged to separate.'[3] It may have suited Augustus to tell his father that his wife's 'imprudent conduct' was to blame for their break, rather than acknowledge that he had tired of her, that he needed a better pension and that he had given up the struggle to have her acknowledged as his legal wife. He was now reconciled to living in Portugal, where he had taken a mistress, and asked the King to find him some employment whereby he could serve his father and his country.

The drive to blacken Augusta's reputation in royal circles was spearheaded by Ernest, Duke of Cumberland and his disgraceful campaign no doubt assisted Augustus's decision to separate from her. Initial suspicions about the timing of her pregnancy may have also played a part. London gossips, quick to denigrate Augusta, said that the Prince did not recognise Emma as his daughter.

Cumberland was two years older than Prince Augustus and therefore in terms of royal succession had nothing to fear from his younger brother or any children he might have but he persisted in besmirching Augusta's name. Fourteen years after her death, Cumberland was perpetuating the calumny, telling Lord Strangford that Emma 'is as much my Brother's daughter as she is mine but [is] Lord Archibald Hamilton's which my Brother was fully convinced of by a Discovery of Letters that were lost by Lady Augusta and was the cause of his separating from her'.[4]

Anyone with the flimsiest knowledge of human gestation knew that the Prince must be the father of Augusta's baby. She was conceived in November 1800 when her parents were living together in London and was born less than eight months after Augustus departed for Lisbon on 19 December, but Augusta's opponents spread the rumour that the little girl was premature and therefore could not be the Prince's child. When her husband left London, Augusta probably did not know that she was pregnant and the Prince himself acknowledged that the child's paternity was not a factor in his decision to separate. He later told George Fincastle that, 'many unfair and untrue reports have circulated since the unfortunate conclusion of my affair with your sister … I have only to state and give my full authority … that my separation from my wife has not been occasioned by any cause of a criminal nature, at all times I shall be ready to declare this'.[5] Still describing her as his 'wife', he acknowledged that his severance from Augusta was not caused by adulterous conduct on her part and he authorised a refutation in his name of all reports of her infidelity 'to his bed' and importantly, cited 'personal differences' as the reason for the split.

In terminating his relationship, he asked the King and the Prince of Wales to help Augusta, 'Now that my separation is decided upon, I humbly entreat your Majesty to make Augusta's situation as little uncomfortable as possible to enable her without splendour to be at her ease as much as from her rank and situation she has a right to expect.'[6] The expense of their second child aggravated her plight and, hounded by her creditors, life in London became insupportable. Lord Dunmore, who might have alleviated her problems, was in debt himself and Augusta knew that the Duke of Sussex was her only chance of financial relief. Rather than lapsing into self-pity, she decided to go to Lisbon to ask him for help and persuaded her sister, Susan, to accompany her.

Having travelled on her own to Berlin, Augusta was undaunted at the thought of the journey to Falmouth and the sea voyage via the Bay of Biscay to Lisbon. She had done it in reverse in 1793 and in equally dangerous circumstances. England was still at war with France on Sunday, 14 March 1802 when she and Susan boarded the *Duke of York* packet, which arrived in Lisbon the next Saturday, having avoided enemy shipping.[7] Augusta's expedition to Lisbon ended in rejection, humiliation and failure. The Duke's equerry, James Trail, delighted in recounting every detail of the disastrous mission but his account, albeit inadvertently, reveals Augusta's mettle and persistence. She had come to ask the Duke of Sussex for help and she would not leave Portugal until she had seen him.

Augusta went straight to the Necessidades Palace, where the Duke was horrified to hear of her arrival. Having communicated to His Majesty his determination to extricate himself from her, he told Trail to inform her that a meeting was impossible. Augusta was not to be put off. 'She pretended perfect ignorance of any letter from the Prince about separation, or that would cause her visit to appear extraordinary,' and was resolute about staying at the palace. The purpose of her journey was to acquire the Duke's signature to an indenture that she had brought with her.[8] This document committed Augustus to paying her £4,000 in quarterly instalments, free of taxes, charges and deductions so that 'Augusta now called the Duchess of Sussex' might be 'better able to support an establishment suited to her rank and station and maintain their said children'.[9] Naturally she had no wish to discuss her financial difficulties with anyone other than the Duke and was certainly not going to take Trail into her confidence.

The equerry went four times between the couple that day. He told Augusta that the Duke would be forced to leave for Gibraltar the next morning if she did not find lodgings elsewhere. Shamed and agitated, she was forced to leave the Necessidades Palace at midnight, the Duke having moved out to stay with the Marquis de Pombal. Next day, a number of letters, at times angry and at times appeasing, coursed to and fro. In one the Duke told Augusta that he could do nothing about her debts until his establishment in England and his pension were settled. He offered to defray the cost of her passage back to Falmouth in the packet that was departing on Tuesday as well as their journey to London – indeed, the subtext seemed to read: he would pay her anything to leave.

On the Monday she told Trail, 'you know, & every body who gives any credit to my assertions <u>must know</u> ... that neither my person or property are safe in England; so that my return under these circumstances is as impossible as was my remaining there'.[10] Events turned farcical when Lady Susan informed Trail that 'it is out of our power to go by the packet tomorrow, for all the clothes we wore on the road & at sea are gone to the wash this morning & cannot be returned tonight'. He retorted that as the packet did not depart until the next afternoon it was possible for them to leave in clean clothes. Augusta took to her bed and Susan delivered the contentious indenture to the Marquis de Pombal's house, but it was returned unsigned with a note saying that it could not be looked at while she and her sister remained in Lisbon.

Hearing this, Augusta roused herself. She had been tried to the limit and now she threatened Augustus:

> I will return to England immediately. This time <u>I know</u> the Duke of Sussex commands it, knowing too my situation. I will suffer myself to be put in prison. ... The Newspapers will tell what has occurred here ... in future it will be through the medium of my brother I shall try to arrange matters with HRH & had he had candour enough to let me know from the first, he had given his word of honour to the King never to see me more, I would have approved of all Mr Trail did to prevent his seeing me.

Numerous creditors were harassing her in London and she had had a long and exhausting journey, but it was unfair of her to imply that she did not know that the Duke was serious about their separation. When Augustus heard that Trail had made arrangements with the captain of the *Prince Adolphus* packet to take Augusta and Susan home, he began to relax, but he was wrong to do so. The fiasco was yet to run its course: Augusta still hoped to induce him to sign her indenture.

Determined to give it one last try, she disguised herself as a Lisbon milliner and went to the Marquis de Pombal's house, where she approached the porter:

> with a bandbox under her arm to be carried to the Marchioness to shew her some new fashions ... She was immediately recognised; & after a long conversation in a detached apartment with a gentleman, a near relation of the Marquis de Pombal's, she was prevailed upon about ten o'clock at night to return in a carriage to her lodgings. While she remained ... a good many ladies who happened to be in the house crowded into the Anti chamber of the apartment where she was with the door half open. When she observed their curiosity she threw aside her cloak walked backwards and forwards with all the grace & dignity imaginable.[11]

After this display a friend of the Duke of Sussex accompanied her home. Still unsatisfied, Augusta 'invited him into the house & charged him with a letter for the Prince which she had brought from England & also with the same papers which he had already seen & had returned unsigned'. Her stratagem failed, the papers were returned and Augustus let it be known that if she did not return to England, he and his household would go to Gibraltar. His threat was unnecessary. Augusta knew that she was defeated and when the *Prince Adolphus* tacked down the Tagus estuary towards the Atlantic, she and Susan were aboard wearing freshly laundered clothes.

The Prince of Wales had been assigned the task of sorting out Augustus's marital and financial affairs, an undertaking for which he had little appetite, and he told William Adam that it was business in which he had been 'uncomfortably intermeddled'.[12] George was in fact encouraging others, including the Duke of Cumberland and loyal Doctor Domeier, to sully Augusta's character.

On her return from Lisbon, not guessing that he was working against her interests, Augusta wrote to the Prince of Wales asking for his protection. She had worked out her argument with care and there is not a single deletion or alteration on any of the seven sheets of writing paper. She reminded him that her trip to Portugal – 'no voyage of pleasure' – had been for pecuniary purposes only and 'the reception she had met with, was the utmost of insult, & ill usage a woman could receive; – never admitted to his presence, – driven from his abode, the sport of his mistress, & dependents, – this too from the man who has sworn, & still swears, ever to call me, & consider me (what he knows I am) his wife.'

Augusta knew that her character was being 'vilely slandered' by Cumberland, who was spreading rumours that she had made the journey 'with a view to concealing a situation which it requires the presence of an husband to support without disgrace'. When she came back from Berlin, she:

> heard reports of a similar nature were then circulated, & believed by some parts of the royal family, – then, with my husband, & under his protection I did not think it my business to interfere, – He was satisfied, he talked to me of these reports, & did not believe it worth his while to pay any attention to them. – I thank him for this act of justice; – now, I am told, that the Duke of Sussex's present assertions, are in direct opposition to his former conviction; that he now disowns the girl for his child; – that by a letter written to the Queen he lends his name to this cruel injustice; – I hear too, pardon my freedom, – that these reports, – if they do not originate with the Royal Family are by them, believed, – repeated, – & spread.

Augusta told the Prince of Wales she had:

> endured nine years of continued affliction, – I have suffered poverty & neglect all along, – I have suffered persecution, & I have encountered duplicity & deceit, – I have borne all this patiently – but this present calamity may possibly reach my children in its consequences, & therefore it is that I rouse myself to the present struggle, & call upon you Sir, by every feeling you ever had friendly to me, to exert yourself this once in my behalf.

She could not believe the reports that Augustus had disowned her daughter but if so, she asked for every particular, reminding the Prince of Wales that his brother:

> has accustomed me to hardship, – has inured me to injury, – has oppressed me with vexation, – has steeped me in calamity, – (let him remember what was my situation in society when we first met, & what it now is, – this sad reverse Sir, is his work ...) this last attack, this flagrant outrage, this last injury without a name, & without limit is more that I can submit to; – I must struggle against this new torture, – I must resist this fatal blow, which is to murder my reputation by the ruin of my child.[13]

It was a powerful letter but the battle to clear her name would be arduous. With the Duke of Sussex safely in Lisbon, it was easy to put words into his mouth, and although she did not believe that Augustus had denied paternity of her daughter, there were plenty of people who thought he had.

By the time Augusta and Susan arrived back in Falmouth, Britain was no longer at war with France. Peace had been secured at Amiens on 25 March 1802, so the Prince of Wales encouraged Augusta to seek refuge in Paris from her creditors. Financial problems however, continued to beset her. Although she had been assured her debts would be paid, when asked to separate her own and the Duke's debts, she told William Adam in November that 'the jobman, the butcher, the linen draper, the wine merchant, the grocer, the chandler, the coal merchant [and] the tax gatherer, have either sent me writs, or attorney's letters' for non-payment of their bills and that since March 1800 she had been without any income.[14]

Tender-hearted Augusta felt responsible for the financial hardship endured by those who had willingly given her credit, and had hoped that the Duke would return and reconcile their bills. She told William Adam that she had left England believing, as the Prince of Wales had intimated, that her affairs would be settled while she was away, otherwise she would have preferred to have stayed in London to face the consequences of a custodial sentence than seem 'to desert the cause of tradespeople' and she had expected to return from France 'to the comforts of a [debtors'] prison'.[15]

Meanwhile, Augusta's family continued to be supportive. They were unified in their attempts to redeem her reputation, as well as trying to shore up her finances while the provision she had been promised failed to materialise.

In the autumn of 1802, Augusta's brother, Jack, sailed to Lisbon intending to obtain the Duke's signature to his sister's indenture. Taking the precaution of using an alias when he arrived, Captain Murray wasted no time in presenting himself at the Necessidades Palace, pushing past sentries and servants until he encountered the Prince's groom, to whom he gave his real name. When the Duke refused to see him, Jack let him know that he had made the journey specifically to see him and he would not go back without an audience. On being admitted, Jack required the Prince 'to disavow certain things to the injury of his sister's honour which his Royal Highness had been represented to have said of her'.[16] Captain Murray obtained the disavowal and Augustus's signature to the bond, having informed him that he had heard that the Duke's financial situation was about to improve. After a few days Jack returned to London. He had acquired the signature to his sister's document but in the end his Portuguese trip made no difference to her fortunes.

The autumn of 1803 was depressing. War with France had resumed in May, the law of Habeas Corpus, whereby a person cannot be detained without trial, had been suspended in Ireland, and the English were living in fear of invasion. Against this uneasy atmosphere, Augusta was arrested for failing to pay her son's writing master and faced incarceration for debt in the Fleet Prison. John Howard, the penal reformer, had reported in 1777 that the Fleet was filthy and riotous, crawling with drunks, the helpless and the hopeless, but his recommendations were ignored. The possibility of imprisonment was so appalling that Augusta's gratitude overflowed when one of her brothers, probably George Fincastle, paid the writing master's invoice at the last moment. Having prevented his sister's imprisonment, the same brother assembled all her creditors and gained her some respite until the New Year.

When Lord Dunmore returned home from overseas at the end of October, Augusta asked her brother, Alexander, 'to come to Town directly', and signed the letter with her family nickname, 'Goosy.'[17] She wanted his support in persuading their father to speak to the King at the levée the next day. Levées, which were held at St James's Palace, were for men only and started at midday on Wednesdays and Fridays when George III was in London.[18] Although invitations were not extended, the King had an opportunity to speak briefly to all his visitors: ministers, ambassadors and supporters of the crown in both houses of Parliament, and he expected members of his family to attend. Everyone wore military uniform, or court dress, which comprised matching tailcoat and waistcoat, breeches, lace cuffs, a jabot and buckled shoes.

Among the group in attendance on Wednesday, 29 October, the King noticed the Earl of Dunmore, the father of that troublesome young woman, Lady Augusta Murray. He welcomed the former governor of the Bahamas and learnt that he had requested a private audience. Having worked his way round the guests in the privy and presence chambers, the King made his way to his closet, where he held confidential meetings. Lord Dunmore was waiting outside and before he was admitted the Prime Minister, Henry Addington, asked him to be 'as moderate as possible on the subject he was about to bring under His Majesty's consideration – as it was one to which he was most particularly alive'.[19] The earl dismissed the request: Augusta's father was not in a conciliatory mood. His blood was up and he intended to ask the King to provide a permanent settlement for his daughter and her children. He had come to court specifically to fight her cause, as well as those of the two grandchildren that he shared with His Majesty. When shown into the royal presence, etiquette demanded that he knelt before the King and, straightening up, the elderly peer readied himself for a clash. His vigour undimmed, he was well aware that what he was about to ask would not please his monarch.

After his audience, Lord Dunmore went home in the early afternoon 'in a most famous rage' and found Augusta, Jack and Lady Dunmore waiting on tenterhooks.[20] The moment he arrived they could see that the meeting had gone badly but Jack's description of what happened at St James's Palace that afternoon, written for his brother 'while fresh in my recollection', reveals the extent of the calamity. Having referred to the two marriages, Augusta's beloved father expatiated on the treatment that she had received from Prince Augustus, who had:

> left her penniless and subject to all the misery of being arrested and of having her house daily beset by Creditors asking and demanding payment of her for things which had been furnished while her husband was living with her and many of which he had taken with him to Lisbon, leaving her without a shilling to provide for herself or his family.

To all this the King listened with restraint but when the earl mentioned the Prince's unfeeling conduct to his children which left them destitute, Jack told his brother:

> the King broke out into a rage, calling them 'Bastards! Bastards!' To which our father replied by observing, 'yes, Sire, just such Bastards as yours are!' On his stating which the King … became as red as a Turkey cock, and going up to him repeated, 'What, what, what's that you say, My Lord?' 'I say, Sir, that my daughter was legally married to your son and that her children are just such Bastards as Your Majesty's are' – on hearing which the King stared at him – as if in a violent passion and then without uttering a word retired into another room and thus terminated the interview.[21]

At the conclusion of his tale, Lord Dunmore exploded with rage, vociferating, 'God damn him – It was as much as I could do to refrain from attempting to knock him down – when he called them Bastards!' Jack told his brother that 'really the Old Cock (tho' in the seventy second year of his age) looked at that moment as if he could have done [it] without much difficulty, and which if I am to judge from the grip which he can yet give with [his] paw – He is yet equal to have done.'[22]

The vision of the two irascible grandfathers sparring with each other horrified Augusta. Her father, not known for his even temper, had committed lese-majesty and in doing so had forfeited any chance of the King's help. His lack of control had made matters worse and as the claims on her finances became more pressing, Augusta had to think of another strategy.

After nine years she was still being pursued for legal costs for the case that invalidated her marriages. In the Duke's absence she had been forced to pay the rent on their house in Lower Grosvenor Street and creditors continued to harass her for bills incurred when Augustus was living with her in London. The failure of a satisfactory outcome from Lord Dunmore's audience with the King forced Augusta to resort to the courts and her trustees filed a chancery case against the Duke of Sussex, the foreign secretary and Thomas Coutts for non-payment of the annuity of £4,000 agreed on her return from Lisbon. Undeterred, she fought on with tacit support from an unexpected quarter.

Edward Livingston told William Adam in 1802 that he thought Lady Augusta had been wronged in being brought to court for debts which properly belonged to the Duke. She had given Livingston authority to state in front of her brother, Lord Fincastle, that she was willing to give up all pretensions to royalty. However, considering the way in which the Prince had 'brought her forward in his family, commanding all his domestiques to treat her as his wife', Livingston thought that the Duke of Sussex should pay all her just debts and he hoped 'for the honour of the Royal Family she may be treat[ed] with becoming generosity'.[23]

When he heard of the chancery case at the end of November 1803, Livingston offered her help. He wrote to William Adam, telling him that:

> perhaps you are not aware that I received when sent to Weymouth by HRH the Prince of Wales on Lady Augusta's business, express commands never to mention Lady Augusta's name to the King nevertheless if you think I can render any service to that unfortunate lady I will not hesitate to go to London as soon as possible … it will give me great satisfaction if I can contribute to relieve poor Lady Augusta from her present distressed situation.[24]

While he pitied her predicament, Livingston thought her ill-advised and deplored her decision to fight the Duke in court.

Two days after Christmas he wrote to Adam again, concerned that:

> if the cause comes to be heard in open court, & a publication of letters etc follow, the breach will be irreparable and her children ruined for ever, I wish it was possible to save her, and the poor infants, her Counsel may still have it in their power to prevent publicity but I am afraid she is not very prudent, a gentleman of great respectability told me yesterday that we were threatened with another publication and he believed my Prince would be the hero of the piece I answered I would be sorry for it.[25]

The Duke, still in Portugal, was astonished to hear that Augusta had brought a chancery case against him. Litigation between them dragged on without resolution. Augusta commented that a lawsuit is 'like an adventure in a gaming transaction, – the mind is always on the stretch, the affair from day to day assumes a new face, hope & fear dance an alternate measure before the eyes, – now sanguine with expectation now speechless & dejected with intolerable despair.'[26] Two and half years later her affairs were still in disarray when Lord Fincastle stood bail for her in May 1805. By June the butcher and baker were refusing to supply her, and, expecting to be gaoled daily, she asked a friend to investigate rooms for herself and her children 'within the walls' of the King's Bench Prison for debtors.[27]

It was not until 1806, the year in which William Pitt, Charles James Fox and the Duchess of Devonshire died, that Augustus and Augusta reached a settlement. After lengthy discussions with William Adam she agreed to give up using the title of the Duchess of Sussex and on 15 October 1806 His Majesty authorised her to take the name of D'Ameland, one of the titles of the House of Orange, with which Lord Dunmore's family was connected.[28] Before making her choice, she had suggested other titles. She proposed Lady Augusta de Bourbon or Lady Augusta de Nassau, but Adam wittily deflected her by quoting the final line of Matthew Prior's *Epitaph Extempore* 'Can Bourbon, or Nassau, go higher'.

On the last day of October the Duke of Sussex told the Prince of Wales that the disagreeable business with Lady Augusta had been concluded. Her debts of £26,457 would be paid by the Treasury if she accepted three conditions: she must drop the chancery case, she must not bear the Duke's coat of arms on her carriages and her servants must not wear his livery.[29] The Duke would settle all her debts incurred before 25 March 1802 and from that date she was entitled to £4,000 per annum, deemed to be £16,000, until the time of their settlement.[30] Thereafter she would enjoy an income of £4,000 a year, of which her existing pension of £1,200 was to form a part with £700 per annum granted for the maintenance of the children. Augusta had been struggling with debts for thirteen years but by January 1807 she was finally solvent and indeed for the rest of her life was generously provided for.

After years of wrangling and worry, the resolution was a relief for both families. Throughout her daughter's trials, Lady Dunmore had supported Augusta, but Queen Charlotte, no doubt at considerable cost to her own maternal feelings, had been obliged to estrange herself from one of her favourite sons. On 1 November 1806 just before the general election, the Queen wrote to Augustus the moment she heard that the arrangement had been reached. He had been suffering from his old complaint and she congratulated him on 'having settled an affair so tedious & so ruinous to your Health … it is very much my wish to come and see you but at this present moment when every town and village are in a bustle I think it is better to wait a little longer … I shall not fail to communicate the contents of your letter to the King, I am sure he will be happy to hear that you are … better.'[31]

Stress had always been a factor in Augustus's health and when he returned from Lisbon, he had asked his father for an establishment near the centre of London, but away from its foul air. He had often dreamed of moving into his own establishment with Augusta but it was not to be. He was now installed in a suite of rooms in Kensington Palace, where he settled down without his once-adored wife and began to amass his famous book collection.

Part III

26

Dear Ramsgate

Before her 1806 financial settlement, Augusta had found sanctuary from her London creditors in Ramsgate; her health always improved when she was by the sea. Properly provided for at last, she entered a new and independent phase of her life and, having sampled a number of coastal resorts (including Margate, Bognor Rocks and Brighton), chose Ramsgate as her second home. Once a fishing hamlet situated in the gap between the East and West Cliffs, like Teignmouth the little town had benefited from the vogue for sea bathing. While she was resident, Ramsgate expanded and many of its distinguished Georgian buildings, including the Obelisk and the Clock House, both visible in William Powell Frith's painting 'Ramsgate Sands', were erected. Janus-like, the town looked two ways. Its civic aspect faced Sandwich, the Cinque Port with which it had been associated since the fourteenth century, and for religious purposes, Ramsgate turned inland to the Norman parish church of St Lawrence.

The duration of Augusta's stays in Ramsgate did not follow a specific pattern and as she aged, she spent less time shuttling to and fro London, preferring to pass longer periods in both places. The journey from London took two days with a night in Sittingbourne. As far as Canterbury her route coincided with the busy Dover road, a swindlers' nirvana. Charles Dickens, a frequent traveller to Broadstairs, wrote from personal experience when he described the tribulations of Mr Dorrit, who 'was waylaid at Dartford, pillaged at Gravesend, rifled at Rochester, fleeced at Sittingbourne, and sacked at Canterbury'.[1] After such a journey Augusta's heart lifted whenever she drove down the hill towards the harbour and arrived once again in 'dear Ramsgate'.

The mill house that she bought on the East Cliff had splendid sea views. It was a breezy location, away from the rest of the town, beyond the common where the military encamped before embarking for France; its seclusion appealed to Augusta and provided her with welcome respite. In 1807, with characteristic determination, she began to acquire parcels of land around her house, lot by patient lot. Eventually she had purchased a small estate (she was still acquiring land in the 1820s) in which she took pleasure for the rest of her life, planning and planting, designing and decorating to her heart's desire. After her death the sale particulars described her house and grounds as being 'surrounded with 16 Acres of extensive Plantations & Shrubbery in a high state of luxuriance extending to the Cliffs, properly fenced in, & commanding a fine full and uninterrupted Sea View. The whole is in excellent repair; no expense has been spared by the Proprietor in adding to the comforts, convenience, & beauty of the Pleasure Grounds in particular.'[2] Her estate, conspicuous for its size, open spaces and dense plantations, is shown in its maturity beneath the compass on the 1822 'Map of the Town and Royal Harbour of Ramsgate'.

The double-lodged entrance to her personal Elysium left Ramsgate residents in no doubt that the owner was a person of consequence. Iron gates pierced the curved brick wall on King Street, and a wide avenue led up the hill to the former mill house, which Augusta enlarged and renamed Mount Albion. In 1811 the Grant family from Inverness-shire moved next to Mount Albion and according to Elizabeth Grant, Augusta had 'turned the whole ground floor into one room, a library, and built a large dining-room out behind. The drawing room floor was her own apartment, containing bedroom, sitting-room, and her maid's room; the floor above was equally divided between her son and daughter.' Augusta did not keep horses 'for she never drove out' and 'passed most of her time in a very large garden, well walled in, which covered a couple of acres or more and extended all down the slope of the cliff to the town'.[3] Informed by Humphry Repton's writings, Augusta followed the latest fashion in landscape gardening and divided her grounds into different parts. A palisade and iron gates by the cliff enclosed the park, which supplied the annual hay crop. Nearer the house she laid out the pleasure grounds with irregular plantations and shrubberies interspersed with serpentine walks.

In 1810 her brother, George, sent her some trees. They were shipped from the little dock at Dunmore, transported along the River Forth, then taken by sea down the east coast to Ramsgate. The next year she built a wall for the kitchen garden located between the pleasure grounds and the top of the drive. It cost her £70. She kept a full-time gardener, who also managed her pigs, and when she needed extra help with the flowerbeds, she employed 'little weeding girls'. On 28 June 1815, the day that Queen Charlotte received the Duke of Wellington after the battle of Waterloo, Augusta paid a Mr Marshall £3 10*s* to thatch her summerhouse, which is visible in the painting of Mount Albion dated about 1850.

Augusta took her own and her children's health seriously. Ramsgate's reputation as a watering place was one of the reasons that she had chosen to live there and Mount Albion was convenient both for the town's warm water baths and for bathing on Ramsgate Sands, a ritual amusingly described by Elizabeth Grant. Entering the roped off enclosure at the town end, those determined to brave the briny signed a book before being conducted to the bathing machines, 'roomy boxes upon wheels', with a horse at one end and a canvas hood at the other. Once the horse had pulled the machine into the sea, the driver turned the carriage so that the hood faced the water. He then unhitched his horse and left the shivering bather to the mercy of the 'guide' or 'dipper'. This character, 'a middle aged woman in a blue flannel jacket and petticoat and a straw bonnet … soon waded into view from a neighbouring machine', lifted the hood and stood 'ready to assist the fearful plunge', ducking her victim before the chilly gusts blew away their resolve.[4]

Augusta was a keen bather and as a younger woman had visited Margate from time to time. After watching her in the water, a male devotee wrote her a verse:

Too lovely Scot what would you crave
From yonder heav'n directed wave?
Not health she loves & graces cry
Hygeia beams in either eye!
Not beauty for the rose's hue
The rose's fragrance dwells with you.[5]

Possibly the same seaside swain, 'Mr B–d', wrote a poem marvelling at her grace in 1791, entitled 'To Neptune' 'on my bathing at Margate':

The Water gave unto her skin
A snowy whiteness still more bright
Like Venus springing from the surge
In all her charms she did emerge
More lovely than the Queen of Night

which ended with the lines:

Augusta's on the Margate shore
And should be call'd great Neptune's Queen.[6]

In Ramsgate she bought an expensive new bathing bonnet shaped like a beehive, which she tied with a ribbon beneath her chin to prevent the escape of any errant strands of hair. She wore a loose flannel gown, which covered everything from her ankles to her wrists, because modesty in the water was paramount.

In 1820 a lady bathing alone was charged 1*s* 3*d* including a guide, so Augusta's bathing bill of £9 in 1808 indicates the frequency with which she and her children took to the water.[7] The bathers did not swim so much as gambol, dip and splash, believing that they were doing themselves good. Alarmingly, bathing in the winter was considered more efficacious than the summer and some brave souls went in when the waves were high, holding on to the ropes laid out by the dippers.

Augusta encouraged Emma to bathe in the hope that it would prevent winter colds and other ailments, and the Grants often saw their friend, 'the little Princess', when they ventured down to the beach. It was a charming scene; when the tide was out the 'sands were very firm, and of considerable extent' and there was always something to watch: crab hunters, shrimpers, and shipping of all kinds, 'little boats, larger craft' and 'huge merchantmen, all moving across the face of the waters'.[8]

It did not bother Augusta that bathing was forbidden after ten o'clock on a Sunday because she was rigorous about attending church. A painting of 1850 shows the interior at St Lawrence before the Victorian alterations. Light streams through the clear glass windows, the brick floor of the nave is worn and uneven and Lady Dunmore's hatchment is discernible above the north aisle; there is a three-decker pulpit in the crossing and a gilt chandelier hangs before the altar. How the god-fearing inhabitants of the parish must have stared the first time they saw the *soi-disante* Duchess of Sussex walk down the aisle and enter one of the box pews, for which she paid a pew-opener 7*s* per annum.

The proximity of her parents was another reason why Augusta chose Ramsgate. The Earl and Countess of Dunmore had retired to the south of England, where life on the Kent coast was congenial. They bought a pleasant five-bay residence, Southwood House, near St Lawrence church, with sea views from its cast-iron balcony. The former governor, accustomed to the warmth of the Bahamas, found the Kent climate kinder to his elderly bones than the damps of the River Forth.

He had been absent for much of Augusta's young life and, as she entered her forties, it was a comfort to have him living nearby. She took a close interest in his health, and writing from London one day, asked Emma to 'tell dear Pappy that I hope he drinks his glass of sweet wine every day at 12 o'clock; as he was so good as to promise me, he would do'.[9] According to the St Lawrence burial register, the earl died of 'decay' aged 76 on 25 February 1809 and was buried in the church, where his memorial states incorrectly that he died aged 78. The year after, Augusta asked the London artist, Mr Leeming, to paint 'my loved father's picture to go to Ramsgate'.[10] Lord Dunmore did not leave a will and it was left to Augusta to mediate between her mother and George after their 'late differences' concerning the payment of his funeral costs.

Augusta was close to her eldest brother and admired his wit, sensitivity, and honesty. After the death of their father however, she had to appeal to his sense of duty and wrote him a sympathetic and conciliatory letter explaining her position:

> I always must feel, that old parents (unless they have been particularly unkind) claim from their children <u>much</u> affection & duty. My loved father has endeared to me every grey headed old man I see, & when I reflect on my mother's age, – I excuse most of her faults, & ask myself, – whether added days & lengthened years may not make my love of money much beyond what hers is; – & when I believe her about [to] go, – I admire her good spirits her happy turn of mind which gives her comfort ... I think my dear Fin still you ought to pay the Funeral without waiting for the selling of the assets.[11]

Life in the seaside town was relaxed and convivial, and Augusta enjoyed its parties and soirées. Accompanied by Virginia and Augustus, she went to dinner at Waldershare Park, the family seat near Dover of her old admirer from Rome, Mr North. At Kingsgate, the house Lord Holland had built on the coast between Broadstairs and Margate, she lost 2*s* 6*d* playing Pope Joan, a family card game with moderate stakes. She enjoyed the game so much that the next time she was in London she bought a Pope Joan table for 16*s*. Persona non grata with the Royal Family, Augusta was shunned by polite society in London, but in Ramsgate she could enjoy an active social life for the first time since her marriage.

In 1807 Marianne Stanhope told her brother that she was going to Lady Conyngham's in Ramsgate, where she would meet '*everybody*, for you must know that even in this small society there is an improper set. Lady Dunmore & her daughters, Lady Virginia Murray, and the married one, Lady Susan Drew, sisters of the Duchess of Sussex … are visited by very few *proper* people but both these houses are *rendez-vous* of the officers.'[12] Ramsgate was the chief port of embarkation for troops going to the Napoleonic wars and, as at Meryton in Jane Austen's *Pride and Prejudice*, officers were welcome at gatherings and assemblies when their regiments were in town.

Napoleon proclaimed himself Emperor of France in May 1804 and three months later when Joseph Farington was staying in Ramsgate, the Herefordshire Militia was stationed there. At the Ramsgate Assembly Rooms Farington encountered Augusta, her son, Virginia and Lady Hamilton, who was staying with her friend, Lady Dunmore. If he is to be believed, Augusta was beginning to lose her looks. He described her as having 'a very singular shaped face. The Lower part from the Nose falling as if shaved off. Her Sister still more plain.' He thought them both 'coarse & confident looking women', and added that Augusta 'entered Herself in the subscription book … *Duchess of Sussex*.' He thought Augustus was 'a fine boy … & very like the Royal family' and 'said to be called the *Prince*'.[13]

Farington also met Lord Keith, the Commander-in-Chief of the North Sea, at the assembly. As George Elphinstone, Keith had been one of the three naval captains whom Augusta had encountered with such pleasure outside Toulon in the summer of 1793. On being appointed commander-in-chief, he made his headquarters at East Cliff Lodge, a Gothic castle 'with battlements and towers, and a curtain [wall] flanked by turrets, and a moat'.[14]

Augusta was delighted when another kinsman in the Royal Navy called on her in 1811. Her cousin, Lord Cochrane, was spending the summer in Deal and persuaded her to join him for a day at sea. He brought round his barge, comfortably fitted with cushions, for the short trip to his ship, where he had prepared refreshments for her. After their expedition, he presented her with a pair of French gloves, a gift much prized during the Napoleonic Wars.

Eliza Grant recollected that 'Our two families soon became intimate, the younger ones especially passing the greater part of the day together, a friendship beginning then which never entirely ceased.'[15] Although Augusta was generous to the Grant children, often tipping Jane, William or little John, she remained polite but remote. One evening soon after the Grants arrived, Eliza recalled that Emma, in a 'large leaved Tuscan hat thrown back off her dark close cropped hair, and her fine countenance brightened by the blush of girlish modesty … held up a small basket full of fine peaches, an offering from her mother'. Mrs Grant made the requisite visit of thanks and a few days later Augusta asked Jane to tell her mother that she had returned her call when unfortunately Mrs Grant had been out, but she hoped that they would be good neighbours. 'On this hint we all acted. We never expected H.R.H. to call nor even believed in the first reported call.'[16]

In 1811 night after night Ramsgate residents watched the Great Comet rise over the town and pass on slowly. The comet was at its brightest in October and that month Augusta put on a children's performance of *Macbeth* to amuse 10-year-old Emma and the four Grants. Eliza was not surprised by Augusta's choice of play because she was 'a Scotchwoman, one of the Dunmore Murrays, and very national … she was besides … very proud of the beauty of her daughter'. Perhaps with her Scottish home in mind, Augusta painted the backdrop featuring 'a bit of an old tower and some trees'. Mrs Deadman, her maid, was in charge of the costumes and Mr Grant was the prompter. Although she 'ranted a little' Emma looked the part of Lady Macbeth and 'a very respectable audience of dowager peeresses and other visitors and residents applauded every speech' given by the young actors.[17] Between the acts the music master played martial airs on an old piano. Afterwards there was a generous supper and a merry dance so that everybody left in high spirits at the end of a successful evening.

The performance of *Macbeth* took place in Augusta's library, which made an excellent home theatre. It was the room where she spent many hours reading and where she found both mental stimulation and repose. She had inherited a love of books from her father, who had been encouraged to read by his mother. Knowing her eldest son loved reading, Catherine, dowager Countess of Dunmore left 'what books of mine he may choose' in her will. In Williamsburg, John Dunmore had a large library, which he had to abandon when the family fled. Augusta's brother, George, was also a bibliophile and at Dunmore Park, the house that he and his wife commissioned from William Wilkins, there was a much-loved library. Their son, Charles Murray, paid a visit in 1882 when the house was unoccupied and described the library, 'where the old books repose on their old shelves, uncovered by glass or paper, and many of them exactly in their old places; so that I could see the book which my father took down and read by the fireside'.[18] Lady Dunmore's family on the other hand did not seem to be literary. The library at Galloway House, her childhood home, was kept locked. When James Boswell was staying, he asked for the key while the rest of the party were at cards and found 'a very good collection in very good order … not much hurt by being used'.[19]

Augusta frequently bought books and she listed them at the back of her commonplace book as she filled the library shelves at Mount Albion.[20] She grouped the volumes methodically by size: folios, quartos and octavos, with the smallest books, duodecimos, being the most numerous. By any standards, the size of her book collection was impressive: at more than 1,200 volumes, it was nearly as large as the one her father had to leave behind in Williamsburg.

Augusta's inventory is precious for two reasons. While we know that Georgiana, Duchess of Devonshire, was a bibliophile and both Princess Elizabeth, Prince Augustus's sister, and Queen Caroline, the consort of George II, were book collectors, little has been written about women and books in the Georgian period. Augusta's list and her accounts, studded with payments for volumes acquired in London or Kent, reveal the type of book that a clever woman of her age and background acquired and read.

In December 1807, for example, absorbed by the world of ancient Rome, she bought six volumes on the emperors, a book on Roman gems and some works by Julius Caesar. On 26 September 1821 she purchased volumes on topography and art from Mr Jones, the bookseller at Margate, including *The Border Antiquities of England and Scotland* by Walter Scott, *Woodburn's Gallery of Rare Portraits*, and *A Graphic Illustration of the Metropolitan Cathedral Church of Canterbury* by W. Woolnoth, 'all most beautifully bound'.[21]

Augusta's inventory also helps us to understand her aspirations, character and mind, and the diversity of books in her library supports Eliza Grant's observation that she was 'intellectual and intelligent, as all her pursuits evidenced'.[22] To modern eyes the number of volumes in French is striking but Augusta spoke and wrote the language fluently, as is verified by her letters to Lady Stafford, which often lapsed into French. The highest echelons of British society conversed in French among themselves, something that surprised Richard Rush, the American Minister appointed to the Court of St James in 1817. He wrote that 'There is scarcely a well-educated person in England who does not speak in French, whilst thousands among the best educated in France are ignorant of English. In the competition between these great nations, this gives England an advantage.'[23]

Augusta was convinced that the ability to speak French with grace and ease would be the difference between success and failure in her son's struggle for royal recognition. She attached supreme importance to the language, as is shown in the letter she wrote to young Augustus in America during the War of 1812:

> I do hope you feel the necessity of learning french, and that you will avail yourself of whatever opportunity occurs of taking lessons and of speaking it; you see my Love, our pretensions are not empty ones, that the time will come, when they ought to be enforced, if not in England in other courts of Europe; and what can you do for yourself if you cannot speak french? Upon my word, it appears to me, that on that single thing, may rest your chance of success or defeat; can the Emperor like a person to whom he cannot speak, one, who must (from that airy circumstance) appear uneducated, consequently beneath his notice. Nowhere on the continent, can you be received but as an incumbrance, if you cannot speak french, it is the language of every court, of every gentleman, and it argues, such absence from good company not to know it, that it amounts to disgrace to be ignorant of it; do pray my love consider this seriously.[24]

She herself had seventy volumes of Voltaire and one of her commonplace books was devoted to extracts from his plays; his best known work, *Candide*, published in 1759, had been influenced by events such as the execution of

Admiral Byng and the Lisbon earthquake. Furthermore, she had books of French memoirs, poetry and letters, as well as novels. One of these, *Julie ou La Nouvelle Héloise*, a study of the concept of authenticity by Rousseau, took the form of an epistolary novel, of which many were published on both sides of the Channel in the second part of the eighteenth century.

Augusta saw it as her maternal duty to keep abreast of current theories in education, one of her greatest interests. She bought the works of Madame de Genlis, the liberal teacher of the future King Louis Philippe. She read Maria Edgeworth's *Practical Education*, a defence of the education of women, published in 1798. She also read older works on the subject including François Fénelon's *Traité de l'éducation des filles* of 1687 and she read *Some Thoughts Concerning Education* by the philosopher John Locke.

We might foresee on her shelves Nicholas Culpepper's *Complete Herbal* or Dr Johnson's *Dictionary*, but dictionaries of chemistry and heraldry are unexpected; Edward Gibbon's *History of the Decline and Fall of the Roman Empire* is anticipated, but not the *History of Turkey* or a book on rambles in Holland. Knowing of Augusta's faith, we are not surprised that a number of volumes of sermons and religious tracts should appear in her library as well as a book on the Bible by Sarah Trimmer, authoress of improving children's books and promoter of Sunday schools. Augusta learnt about the French enlightenment from the works of Montesquieu. She read classical writers including Ovid, Homer and Seneca and, having spent so much time in Italy, she was at ease with poets such as Ludovico Ariosto and Pietro Metastasio. She did not neglect the works of English writers – the poet Samuel Rogers was a family friend – and she read the plays of Vanbrugh and Garrick. She owned a number of editions of Shakespeare and enjoyed the poems of Addison, Milton and Gray. Chaucer's *Canterbury Tales* held a certain local appeal.

Her interest in the rights and identity of women is represented throughout her book collection. As a single woman, whose marriage had not been recognised, she had to fight for what she saw was her due, such as the right to keep her children, and she did not shirk from the challenge. While she owned *The Whole Duty of a Woman: or a Guide to the Female Sex*, a manual of correct conduct written by a 'lady' at the beginning of the eighteenth century, Augusta embraced the works of Mary Wollstonecraft, her contemporary. Wollstonecraft's *Vindication of the Rights of Woman*, published in 1792, was both controversial and influential. It emphasised the importance of physical strength and disdained female 'innocence' as well as the practice of girls being educated only to please the opposite sex. Her copy of *Secresy* by Wollstonecraft's friend, Eliza Fenwick, which addresses gender and class, is now in the Royal Archives. Augusta also owned the works of Etta Palm d'Aelders, the Dutch feminist, who spied for the French and advocated the importance of the role of women in a free government during the Revolution.

She could forget her problems by taking up a novel and read Tobias Smollett's *Humphry Clinker*, an amusing tale by a fellow Scot, who held trenchant views on the Union of Scotland with England. With her experience of life in Virginia just before the Revolutionary War, she enjoyed *Emma Corbett*, Samuel Jackson Pratt's story of a family divided by the conflict in America. She liked to keep up to date with recent publications and was an early reader of both Fanny Burney's *Camilla* and Matthew Lewis's Gothic romance, *The Monk*, both of which appeared in 1796. She recommended another horror story, Mrs Radcliffe's *Mysteries of Udolpho*, to Augustus when he was at Harrow. Some years later Jane Austen satirised Mrs Radcliffe and the Gothic genre in *Northanger Abbey* but we can be sure that Augusta agreed with its hero, Henry Tilney, who declared that a 'person, be it gentleman or lady, who has not pleasure in a good novel, must be intolerably stupid'.

It was unusual for a lady to have a library, a room usually regarded as the domain of a gentleman. There were however, a few exceptions. Elizabeth Montagu had one at her husband's Berkshire house, Sandleford Priory, and in 1752 Lady Isabella Finch, the unmarried sister-in-law of the royal governess, was the only woman at court to have her own library.[25] The most notable exception was Queen Charlotte. James Wyatt built her a large library at Frogmore where she employed a full-time librarian. She also had a botanical library and a 'Small Library' in two other rooms, as well as a printing press and bindery. Without the demands of a husband and with her own means, Augusta, like Isabella Finch, could indulge herself in her precious library, the private sanctuary she could arrange to suit her personal comfort. She spent her leisure reading her own choice of books and the size of her collection is proof of the diversity of her interests, while its breadth is testimony to the quality of her intellect.

27

An 'Accidental' Son

Augusta's third child was her illegitimate son, Henry Hamilton. After the disastrous trip to Lisbon, when it was clear that reconciliation with the Prince was impossible, Archibald Hamilton rekindled their affair. They may have been unofficially engaged a decade earlier but when she was in Rome she heard that Archibald was to marry someone else. That marriage did not take place and at the beginning of August 1802, Archibald asked Augusta to marry him. In a passionate poem of four verses he included the lines:

> Ethereal fire hath surely form'd that love
> Whose fondest hope is still to call thee Wife.[1]

Augusta was vulnerable and alone but she was not easily wooed. Although unacknowledged as the Duchess of Sussex, she was unwilling to become Lady Archibald Hamilton. (Archibald's father had succeeded to the dukedom of Hamilton in 1799.) Her religious beliefs would not permit it. Marriage to Archibald would be tantamount to accepting that her marriages to the Duke of Sussex were null and void and that her two children were illegitimate. She would not condemn her own children to bastardy and she believed that Archibald's proposal came from a sense of duty resulting from his past rejection. Her soul shrank from such a thought. If she married him, she could not expect any of the happiness that they had once anticipated. Recalling with pleasure Augustus's cultural interests – music and archaeology – Archibald seemed to have no intellectual life. She knew that living with him on a permanent basis would be trying, not only because he was deaf but also because he could be demanding.

Archibald did not give up hope. From another love poem that he wrote on her 44th birthday in 1805, it appears that she had become his mistress and he was even more determined to make her his wife, asking her to:

Let me the gifts of birth & marriage view
As this day ripen'd & compriz'd in you;
Deem all the past a wanton waste of Life
'Till Friend & mistress soften'd into Wife;
Till ties of fondest love, & name & Friend
In closer union did propitious end. –
Let me this day, my day of marriage see
Since marriage were divorce unless to thee
Let me this happy day, – a Husband prove
And bless the magic mysteries of Love.[2]

It has been suggested that their son, Henry Hamilton, was the result of their earlier liaison. However, it is unlikely that Augusta was Archibald's mistress before she went to Naples and recent research suggests that he was born after her break with the Prince. In 1811 Elizabeth Grant spoke of Henry as 'a fine boy'.[3] The year before, Augusta referred to him in her accounts as 'little Henry Hamilton' when she gave him a present of five shillings. If he had been born in or before 1792, 'little' is an inappropriate epithet for a young man of at least 18 years of age. Countless monetary gifts to 'little Henry Hamilton', the son she could not acknowledge, appear in Augusta's accounts but it is noteworthy that she had dropped the adjective by 1818.

References in her account books and her Book of Cures imply that Henry Hamilton was probably born in the dying days of 1805 when Augusta was nearly 45.[4] She paid two guineas for a midwifery subscription on 8 December that year. On Christmas Day she copied out Susan's prescription from Dr Denman, one of London's leading man-midwives, who was one of the first to advocate induction of premature labour in cases of contracted pelvis.[5] For 'a good opening medicine for the womb', Denman recommended two or three tablespoons to be taken two or three times a day of a concoction of syrup of mulberry, spirit of mint, infusion of roses and Epsom Salts.[6] On 30 December she paid two guineas to Dr William

Rowley, another highly respected man-midwife, and the next day she paid him a further guinea.[7] Uniquely, there are no entries in Augusta's accounts between 2 and 16 January 1806 but at the end of the month Dr Rowley was paid a guinea, which may have been for a postpartum check.

Augusta later described Henry elegantly as the 'accidental' son of Lord Archibald and it was evident to those close to her that she adored the boy who she could not acknowledge as her own. According to Eliza Grant, Archibald spent most of his time with his cousin Augusta and '*his* son Henry Hamilton, a fine boy then'. She also noted that there was 'scandal going about the extreme attachment of the Duchess to this handsome lad' and recounted an episode that she heard discussed by her parents:

> Lord Archibald, one day talking of this dearly beloved son of his, consulting Lord Lauderdale about his destination and thinking himself but coldly listened to, said rather testily as an addition to whatever argument he was using 'I can assure you he has in his veins by both sides some of the best blood in Europe.' 'I never heard it doubted,' replied Lord Lauderdale gravely and with a low voice. 'The blood of Princely Hamilton we all know sufficiently to value. The Murray blood of that one family is purer still, more ancient and more of royalty in it.'[8]

Eliza noticed that there was a strong family likeness between Henry and the Murrays.

There seem to be few references to Henry Hamilton, but Robert Brown, the factor at Hamilton Palace, mentioned him in a letter of August 1816. Brown described a grouse shoot that Archibald organised in Arran when the other guests were the Duke of Portland and his heir, as well as Lord Archibald's 'own son, Mr Henry Hamilton', and Augustus, 'son of the Duke of Sussex'.[9] Henry died in December 1824 and Archibald three years later, aged 57. He had never succeeded in softening Augusta 'into Wife' but they had enjoyed companionship both in Ramsgate and London and he had helped her with financial affairs, lawsuits and property transactions.

As Archibald instructed, he was buried unostentatiously at Hamilton, the ducal seat in Lanarkshire, a few miles south-east of Glasgow. Robert Brown arranged the funeral and informed Archibald's brother, the tenth Duke of Hamilton, that everything had been carried out 'in the most respectful way to his Lordship's memory'.[10] Augusta's brother, George, by then Earl of

Dunmore, and her nephews, Lord Fincastle and Charles Murray, were in attendance. Her former lover left her a mourning ring to the value of £5 and exceptionally generous legacies of £5,000 to Emma and Augustus.

Despite Brown's careful arrangements, Archibald did not rest in peace. His remains were removed to the gigantic mausoleum at Hamilton Palace that his brother completed in 1858. When the palace was given up, the Dukes departed and the mausoleum had suffered from flooding as well as mining subsidence, Archibald was disturbed a second time. In October 1921, a lorry containing the Hamilton coffins taken from the mausoleum trundled across town to the municipal burial ground on Bent Street. There on the edge of the cemetery, haunt of the homeless, Archibald lies with his father, mother and older brother, Alexander, known as *Il Magnifico*, who would have accepted the crown of Scotland had Napoleon been victorious. The 'Most High and Puissant Princes' of Hamilton have ended up in a communal tomb amidst broken bottles and discarded crisp packets. If Henry Hamilton, the 'accidental' son of Augusta and Lord Archibald, also sleeps in that dismal grave, the colossal epitaph does not record it.

28

Keeping Account

Augusta's account books are invaluable. Not only do they provide clues to the date of Henry Hamilton's birth, they give us myriad details about Augusta's domestic life. They inform us about her spending habits, where she went and with whom she spent her time. Her payments and the adjectives she used to describe the recipients illustrate the extent of her charity and her sympathy for those less fortunate than herself. They also reveal the kindness she showed to her extended family. As a beneficiary of a government allowance, she feared that her finances could be scrutinised at any time. This did not, however, curb her natural generosity; she spent freely on her loved ones as well as herself. Sometimes the accounts disclose her opinions, emotions and mental attitude; dates such as family deaths and sundry addresses are faithfully chronicled. The first surviving book dates from 12 August 1805 and belongs to Harrow School[1] but most of the carefully detailed ledgers are held in the National Archives at Kew.[2] Augusta made her last entry two days before she died.

When the accounts begin in 1805, Augusta was in Ramsgate. In September she went on a shopping spree to Margate with her mother and bought a telescope for 'P. Augustus' for £2 8*s* 6*d* and a purse for Susan's son, John, costing 3*s* 6*d*. In contrast to this pleasant outing, Augusta recorded the death of her younger brother, Captain John Murray, in the margin further down the same page.[3] Jack died on 4 July 1805 but the family did not learn of their loss for three months. On 7 October Augusta logged £18 12*s* 'for mourning for my most beloved, & most regretted Jack', the loyal sibling who had travelled to Lisbon to obtain Prince Augustus's signature to her indenture. She also paid £22 9*s* for 'Mourning ditto the children and servants' and splashed out on a black pelisse, a long cloak of satin or velvet, sometimes lined with fur. Aunt Susanna's fear that Augusta's marriage would affect Jack Murray's naval career proved unfounded and he commanded seven ships before his final appointment as captain of HMS *Franchise*, a frigate captured from the French. According to *The Gentleman's Magazine*, he died during the blockade of the Dutch island of Curaçao. He had gone ashore to speak to one of the principal inhabitants when he 'caught a cold, that brought on a fever, of which he died in 3 days'. His remains were interred on the uninhabited island of Little Curaçao and it made Augusta melancholy to think of her brother dying with no relative at his side.

Her accounts inform us of another family death, that of Augusta's niece, Charlotte Tharp, who died on 13 February 1809, just before Lord Dunmore. Later that year, we learn that Susan married for the third time on 'il giorno del matrimonio' (the wedding day).[4] (After the death of her first husband, Susan had married John Drew and they had two daughters: Lucy and Georgiana.) After the appropriate period of mourning, Susan wed the Reverend Archibald Douglas, a handsome Irishman, described by Eliza Grant as 'quite a crack preacher, all London flocking round any pulpit he consented to mount'.[5] Augusta gave her Drew nieces 6*s* on the day of their mother's third wedding and a year later, at the age of 43, Susan became a mother again when she gave birth to Augusta Mary Douglas.

Augusta's account books testify to the frequency with which she gave her family presents. She treated her children, including 'little Henry Hamilton', indulgently and in November 1809, paid 2*s* a month in pocket money 'to my loved little mad cap', Emma, aged 8. Almost as often as the pocket money and gifts she gave the young people in her family, she bought grapes and strawberries for her mother, who loved fruit of every kind, particularly pineapples. She often donated charitable gifts to the needy that she encountered on the streets of London and Ramsgate. Touched by the woes of those she saw, Augusta taught her children to do the same and on one occasion Emma gave a shilling to a man with a 'dancing bear'. There are payments like 7*s* to 'the poor little family of Chandler Street'; 2*s* 'to four little sweeps'; 7*s* to a 'poor Morocco slave'; 12*s* 'to Mrs Summers, a poor woman whose child was run over', and 7*s* to a man who fell from a scaffold. Augusta was often moved by the predicament of British veterans of the Napoleonic wars and offerings such as the one of 5*s* 6*d*, which she gave to a 'Scotch soldier' in London, are recurrent.

In 1808, the year in which the Peninsular War began, Augusta moved to Connaught Place, named after one of the titles of William, Duke of Gloucester. The Duke, whose mother had also been ostracised by George III, sympathised with Augusta's plight and bought her the first house built in the new terrace overlooking Hyde Park. Augusta was not sufficiently brazen to remind the world of her connection to the Duke by naming No. 1 Connaught Place, 'Sussex House', but she did the next best thing and called her residence 'Arklow House'. Earls, baronets and a bishop soon came to join her, buying houses in the terrace, and in 1814 Caroline, Princess of Wales, took up residence at No. 7.

In furnishing Arklow House (demolished during the widening of Edgware Road), Augusta patronised the best firms. She bought a piano from Mr Broadwood and she had an account with Marsh & Tatham, cabinetmakers to the Prince of Wales. Her silver came from 'Mr Garrard' and she bought silver candlesticks from Rundell & Bridge. Let us hope that the provenance was reliable and she was not cheated when she paid £2 2*s* for the desk of 'Cardinal Wolsey'.

Augusta was a good employer and kept her staff for long periods, although she did pay off one cook 'whom I never again will employ'.[6] Many of her servants worked for her for years, such as Mrs Deadman, known by the family as 'Deady', whom Eliza Grant described as a 'very strange looking elderly maid'.[7] Mrs Deadman was particularly fond of Henry Hamilton and whenever any of the children offended her, they sent him to make peace with her and 'never unsuccessfully'. Possibly Deady had been with Augusta since Henry's birth and knew the truth about his paternity, which may explain why Eliza noticed that 'her influence was great even to our young apprehensions'.[8] There were times however, when Deady tried Augusta's patience. In an era when water was undrinkable, beer money was a necessary expense for servants but she was not pleased to return from France in 1815 to find a chit for £4 15*s*, Deady's 'most cheating bill for beer money while I was abroad'. Nevertheless, mistress and maid stayed together until Mrs Deadman's death in 1827.

Another of Augusta's faithful servants was her footman, memorably named Ransom Lemon and described as 'a man of colour native of Virginia late in the service of the Right Honourable Lady Augusta Murray, a bachelor and a bastard'.[9] She valued his services and in 1805 presented him with a gift of £5. Although he died in 1808, Augusta did not forget his mother, who was by then living in Somers Town and to whom she was still giving gifts of £5 as late as 1825. Like George Murray, '*le nègre de mes chèrs parents*' who lived off Edgware Road, Ransom Lemon probably came to London when the Dunmore family returned from Williamsburg.[10] An Italian, Grifoni Donato, came to work for Augusta in Ramsgate in February 1809 with an annual salary of £40. He was still with her in 1817 when she was paying him £52 including beer money. Along with Samuel, who received £60 with beer money, Donato was one of her highest-paid servants, so the two men were probably her butlers in London and Ramsgate.

In 1812, the year that war was declared with America and London society was shocked by the assassination of the Prime Minister, Spencer Perceval, Augusta's annual expenditure amounted to £3,034. In London she was employing a butler, a coachman in livery, a gardener, two footmen in livery, a groom, a porter, a housekeeper, Mrs Deadman, a scullery maid, two other maids, 'Mary', and Mrs Van, who lived in South Audley Street. Her expenditure that year included servants' wages, expenses noted in the housekeeper's book, and the cost of her carriage and horses. There were food bills to pay from the butcher, butter-man, grocer, milkman, fruiterer, poulterer and fishmonger. The accounts contained payments to the chandler and the coal merchant, for laundry and for wine as well as for taxes and insurance. On top of all this she had to buy her clothes but fortunately the Duke of Sussex was responsible for all the children's expenses.

29

My Two Treasures

Augusta was the first to admit that her role as a mother preserved her sanity. She acknowledged that:

> maternal love has been my guardian genius … & even in that perplexing moment, when the waves ran high about my little shattered bark, while the Harpies of poverty, famine, & despair, screamed & flapped their heavy wings as they rode upon the whirlwind, – her angel form, adorned by the breath of hope stood beckoning to the haven, animated my spirits & gave the genial glow of comfort to my heart.[1]

Deprived of a husband to love, Augusta bestowed on her children the excess of her abundant affection. Their indulgence was recompense for the loss of a husband.

Two of her notebooks, 'Dr Rowley's prescriptions for the baby 1794'[2] held at Kew and her 'Book of Cures'[3] in the Royal Archives demonstrate the care that Augusta lavished on her own and on her children's health. William Rowley prescribed a number of remedies, some of which sound horrifying today. His preparation 'to stop my Treasure's purging' (emptying the bowels) when Augustus was 2 years old contained a mixture of chalk and opiate,[4] while Rowley's advice that all fruit, greens and salads should be avoided 'for the first three or four years of infancy' because they caused wind and impeded the digestive organs, sounds like a sure recipe for constipation.[5] His recipe 'for a baby with green stools' including magnesia and a small quantity of rhubarb stirred with dill and water is more reassuring.[6] There are treatments for sourness in the stomach and convulsions, and St Anthony's fire – a violent red inflammation on the skin – was to be cured by senna tea and soluble tartar. There was a particularly alarming section in the book on opiums, laudanum, 'syrop of poppies' and hemlock.

In April 1806 4-year-old Emma appears to have been given a series of prescriptions from Dr Home 'for a young person growing crooked'.[7] She had to wear supportive stays and a raised boot on her left foot; she was required to bathe in the sea three times a week in the forenoon, and to go to bed early and rise late 'so as to shorten the day'. After dinner she lay down on the floor for an hour and if she sat, it had to be on a hard flat chair. When writing or drawing she was to stand at her desk but 'no two days with light on the same side' and she was not permitted to take any medicine in the morning. There was one part of this strict regimen that may have pleased her: she was not allowed 'to take any lesson of music above half an hour'. The uncompromising guidance must have worked. Five years later Eliza Grant noticed Emma's healthy good looks and made no illusion to a curvature in her spine.

Another credence of the times was the efficacy of alcohol in prescriptions for all ages and when she was 4 years old Emma was prescribed wine or malt liquor with meals. Two of Augusta's prescriptions for gargles to relieve sore throats included similar amounts of port wine as sage tea and vinegar, and a receipt for a sore throat 'from cold' recommended half a cup of milk to half a cup of brandy. As the children grew older, Augusta filled her notebooks with remedies for adults as well.

She recommended an excellent mixture 'pour les règles' including tincture of castor, a preparation made from the gum of acacia, syrup of saffron, and laudanum.[8] Augusta was careful to include rudimentary instructions for resuscitation and emphasised that for the sake of propriety, the giver must be 'a healthy person of the same sex'.[9] Should the treatment become necessary in the sole presence of the opposite sex, no advice was forthcoming. Augusta also wrote down prescriptions of a more mundane nature. She found that mustard was efficacious for rheumatism and strong ginger cakes calmed the stomach. She recorded the way to take castor oil prescribed 'for my beloved mother', who found it more palatable if mixed with egg yolk, brown sugar and cinnamon water. A prescription for pills to counteract Augustus's 'flatulency' included directions written in Latin: the soda sub carbonate and extract of aloes to be taken 'ante prandium quodtidie', or before lunch every day.[10]

Having nursed her children through various childhood diseases and brought them up to the best of her ability, Augusta was continuously frustrated that however much she cherished them, polite society would not accept her son and daughter. The arrangement of 1806, by which she received an annuity from the Duke and a pension from the King, was made on the condition that she gave up all pretence to the titles of 'Duchess of Sussex' for herself, and 'Prince' and 'Princess' for Augustus and Emma. But Augusta was defiant: in private she refused to keep to her side of the bargain. She did not discourage the use of the Duchess of Sussex, by which her friends, acquaintances and the residents of Ramsgate knew her. Augusta called her son 'Prince Augustus' in her account books and although she herself was careful to call the children 'my boy' and 'my girl' in public, to the servants and everyone who visited Mount Albion, Augustus and Emma were the Prince and Princess. She continued to address her letters to her daughter as 'Princess Augusta of Sussex at the Dss of Sussex's'.

News of the way that Lady Augusta was raising the two children reached the Royal Family. Referring to Emma in 1808, Princess Amelia told Lady Harcourt, 'You may be sure that she has been educated with very *high ideas.*'[11] Similarly, Eliza Grant noticed that the two children 'fine, large, handsome young people' were '*un*duly imbued with the grandeur of their birth'.[12] The Grants were amused that despite their informal friendship with Emma, when they saw her on their bathing trips she would walk 'right royally' in front of her maid, and in the subscription book, she would 'dash down a very flourishing "P", the single letter that served to mark her name; then she would smile most courteously upon us, but never came near or spoke on these public occasions.'[13]

The children of a well-travelled and cultured mother, Emma and Augustus had cheerful childhoods despite their confused identity. The Dunmore Murrays were a close family and the two children enjoyed the society of grandparents, cousins, and aunts and uncles. Eliza Grant described George, fifth Earl of Dunmore, as 'very nice, and his wife too … Fincastle and Charley Murray charming boys'.[14] Of Susan's daughters, Georgina Drew was Emma's direct contemporary and her sister, Lucy, was three years older. After Susan's third marriage, the Drew girls lived with their grandmother, and later were brought up by their aunt Virginia. According to Eliza Grant, Virginia 'had the ugliest face I ever looked on, seamed, scarred from the small pox, her figure perfect, and her general kindness unfailing'.[15] The sobriquet given to Virginia as a little girl, 'the Virgin', turned out to be prescient.

Lord Archibald Hamilton helped to make up for the absence of Emma and Augustus's natural father and was affectionate to both children. Their half-brother, Henry Hamilton, was a cherished member of the family circle. Henry was often included in the family's annual trips to Astley's Amphitheatre, one of Augusta's favourite expeditions. Sitting on the edge of their seats, the children marvelled at the acrobats, chuckled with the clowns and thrilled at the riders performing headstands in the saddle, one of the equestrian stunts for which Astley's was famous. Augusta took the children to plays; she hired a box at the opera and she and Emma attended exhibitions at the Royal Academy in Somerset House. In the winter she taught them how to play backgammon and chess. Augusta herself was a wily chess player and in earlier days had transcribed a poem written 'By Mr XXXX upon my having beaten him several times at Chess', beginning with the lines:

Too often foil'd (fair Victress) now I yeild [sic]
The proud & well-earned Laurels of the field

The 'fair Victress' carefully noted winning chess moves in her commonplace books.[16]

The family went to Margate on shopping expeditions and there were boat trips in Ramsgate; Augustus went fishing and took fencing lessons, while Emma attended dancing classes. Pets were always part of the family; Emma kept a caged bird and a beloved border terrier features in a typically border terrier pose at the centre of the large portrait of the two children. Sweetness infuses the picture and it is clear why Augusta adored her handsome 'treasures'. The children and their dog are painted close to the bottom of the canvas, which gives immediacy to young Augustus's direct gaze while Emma looks up at her older brother affectionately. The girlish femininity of her white dress, frilly pantaloons and matching pink slippers and sash are contrasted with Augustus's military uniform decorated with braid and epaulettes. The children's cheeks bloom, and in later years when the gods of health had deserted her son, Augusta must have looked at the picture and wept. Although the artist has not been identified, the society portraitist Thomas Phillips, who often included dogs in his portraits of children, is a likely contender. Whoever the artist was, the commission was undertaken with sensitivity and virtuosity. Emma appears to be about 3 years old so it can be dated to around 1804 when the family took up residence in Ramsgate.

A few days after they had moved to the Kent coast, Augusta arranged for an army sergeant to give Augustus lessons. Three years later it was time for him to go to boarding school, and although Eton, where the Murrays were usually educated, might have seemed an obvious choice, it was not an option. George III had a special fondness for the famous school and took a closer interest in its welfare than any other monarch since Henry VI, its founder. He knew many of the masters and boys personally and the provost was a royal appointment. The King and Queen often visited Eton and enjoyed entertaining its pupils at Windsor Castle, where the boys' youth, fun and frolics enlivened their parties and picnics. A chance meeting between the royal grandparents and Augustus, their estranged and bastardised grandson, was unconscionable.

Consequently in 1807 at the age of 13, Augustus went to Harrow, a circumstance that prompted a delicate question. By what name should he be known at his new school? Augusta did not consult the Duke on the choice of school and she forbore to discuss the question of his surname, so it was 'Augustus Douglas' who joined Mrs Armstrong's boarding house on 24 February. Why she chose the surname Douglas is a mystery but it sounded undeniably Scottish.

Lady Augusta knew that if Augustus's claim to what she regarded as his rightful inheritance as the grandson of the King was to be taken seriously, he must appear in society as accomplished and urbane. She therefore showered him with a series of instructive letters, which were 'not such as would render his mental outlook quieter'.[17] Her correspondence stressed that her happiness depended on her son, an onerous responsibility for an indulged 13-year-old. As soon as Augustus had departed for the autumn term at Harrow, Augusta whisked away her tears. Hastening to her desk, she began her campaign. 'Crying at parting is the way Women shew their love,' she wrote, 'a manly, noble Boy shews his love in a more noble, manly way, – he says to himself "My Mother shall see how much I love her ... by making myself *equal* to the hopes she entertains of me ... and my own loved and loving Mama *shall be happy thro' me*."' Heaping on the pressure, she added that through him, his mother and Emma 'shall meet with the respect they deserve, – they have no Man now to protect them.'[18] She urged him to cast off his natural volatility, thoughtlessness and lack of application and made him promise to be in bed by ten o'clock having taken his two glasses of cinchona bark, a source of quinine, ground down and taken in water.[19] Echoing Queen Charlotte's advice to Prince Augustus in Göttingen, Augusta cautioned her son against weakness and idleness.

His upbringing – pampered by an adoring mother – ill prepared Augustus for the merciless regime of an early nineteenth-century public school. Augusta attempted to smooth her son's path by scattering largesse. Having sweetened the pill of severance by giving him two guineas, she proceeded to tip three senior boys and the boys' maid a guinea each, for she rightly suspected that her son would not fit in easily. By smothering him with affection and implanting unrealistic aspirations, Augusta's nurturing had done nothing to help Augustus make friends in a boys' boarding school and after five terms at Harrow, the Duke of Sussex stepped in and removed him at the end of the summer term, 1809.

Alarmed at the royal pretensions of their mother, he unsuccessfully applied for legal custody of Augustus and Emma. To be deprived of both her 'treasures' would have broken Augusta and although the Duke's friend, Lord Moira, officially became their guardian, both children remained in their mother's care. Unsuccessful in wresting them from her influence, the Duke managed to exert his will elsewhere. At the beginning of September before starting a new school, young Augustus received a life-changing but kindly letter from his father that further shook his fragile sense of identity. His son was starting out on 'a new system', the Duke wrote, so:

> it is best that you should at once take the name by which you are to be known hereafter. Not being able to give you that most congenial to my wishes and feelings [I have chosen] one of the names of my family which is <u>Este</u> by this I shall in future call you; it is one you need in no ways regret & which marks who you are, to <u>whom</u> you belong & with whom you are

connected. I expect therefore ... that when you write to me you will sign your name Augustus Frederick Este.[20]

At the end of the month Augusta received a letter from her lawyer explaining that 'the Duke thought it proper to drop the fanciful title of Douglas'. Their son 'should have a name by which he might trace his origins – & that Esté had been selected as belonging to the Queen'. Importantly, no possessions, which might cause future conflict, were attached to the title. Augusta's lawyer believed that 'throughout this dispute the Duke has only been contending with your Royal Highness for precedence in establishing the very point at issue', but on the matter of giving their children a lasting surname, the Duke was victorious.[21]

Turning his mind to the second part of Augustus's 'new system' – a different school – the Duke chose Winchester College. One of its attractions lay in its distance from both Lady Augusta's homes in London and Ramsgate and in the autumn term of 1809, Augustus Este was enrolled at Mr Urquhart's house in College Street. Everything was confusing for the boy and his Winchester notebook confirms his unfamiliarity with his new name, which is practised countless times among the blots and scribbles.[22] It is poignant to see that while he laboured on lines from Virgil and Xenophon, he was inscribing 'Este' on page after page, trying it out in upper and lower case, in pencil and ink, in italics and upright. His father's designation was an unwelcome adjustment: no longer his mother's 'Prince Augustus', he received letters from her addressed to 'Augustus Frederick of Este' and was hence forward known as Augustus D'Este. A change of identity is testing for the strongest personality, but for a 15-year-old, who had been mollycoddled by his mother, it was a psychological disaster. D'Este was forced to suffer the ignominy of being a new boy for the second time, something that the Duke, who had been educated at home and later at the University of Göttingen, had never experienced.

Augustus attended Harrow and Winchester at an undistinguished period in their histories. In 1806 a Harrovian had drowned in circumstances many believed had been caused by bullying and two years later there were pupil rebellions in both schools.[23] In contrast to today's public schools where the pupils' well-being is paramount, those at the beginning of the nineteenth century were inhumane. The behaviour of many of the masters and senior boys was brutal and beatings frequent. The curriculum concentrated on the classics to the detriment of every other discipline, the benefit of team games was yet to be understood and food was often in short supply. The younger pupils were forced to 'fag' for the seniors, which meant being available at all times of the day to run errands such as shoe cleaning, fetching water and preparing breakfast or tea.

D'Este's fellow pupils at Winchester included the nephews of Jane Austen, and Thomas Arnold, later the famous headmaster of Rugby. One of his peers was a scholarship boy, Augustus Hare, the future clergyman and writer. Hare had received the name of his godfather, Prince Augustus, who had attended his baptism in Rome with Lady Augusta Murray in 1793. D'Este left Winchester in 1810 and the next year he was enrolled in the 7th Royal Fusiliers.

Augusta was happiest when her children were with her. On 1 November 1812, starting a new account book, she wrote, 'both my Treasures at home with me, happy and well; I begin this book therefore – with sentiments of gratitude to heaven.'[24] Two years later, D'Este's regiment took him to Jersey, where he enjoyed driving to St Heliers in his mother's latest gift, a Tilbury.[25] The Tilbury was a fast and stylish carriage for two; the same model that John Thorpe drove so recklessly when he terrified Catherine Morland in Jane Austen's *Northanger Abbey*. On 19 April 1814 Augustus met 'many beautiful young creatures' at a ball, and later dined in a tent 'subaltern style'; he went to field days and, cutting a party, he 'bowled away to Bagatelle', the residence of the Duke de Bouillon. On 12 May he spent a 'most quiet day, ate drank and vegetated' and on the last day of the month, he rose and did nothing but spend his time in idleness.[26] Jersey was clearly no hardship posting but within a few months, his life in the army had become deadly serious.

In 1812 President Madison had invaded Canada, tantamount to declaring war on Great Britain. He was exasperated by Britain's interference in American affairs: supporting the Native Americans, pressganging US merchant sailors and imposing trade limitations. Often overlooked in British history books, the War of 1812 saw the White House razed, inspired 'The Star-Spangled Banner' and witnessed the rise of General Andrew Jackson, the seventh president of the United States. When Napoleon abdicated in April 1814 the British could focus their attention on the war with America and one of their objectives was the capture of New Orleans.

The city was strategically important for three reasons: it was the gateway to Louisiana, America's newest state, it was the country's largest slave market and it was the key to the River Mississippi, on which much of the South's trade depended.

In November 1814, as aide-de-camp to General John Lambert, Augustus left England aboard HMS *Statira* for New Orleans. He sailed through the Bahamas and the Gulf of Florida and entered Lake Borgne on 3 January 1815. From there the regiment worked its way up to the creek where British forces had gained a footing on the marshy shores of Louisiana. That night he dined with Lambert and the British commander, General Sir Edward Pakenham, the Duke of Wellington's brother-in-law. Behind the house where they ate, Augustus saw a large orange grove and round each tree the Light Dragoons had made their huts, with a fire at each entrance. It was the first night that he had slept on a bearskin. Far away from the gentle delights of Jersey and about to participate in his first battle, Augustus was afraid.

The irrelevant assault on New Orleans was his only experience of warfare and as General Lambert was placed in command of the reserves, Augustus did not see hand-to-hand fighting. The battle started early on the foggy morning of 8 January at Chalmette on the north bank of the Mississippi River, where General Jackson's well prepared and deeply entrenched army defended New Orleans. The gullies, canals and creeks as well as Jackson's earthworks were formidable obstacles and the encounter was a British disaster. After the death of Pakenham, Lambert was left in command and decided to retreat. Augustus wrote, 'there was no possibility of rallying the troops … I quitted with my General the Field of Action at about two o'clock – The memory of this day to Brittons must be ever melancholy, they lost in this unsuccessful attack at least 2,000 men.'[27] The plains of Chalmette were red with the jackets of the fallen and the blood of the lost. Conversely, the Americans recorded only thirteen men dead, with thirty-nine wounded and nineteen missing. The battle was the last engagement of the War of 1812, sometimes known as America's second war of independence. Although America had seen its capital burnt, it had successfully defended itself against the mother country.

Before the British retreated to their ships a week later, Augustus had time to go alligator hunting up the Mississippi creeks. When he lunched with the 14th Dragoons he took the opportunity to taste some of the meat, which he found 'exorable'.[28] The fleet sailed to Mobile Bay at the beginning of February and the troops set up camp on Dauphin Island, where Augustus enjoyed more shooting before all field sports came to an end on 16 March.

At dinner that night Augustus was disturbed by the arrival of two Americans, Mr Livingston and Major Woodruff, who had come to see General Lambert. They had been sent by General Jackson in New Orleans and brought 'the official document of the signature of the Peace' from President Madison, the battle of New Orleans having been fought two weeks *after* the peace treaty was signed. When General Lambert and the admirals had attended to the documents, the British fleet departed for England on 7 April, with Augustus aboard HMS *Diomede*.

Stopping in the beautiful harbour at Havana to complete provisioning, he could not fail to be impressed by the neatly fortified city, where he dined at Government House. Waking on the morning of 24 April, he was saddened to find that they were lifting the anchor. He had spent a few days so pleasantly in Cuba that reflecting on 'the numberless unpleasant circumstances, that my unpleasant situation forces me to submit to in my own country, I almost regretted quitting this island of apparent calm'.[29] The prospect of homecoming was not one of unalloyed delight.

D'Este's awkward personality made him heartily disliked during the voyage home. He seemed adept at fomenting trouble on board and fell out with his brother officers; Captain Kipping, no doubt maddened by Augustus's airs, threw his pet dog into the sea. Fortunately the animal was 'not drowned or hurt by the occasion'. After five weeks at sea, HMS *Diomede* docked in Portsmouth on 30 May and the unpopular officer spent the evening at the theatre.

His social gaffes, foolish interference, imagined slights and clumsy attempts at friendship elicit sympathy rather than censure. Infuriating company he may have been, but the 'unpleasant situation' in which D'Este was to find himself in England was no fault of his own. He suffered from a crippling identity crisis, that of the unacknowledged grandson of the King, and was forced to make separate social provisions. When he visited the Grant family soon after his return, Eliza recalled that:

> he had not then given up his claim to royalty, therefore there was a little skilful arrangement on his part to avoid either assumption or renuncia-

> tion. He entered unannounced, my father meeting him at the door and ushering him into the room, my mother, and all the ladies on her hint, rising till he begged them to be seated. Otherwise he conformed to common usage.[30]

On one hand Augustus was idolised by his mother, who inflated his sense of entitlement, and on the other, the Royal Family ignored him and his father could not acknowledge him as his legitimate son. D'Este's pretensions, firmly implanted by his mother, would eventually land him in grave trouble.

30

A Very Foolish Young Man in Some of His Ideas

Augustus D'Este came of age on 13 January 1815, a few days after the battle of New Orleans. Determined to mark such a significant anniversary even though her son was absent, Augusta arranged a ball in his honour at Mount Albion, instructing the servants to clear the library of furniture, roll back the rugs, and lay all the fires downstairs. She was expecting a large party. On the birthday itself she told D'Este that, 'I have had the kindest letter this morning from Archibald that you can imagine, – congratulating me, on the return of a day so dear to my heart.'[1] If nothing else, her lover was thoughtful and loyal.

She described the celebrations in a letter to D'Este the following day:

> Your health my beloved was drunk with 3 times 3, cheers, hurra's ... everybody standing up; – how I loved them, – & prayed you might deserve, enjoy, & often welcome deserved greetings similar to these. The usual set were there ... [with] a new cargo of officers, who came from Deal & Canterbury for the occasion. I told poor dear Thorpe that in your stead, he must do the honours ... & when your health was drunk – he was crazy with delight, & joy, he says he has promised you half his fortune & that you shall have it.[2]

His grandfather, 'a gentleman of the first rank in the mercantile world', had left John Tharp a generous legacy: £6,000 a year.[3]

Organising the party exhausted Augusta; while her son's health was drunk enthusiastically, her own was fragile and on 20 January she sustained an inflammation of the lungs. She was relieved that Archibald had 'renounced all intention' of going down to Ramsgate as he 'would have tired [me] very much'. She told D'Este that 'the snow is deep on the ground, & the weather intensely cold, – however this does not prevent young one (Augusta, Susan's daughter) from walking out every day on the Pier with Virginia'.[4]

Augusta's chest infection was the latest in a series of health problems that she faced that winter, made worse by the thought of her son joining the American War and the government's refusal to allow her to go abroad to a warmer climate. In early February her request to go away was turned down again and she told Augustus that 'I look upon that decision as nonsense, all the physicians say I must go, therefore they cannot keep me here, my health is gone, ... there is a total break up of my constitution coming on.' For the last nine weeks she had been 'blistered, bled, starved' and was only just beginning to recover.[5] On 19 February she reported that, 'the Duke of Sussex is positively resolved we shall not go abroad, so that I am obliged to go to London to have a suit in chancery to try whether he can really prevent my going, this is very wearing to my health and spirits, but I cannot help it'.[6]

The Duke probably thought it unsafe for Augusta and his daughter to leave England and a week later the news that Napoleon had escaped from the island of Elba and was gathering support in France put a stop to their plans. D'Este's safe return in May gave Augusta peace of mind and after the battle of Waterloo she was able to go abroad. As she had hoped, the change of climate had a marked improvement on her health.

Augusta arrived in Paris on 1 September at a time of humiliation for the French when the allies were recovering the works of art that Napoleon had stolen. As one of Emma's friends, Lady Edgecumbe, recalled many years later, the restitution was:

> a severe blow to the pride and vanity of the French (or perhaps, more correctly speaking, of the Parisians), but they needed it; they needed this 'great moral lesson,' as the Duke of Wellington called it. The events of 1814 had taught them nothing, and those of 1815 ... and possession of their capital by foreign armies, would probably have passed from their memories in a few years, had not the bare walls of the picture gallery and the empty statue galleries of the Louvre impressed upon their eyes and minds the fact that Europe had at last roused itself, that their day of

spoliation and attempt at universal dominion was over, and that they were no longer conquerors, but conquered.[7]

During the second half of September many of the stolen artworks were removed from the Louvre. Emma Edgecumbe went there frequently, 'to see glorious paintings and statues before they gradually disappeared. And a curious sight it was, workmen busily employed in taking the pictures down and putting them in packing cases, and a number of the English Guards placed at short intervals the whole length of the gallery, to see that they were not damaged either from carelessness or spite.'[8] Augusta would not have missed such an opportunity while she was in Paris.

The most galling act of restitution for Parisians was the removal of the four horses, which had originally come from St Mark's in Venice. Napoleon had harnessed them to a gilt car on the triumphal arch in the Place du Carrousel and for some days beforehand the populace assembled at the arch 'and looked with emotion at the horses as if to take leave of them'.[9] Fearing a disturbance when the horses were lowered, the authorities placed Austrian cuirassiers at every entrance to the Place 'and no carriages were admitted with the exception of those belonging to English persons', so Augusta and Emma may have witnessed the liberation of the famous steeds.[10] Since the allied armies had entered Paris, Jacques-Louis David had turned his full-length portrait of Napoleon to the wall and on 20 November, while Augusta was in the French capital, the Treaty of Paris was signed, completing the vanquishing of the defeated Emperor.

By mid December, she was back in Ramsgate, where she found her family worried about John Tharp's mental health. His behaviour had become more and more erratic and it was thought best that he should terminate his studies at University College, Oxford, and live quietly at the Countess of Dunmore's house at Southwood with his mother, Susan.

In Augusta's opinion, Susan did not pick husbands well. While Augusta had disliked Susan's first husband, she abhorred her sister's third, the Reverend Archibald Douglas, who held a number of livings in Ireland but never seemed to be there. Soon after D'Este's birthday ball, his mother told him to her annoyance that the Douglases were still with Lady Dunmore at Southwood, 'I understand Mr Douglas runs the risk of losing his Irish livings, by remaining absent, & yet he is so thoughtless and improvident and continues to stay.'[11]

Augusta also loathed the way that he bullied his stepchildren. She believed that he had forced Susan to make over Lucy and Georgina Drew to Virginia, their kindly but hypochondriac maiden aunt, and now that John Tharp was of age, Archibald Douglas saw a way of removing his strange stepson from the family circle by finding him a docile wife. Augusta was infuriated by her brother-in-law's unscrupulous behaviour and did everything she could to stiffen the sinews of her besieged nephew 'for Mr Douglas seems to have him entirely under his control, tho' I do all I can to emancipate him from it; and tell him (before Mr D) not to look at him before he answers, not to be governed by his opinions, but to have one of his own; in short I exert my best endeavours to give poor dear Thorpe a little independence of feeling and action, but it will not succeed.'[12] Sadly she was right.

On 1 June she attended a pathetic ceremony that should never have taken place: the marriage between John Tharp, madman, and Lady Hannah Hay, orphan. The brief marriage was disastrous for both parties and soon after their union, the bride sought refuge with her aunt amidst reports of improper behaviour towards her new husband. With the breakdown of his marriage and growing insanity, John's associates applied to the Lord Chancellor to declare him a chancery lunatic. In that way his fortune would be held in chancery and he could not squander it. In November 1816 it was decreed that the lunatic's paternal uncle should run the estates in Cambridgeshire and Jamaica and Lady Hannah was given legal responsibility for the care of John himself, who lived in a series of private asylums until his death in 1863.

Augustus returned from America two days before the Tharp wedding and with his mother's encouragement his thoughts turned to his own marriage. He was good-looking although, like his father, inclined to be stout. Augusta's aspirations for her son were opposed to those of the Duke, who had resigned himself to the fact that the Royal Family would never accept his children as legitimate.

When he was at Harrow, Augusta had unwisely informed her son that some gentlemen believed that he would make a perfect match for Princess Charlotte, the daughter of the Prince of Wales, and the King's only legitimate heir. From that day Augustus had been encouraged to regard Charlotte as a possible wife and he had pestered her before he went to America. As the Princess told her friend, Mercer Elphinstone, D'Este was:

> a very foolish young man in some of his ideas & particularly in his conduct. He is the *mother's favorite* & always has been from his childhood; consequently behaves very undutifully to his father & causes him much anxiety & uneasiness. I should hope for his *own sake* that he will *throw* off his *ridiculous fancies*, & as he is shortly to join the Fusilliers I should hope the *soldier* would *take* [the] *place* of the *spoilt child*.[13]

Although she ignored him, her coolness did not discourage Augustus, who could not believe that she might find his attentions odious. Charlotte understood that it was his 'ambitious mother … that has thus set him on, & no doubt made sure of the Duke & I never resisting'.[14] D'Este persisted in following her in Hyde Park so that when she heard that he was going to war, the young Princess was relieved.

On his return from America he continued his suit and, hearing that Charlotte was in Weymouth, hurried down to the Dorset coast in the autumn of 1815. As she told Mercer, 'His being here & his folly rather keep me in a fuss, & I shall be glad [when] he's gone.' He did depart a week later, having kept her in 'constant *hot water* for fear of some *impudence* or *imprudence*'.[15] Happily for his relationship with his father, and indeed his uncle, the Regent, D'Este's pursuit of Princess Charlotte ended there.

The next year she married Prince Leopold of Saxe-Coburg-Saalfeld and when she died in childbirth on 6 November 1817, the lack of a legitimate heir caused consternation. Both the Prince Regent and his younger brother, the Duke of York, were estranged from their wives and although the Duke of Cumberland had married a Mecklenburg-Strelitz princess in 1815, the three other brothers of the Duke of Sussex: the Dukes of Clarence, Kent and Cambridge, were all bachelors, though the Duke of Kent had taken mistresses and the Duke of Clarence, notoriously so. The actress, Dorothea Jordan, had borne him ten FitzClarences and their eldest son had been born sixteen days after Augustus. The status quo needed to change fast to preserve the royal line.

Augusta watched the start of the race for an heir with interest. She recalled bitterly that unlike most of his brothers, the conduct of the Duke of Sussex had never invited serious reproach. She believed that her marriages to him were valid and that their two handsome children had been declared illegitimate most unjustly. It was hard for her to see Augustus and Emma overlooked at such a critical time. However, a number of articles in the press began to promote their cause.

In December, Sir William Knighton, the Regent's physician and adviser, was busy keeping an eye on the provincial newspapers, which, as he pointed out to his master 'are read locally, and have an influence'. He reported that a journal in Leeds, 'has lately been at work for the Duke of S[ussex]. They … wish to legalise his son, whom they designate by the title of a fine spirited "Prince". They then notice that the Duke was married twice to the Lady, and the last time at St. George's Church, Hanover Square.' Alluding to the Royal Family vying with each other to provide an heir, Knighton added, '*It is all very harmless* but it proves … that they resort to distant provincial papers, for particular purposes. I am very watchful of them *all*.'[16]

The Dukes of Clarence and Kent wed respectively Princess Adelaide of Saxe-Meiningen and Princess Victoria of Saxe-Coburg-Saalfeld, sister of Prince Leopold, in a double ceremony at Kew Palace in July 1818. Princess Alexandrina Victoria, daughter of King George's fourth son, the Duke of Kent, was born in June 1819 at Kensington Palace. Her parents had hurried back from Leiningen for the event, and the Duke of Sussex incurred the wrath of the Prince Regent for supporting the Duke of Kent in his desire for his child to be born in England. Three days later Prince George of Cumberland was born in Berlin, bringing the tally to three heirs in as many months because the Duchess of Cambridge had given birth to a son, also named George, in March 1819.

There were high hopes that the Duke and Duchess of Clarence would follow suit and produce a nursery full of children but Princess Adelaide lost two baby girls and sustained further miscarriages, once with twins. The personal heartbreak for the Clarences meant that the succession focused on Princess Victoria of Kent, who lived at Kensington Palace with her widowed mother (the Duke of Kent having died less than a year after his daughter's birth) and half-sister, Princess Feodora of Leiningen.

Having failed in his suite with Princess Charlotte, in 1825 Augustus D'Este decided to try his luck with Feodora, who seemed a perfect candidate: royal, young and attractive. Although he was aware that courting her might infuriate the Duke of Sussex, Augustus knew that his mother would approve and he started his campaign while he and Feodora were both in Coburg, far away from Kensington Palace. Moreover, he fervently hoped that one day he might prove that the provisions of the Royal Marriages Act were invalid outside Britain.

Feodora was visiting her grandparents and, flattered by an invitation from a handsome soldier, the 17-year-old Princess accompanied Augustus on an afternoon walk to the fortress high above the town of Coburg. It was a fine day in November, the autumn leaves were at their best and as the pair wandered through the woods to the castle, Augustus felt heartened. Although the behaviour of his inamorata at a ball the next day was far from encouraging and made him 'excessively unhappy', he decided to act.[17] Before consulting either of their parents, he proposed to Feodora on 2 December.

Assuring her that he was 'as legitimate a Prince as any to be named in either of our houses', he promised her that he would not cease in trying to obtain those 'rights which the iron hand of power so unjustly has hitherto withheld'.[18] Bewildered and unnerved by the passion she had provoked, she asked Augustus to forget her and told him that it was too hard to give him an answer. Her brother's presence ensured that their farewell was formal when Augustus took his leave. However, he was obliged to return to Coburg, as flooding prevented him from reaching his next destination.

In pursuing Feodora, Augustus showed a pitiable lack of judgement, as well as desperation to be acknowledged. The day before Feodora's 18th birthday, Baroness de Speth, one of the Duchess of Kent's ladies not known for her discretion or common sense, gave Augustus unreasonable hope. Mistakenly the baroness led him to believe that there was no reason why the Duchess would refuse her consent to his marrying her elder daughter. Flushed with optimism, he offered Feodora a wedding ring. She refused it but in return gave him a purse that she had made.

On his return to Hanover he received a devastating letter from the baroness. She terminated his hopes and in a tactless postscript expressed her sadness that he did not appear to have many friends and apologised for misleading him. At a party given by the Duchess of Cambridge later in London, he was handed the gold ring that he had pressed on Feodora with a second letter from de Speth instructing him not to think of reviving the subject of marriage as it would not only distress, but offend, the Princess. When he asked her to explain her sudden change of tone, she reminded him of the number of people opposed to his pretensions. The Duchess of Kent, who had been kind to Augustus and Emma in the past, blamed herself for encouraging the unsuitable connection and rightly regarded Augustus's behaviour as disrespectful.

At the end of February he told Baroness de Speth that for the last fortnight he had been in:

> alternate fits of deep despondency and of violent irritation and anger into which I have been thrown by a most unnatural and insulting letter from my father. To the infirmity of passion carried by a father to any extent a son may be bound by duty to submit, but when a father coolly and deliberately writes purposely to insult, to torture, and to outrage every sentiment of Honor, of moral principle and of integrity in the nature of his son, submission beyond certain limits wd become mean and pitiful … from the receipt of such an other letter I shall be spared

The Duke had informed his son that he wished to break off relations with him.[19] The severity of his father's reaction wounded D'Este's dignity, his humiliation was complete and he made no more attempts at royal marriage.

31

My Dearest Girl

If Augusta idolised Augustus, she adored Emma, a loving, happy and lively little girl with good looks and a healthy constitution. Knowing that she alone was responsible for her daughter's upbringing, Augusta masterminded every detail. When they were parted she asked whom Emma saw and what she ate during her absence. She encouraged her to bathe, to be attentive to her lessons, to say her prayers every day and 'to be good natured to her visitors'. She believed that Emma's education would be the key to her acceptance in society and, as she had Augustus, exhorted her daughter to speak French, not forgetting to learn her verbs and practise the language on her walks.

Augusta was a deeply affectionate mother who enjoyed spoiling her daughter and there are numerous gifts for Emma in her accounts. On her 8th birthday, 9 August 1809, she gave her 'dear little girl' £2 10*s* 6*d*. By 1810 she was paying her daughter half a crown a month pocket money and soon Emma's monthly allowance was a generous £1. Augusta loved to buy her new clothes and spent 10*s* 6*d* on a pelisse, as well as 6*s* on a spencer or close-fitting jacket. There is a mystifying entry on 4 December 1810 when she paid her daughter £1 'for her courage', perhaps for a tooth extracted or a leech applied.[1] To sweeten their journeys to and fro Ramsgate, Augusta brought treats: biscuits or grapes and once, rather impractically, paid 5*s* 6*d* for a lobster. On 1 January 1818 there was a New Year's gift to her 'dear loved girl' of £10, at the same time she gave her son a 'little present' of £24 and sent Susan in Ireland £25.[2] In March 1815 she lost a bet with Emma about George, the Duke of Clarence's eldest son, and had to pay her 5*s* 6*d*.

In 1819 she paid Emma 2*s* 6*d* and noted that it was for '(a bet) to remember I always lose when I bet with her, she being always right'.[3] Augusta never did learn: six years later, on 19 August 1825, she 'paid my girl for a bet abt Queen Mary £5'.

When Emma was of marriageable age, there were payments for gowns of chintz, muslin and bombazine, a corded material of silk and worsted. There were hats, ribbons, shawls and reticules, small beaded or embroidered bags. In 1820 Augusta started taking Emma to Wednesday evening subscription balls at Almack's, the fiercely exclusive Assembly Rooms in King Street, St James's. An entrance voucher cost a guinea and was highly prized – the guest list for each ball was supervised by a different group of noble and fastidious patronesses – but Augusta could be sure that the partners her daughter met in the elegant ballroom would come only from the highest rank of society. That year, at a cost of nine guineas, Emma sat for her portrait with William Fowler, the artist who also painted young Princess Victoria. She had almond-shaped blue eyes, a small mouth and a long nose, all set in a placid round face surrounded with ebullient dark curly hair.

Augusta took Emma to Paris for the winter of 1820 and Augustus joined them in the spring. They were still in the French capital when Napoleon, imprisoned by the British on the island of St Helena, died on 5 May 1821. On their return to Dover Augusta had spent so much money 'a shopping' in Paris that she was charged £26 11*s* import tax.

The coronation of George IV, held on 19 July that year, was a splendid but an unedifying occasion. Queen Caroline had been forbidden to participate in the ceremony and after trying to enter the Abbey, she had been ridiculed by the masses and forced to go home. Three weeks after the coronation from which she had been excluded, the uncrowned Queen was dead. Aged only 53, Caroline had expired from an abdominal obstruction on the night of 7 August.

Nobody was surprised when they learnt that she had given final instructions for her coffin to be laid at her childhood home in Brunswick. Her executors found themselves charged with arranging a funeral procession from London to Harwich, a passage across the North Sea, a voyage down the River Elbe to Stade, and a progress from thence to Brunswick. It is unclear why Emma D'Este accompanied the Queen's coffin on this ill-prepared expedition but she was the Queen's second cousin and perhaps they had become close when they had been neighbours in Connaught Place from 1813 to 1814. Lord Archibald Hamilton, a loyal supporter of the late Queen, may also have encouraged Emma to go.

The published accounts of the Queen's final journey do not record Emma's presence on the journey to Brunswick, thus highlighting her social exclusion and insignificance as an illegitimate daughter of a royal duke. Without her own account, documented in a slim vellum notebook now in the Public Record Office, Emma's participation would be unknown. Although sometimes illegible and often untroubled by the rules of grammar, her closely observed record is valuable in furnishing us with details of this little-known journey.[4] Lady Anne Hamilton, Archibald's sister and Queen Caroline's former lady in waiting, was also one of the party. Lady Anne blamed Augusta for the fact that Archibald had never married and made a point of ignoring Emma, but her rudeness was mitigated by the kindly presence of another traveller on the expedition: Emma's future husband, Thomas Wilde, one of the Queen's executors.

On Emma's return, Augusta took her to Paris in December to buy clothes for her coming of age ball. When they came back in May 1822, Augusta had spent nearly £1,000. She also spared no expense for the birthday celebration itself. The party took place on 28 July at 17 Montague Street, where the ballroom opened on to private gardens behind. Augusta hired plates, china, linen and lamps, booked an orchestra and purchased 'fruit for the dance'.[5] Faithful 'Black George' Murray, her parents' servant from Virginia, was paid £1 to be the Master of Ceremonies.

If Augusta were hoping that Emma might find a suitable husband as a result of launching her daughter in such style, she would be disappointed. Her unrealistic hopes tended to cloud her judgement and having proposed Princess Charlotte as a match for her son, she thought that Charlotte's widower, Prince Leopold, might suit Emma. Potential husbands may have been put off by Emma's height and ebullience, but the uncertainty surrounding her birth was a more powerful deterrent.

Henry Fox told his aunt in January 1828 that, 'Lord Seymour has escaped from the clutches of Lady Sandwich, only however to fall into those of Miss D'Este, very much frying-pan fire-like. She is a brazen, hoydenish, old rouged coquette, and neither her manners or conversation are those of a demoiselle à marier.'[6] The next month, Fox's mother, Lady Holland, who had disliked Augusta since they were both in Naples in 1792, rejoiced, 'at Lord Seymour having escaped the toils of that veteran coquette. I was afraid he might have got into an entanglement with her, as poor Ld Archibald did with [her] mother which grievously affected his whole life, & kept him from marrying another.'[7] Despite Henry Fox's unkind prediction, Emma did get married some years later and her marriage was a happy one.

32

Sad Unhappy Day

Emma was a favourite of her maternal grandmother and in November 1817 Lady Dunmore had told her a secret. In a letter to her 'dear little Princess', the countess wrote:

> In obedience to your request and as you wisely observe that I am under no solemn promise of keeping secret who was the clergyman that performed the ceremony of your mother's marriage I tell it you under the certainty that you will not divulge it – but when necessary – it was the Revd Mr Gun who was then in Rome, – both him, and your father had exacted an oath from your mama that she would not tell.[1]

She then explained that if she had not been blackmailed by the servant who admitted the rector to her house in Rome, she would have 'remained ignorant'. Emma's request was made just in time. Charlotte Dunmore died a year later 'at a very advanced age' on 11 November 1818, which was, as Augusta noted in her account book, a 'sad unhappy day'.

In her final years the countess had become so deaf that she could hear only with the aid of an ear trumpet but the affliction had not dented her spirits and she remained cheerful. As far back as 1804, when Emma Hamilton was staying with Lady Dunmore, she told Lord Nelson that her hostess had 'crowned a "String of Peccadilloes" by turning in her old age to religion.'[2] It is unclear what those misdemeanours entailed, but Charlotte Dunmore was undeniably remorseful. At the end of her life she lived in the former convent of St Mildred on the cliffs at Kingsgate and according to

Eliza Grant, she 'had, like a Frenchwoman, taken to religion … by way of expiating the sins of her youth'.[3]

She left a brief will in 1818 bequeathing her house at Twickenham and all her effects to Virginia. Not wishing to trouble her children, the countess specified that she should be buried in the parish in which she had expired, in as plain a manner as possible, with 'a hearse and one mourning coach only to attend my funeral in order that all unnecessary pomp and parade be avoided'.[4] She died in Augusta's care at Mount Albion and therefore, her remains 'were deposited (by her desire, without parade) in the vault prepared for her late husband in the church of St Lawrence'.[5] Of the five sons she had borne, only one was able to attend her funeral. William and Jack had predeceased her, Leveson was in Madras and, in the absence of George, Alexander was chief mourner. Augusta was not there. Ladies of rank, unwilling for their emotions to be paraded in public, did not usually attend funerals.

Throughout Augusta's life, Lady Dunmore had supported her and their relationship had been exceptionally close. Augusta's marriage to Prince Augustus had turned her mother's life upside down but the countess remained constant to her disgraced daughter and as a consequence was forced to forsake her own place in society. Lady Dunmore's performance at the inquiry into Augusta's illegal marriage was nothing short of bravura. Once the toast of Virginia and a habituée of the court of St James's, after the disastrous marriage the countess was excluded from royal circles and shared Augusta's disgrace and isolation. She supported her daughter financially and became so poor that she was forced to give up her carriage. She faced a lasting rift with her sister, Susanna, to whom she had been warmly attached and to whom she was obliged for forwarding the career of the Earl of Dunmore, but Charlotte Dunmore never disowned her daughter. Prince Augustus himself had regarded her as his second mother when they were in Italy and held her in great affection.

Two days before her death, Lady Dunmore's older sister, Lady Euphemia, expired in the Scottish Borders. Their father, the Earl of Galloway, had been solicitous in advancing his daughters' prospects through good marriages but he faced a challenge because their fortunes were unequal to their birth. He was, however, a formidable tactician and assisted by his daughters' personal attractions, succeeded in organising alliances for five of them. Only kind-hearted Euphemia had remained single and was therefore in a position to support her nieces and nephews whenever required. Augusta's estranged aunt Susanna had died in 1805 and with the death of Charlotte and Euphemia, the six daughters of the 6th Earl of Galloway and his second wife were no more.

It was a melancholy time. Queen Charlotte died on 17 November at Kew Palace after a long illness. Whenever her role as royal consort had permitted, she had helped Augustus and acted as go-between and peacemaker in his troubled relationships with the King and the Prince of Wales. No doubt she had suffered intensely at the rupture between her husband and child.

Seven months before the Queen's death, the marriage took place between Augustus's sister, Princess Elizabeth, and the Prince of Hesse-Homburg in the throne room at St James's Palace. In marked contrast to both of Augustus's hole and corner weddings, the Cabinet, officers of the royal household, two archbishops, the bishop of London, the Lord Chancellor and the Lord Chief Justice were in attendance. Ambassadors and foreign ministers were present at the Queen's invitation and it is clear from his description of the ceremony that Richard Rush, the American Minister, was impressed:

> Before the throne was an altar covered with crimson velvet. A profusion of golden plate was upon it. There was a salver of great size on which was represented the Lord's Supper. The company being assembled, the bridegroom entered, with his attendants. Then came the Queen, with the bride and the royal family ... Her Majesty sat; the rest stood. The Archbishop of Canterbury read the marriage service and the Duke of York gave away the bride. The whole was according to the forms of the Church, and performed with great solemnity. A record of the marriage was made. When all was finished, the bride knelt before the Queen to receive her blessing.[6]

Rush was touched by the elderly Queen's conduct at her daughter's wedding reception. He wrote:

> This venerable personage, the head of a large family – her children then clustering about her; the female head of a great empire – in the seventy-sixth year of her age – went the round of the company, speaking to all. There was a kindliness in her manner ... No one did she omit. Around

> her neck hung a miniature portrait of the King. He was absent, scathed by the hand of Heaven; a marriage going on in one of his palaces; he, the lonely, suffering tenant of another. But the portrait was a token superior to a crown! It bespoke the natural glory of wife and mother, eclipsing the artificial glory of Queen. For more than fifty years this royal pair had lived together in affection. The scene would have been one of interest anywhere. May it not be noticed on a throne?[7]

King George III, the 'lonely, suffering tenant' of Windsor Castle, was in no state to comprehend the death of his loyal wife. Not long afterwards the pathetic old man, who had lived for so many years in a world of his own, was released from further indignity and pain. He expired in the evening of 29 January 1820. Neither he, nor his Queen, had ever met their grandchildren, Augustus and Emma.

33

I Very Ill

The number of payments that Augusta made at the beginning of 1823 to Sir Henry Halford, one of the late King's physicians, indicates the deterioration in her health. She took regular baths in Harley Street and was often bled. She was open-minded about alternative cures and paid Mr La Bourne £1 for three sessions of galvanisation, an electrical current treatment sometimes used for paralysis.

In September 1823 Augusta made a poignant visit to Fonthill Abbey, designed by James Wyatt for William Beckford. It was the only time she would see the bizarre house that had replaced Fonthill Splendens because the tower collapsed for the final time in 1825 and the abbey was demolished soon afterwards. With hundreds of others, Augusta bought a ticket to preview the sale of Beckford's 'Magnificent, Rare, and Valuable Library' of 20,000 volumes. She spent a day viewing her old friend's books and on her way back to London recalled the fireworks, music and dancing at his coming of age party in 1781. Then she had been 20 years old, the toast of society with all her life ahead of her. Now she was a sickly old lady of 63, unwelcome in polite circles. It was a melancholy comparison and four days later her spirits were lowered further by the departure of D'Este to his regiment in Ireland.

The proximity of Ramsgate to France enabled Augusta to make frequent trips across the Channel to visit her sisters and cheer herself up with a little shopping. She also took shorter trips to Calais, where she bought white gloves by the dozen, satin shoes and handkerchiefs, a reticule and 'trois fichus'. At the end of September 1825, Augusta and Emma took a steam packet across the Channel for the first time.

They were visiting Susan and Virginia, who had been living in the French capital for the last six years. Augusta rented a house in Paris and straight away began to shop, paying a 'cheating Mantua maker 45 francs' and buying a table for her relative, Madame de La Trémoille, for 50 francs. Early in the New Year Augusta was suffering from asthma and gave Dr Mellingen 20 francs for a new treatment whereby the inhalation of gas widened the pulmonary vessels. She continued her acts of charity in France and on her 65th birthday in 1826 gave a man without legs 2 francs.

While in Paris she paid for Emma to learn hairdressing and the alarming payment of 26 francs for 'blonde' was probably for her daughter; she also lent her 'naughty girl' 100 francs. On 14 March she purchased night lamps and bedpans for Susan, who was gravely ill. Two days later her treasured sister died. It was Augusta who paid the interment expenses, giving Lucy Drew a present of 1,000 francs for 'dear Susan's funeral'. Augusta and Emma returned to England in early April 1826.

Susan's death reminded Augusta of her own mortality and roused her to make another attempt at extracting her wedding certificate from elderly Mr Gunn, who now lived at Smallburgh in Norfolk. She had relinquished hope of young Augustus being recognised as legitimate at home but believed that the possession of his parents' wedding certificate would facilitate his acceptance abroad. With characteristic persistence she had tried unsuccessfully to secure it a number of times. Soon after she returned from Berlin in 1799 she visited the rector, who would not relinquish the document but implied that when her son was 21 he would comply with her request. At the same time Prince Augustus had written asking for the certificate 'which is greatly important for us, as it regards the future fortune and legal pretensions of our child'.[1] The Prince suggested that if Mr Gunn felt unable to hand it over, he should put it in a safe place and instruct his executors to give it to the Prince at his death.

When Lady Dunmore's health was failing in May 1818, Augusta wrote to Gunn again and informed him that before her illness, her mother:

> thought it right to inform my children of the name of that person who alone could give them legal claims (their due) upon the family of their father, – & equally did she think it her duty to inform my brothers of that

> name (which I had never revealed) but which ultimately could assure to the world the real situation of her daughter; – you must believe me dear Sir that the doubtful character under which I have so long laboured, has been very trying to my feelings.[2]

Soon after, she despatched her brother, Alexander, to Smallburgh on the same mission. The rector's obduracy in refusing to help elicited a cross letter from his visitor, who told him firmly that 'you are by the sacred obligation of your religion obliged to give that document that will relieve my innocent relatives from a stigma which you alone can remove from them and which you are in every moral point of view injuriously called on to [release] them from'.

Alexander absolved his sister from breaking her word to the rector and told him that it had been at his mother's wish that he had made the journey to Norfolk; the Duchess:

> only acquainted me with your place of residence at the express entreaty of a mother who lying on a couch near her from which she never expected to be able to arise & at whose desire she also gave me a letter of introduction to you … it was at the express desire of that mother that I called upon you for the certificate.[3]

Three days later, Dr Henry Bathurst, the liberal Bishop of Norwich, who had been pro-Napoleon and supported both Roman Catholic emancipation and protestant dissenters, became involved; he told William Gunn that he believed there was no 'risque' in him giving Colonel Murray the contentious document. Despite this Gunn was immoveable.

In August 1823 the bishop wrote a letter to Gunn introducing Captain D'Este, a young man for whom he had 'a very sincere regard' and hoped that Gunn would do everything in his power to meet his wishes. D'Este was no more successful than either of his parents or his uncle and came home empty-handed. Now Augusta decided to have another attempt herself and, despite feeling unwell, she left London on Thursday, 11 May 1826 and that night reached Colchester, where there were 'good people but an old dirty inn'. She slept the next night at Scole and, having made good time, arrived in Norwich and left her luggage at The Swan.

Still poorly, she determined that nothing would prevent her from making the 14-mile journey to Mr Gunn the same day. The route to Smallburgh took her along the edge of the Norfolk Broads and she crossed the River Bure at Wroxham. She saw the boats lining the river, a warehouse, a mill and the parish church on the hill. She looked at the flint cottages with wavy pantiles and felt sick with nerves. Everywhere the countryside looked glorious: bluebells were in flower; hedges cascaded with hawthorn blossom; crab apple petals, the colour of strawberry ice cream, drifted across the lanes and cow parsley and pink campion burst from the verges but Augusta felt uneasy. She had not seen Mr Gunn for many years and wondered what sort of reception she would receive from the elderly cleric. As her carriage drove along she rehearsed once again her plan to procure her wedding certificate. First, she would appeal to Gunn's better nature. She would explain how the document could prove her son's legitimacy abroad, and second, she would assure him that they would never use the document in England.

With her case in order, Augusta was admitted to Smallburgh Grange but her powers of persuasion did not move William Gunn and he would not relinquish the document. Nothing daunted, she informed him that she would return on Tuesday when he had had more time to consider her request. Her second attempt was also unsuccessful, and like each of the previous supplicants, Augusta left Smallburgh without the certificate.

She had made the expedition from London at great cost, and her failure to extract the document affected her health. She returned home at a gentler pace, spending three nights on the road, staying the first night at Thetford, 'a pretty place', the second at Chesterford, where she noted 'I very ill', and the third night at Epping, where she was 'much worse'. On arrival in London on 21 May, she retired to bed, physically and emotionally spent. Even then she did not give up and at the beginning of June the Bishop of Norwich was writing to Gunn again asking him to give up the 'papers relating the marriage of the Duke' and he concluded wearily that 'as soon as we get entirely rid of them, we shall neither of us have any further trouble upon the subject – adieu!'[4] The marriage certificate however, remained in Gunn's possession.

After her visit to Norfolk, Augusta began to consult Dr Joseph de Courcy Laffan, physician to the late Duke of Kent. When Laffan informed her that he was spending the summer on the Isle of Wight, she had so much faith in his ministrations that she asked to continue her treatment on the island where the climate was deemed beneficial to those with weak lungs. Augusta was an early Isle of Wight tourist. She was in the vanguard of a sequence of visitors, which included John Keats, who had discovered the delights of the diamond-shaped island in 1817 when he stayed at Carisbrooke and returned two years later to stay in Shanklin. Lord Tennyson, the poet, and Julia Margaret Cameron, the photographer, made their homes on the island, as did the family of another poet, Algernon Swinburne, at Bonchurch, the village where Charles Dickens wrote part of *David Copperfield*. Queen Victoria first visited the island in 1831 and enjoyed it so much that she built Osborne House, her Italianate palace at Cowes, where she died in 1901.

The Royal Mail Steam Packet Company's introduction of a paddle steamer between Southampton and Cowes in 1820 made the Isle of Wight more accessible than before and Augusta and Emma took advantage of the new service when they embarked on the *Prince Coburg* at midday on 27 July 1826. As they steamed down Southampton Water into the Solent, we can assume that Augusta told Emma about her last visit to Cowes, from where she had embarked for Virginia just before the American War of Independence. The small port now supported an American consulate, which had opened in June 1790, the same month as American diplomatic missions in Liverpool and London.

Augusta and Emma stayed in Cowes and Augusta kept regular appointments with Dr Laffan. As she had hoped, hot baths and marine air expedited a recovery and soon she was strong enough to begin a full programme of sightseeing. On 8 August they drove to Newport, the island's social centre, which had recently been embellished with two neoclassical arcaded buildings: John Nash's town hall and the Isle of Wight Institution. Augusta bought a chessboard and pieces for their evening entertainment and they visited Charles I's final prison at Carisbrooke Castle. On 16 August they took the ferry from Cowes to the new pier at Ryde, where they had dinner and purchased a spyglass. They hired a 'little carriage' to take them to the sands at Shanklin on the east coast of the island, and they dined at Ventnor, 'a lovely place', built on terraces above the sea. They admired Lord Yarborough's collection of Italian paintings and Roman marbles at nearby Appuldurcombe, the grandest house on the island, landscaped by 'Capability' Brown. When they steamed back to Southampton, having first settled their marine library subscription in Cowes, Augusta and Emma had seen the chief sites on the island. On their way to London, they visited Windsor Castle, where the charge was 10*s*, rather than the 2*s* they had paid at Carisbrooke. It is a measure of Augusta's strength of mind that she was able to take her daughter to see Windsor Castle, which in happier circumstances the two of them might have regarded as home.

While they had enjoyed their visit to the Isle of Wight, its benefits did not last. Augusta was now 65 years old and her health was poor. Unwilling to spend another winter in England, she said farewell to Ramsgate and, accompanied by Emma and Mrs Deadman, was back in Paris by the end of September 1826. After visiting Virginia and Lucy and Georgina Drew, Augusta made preparations for the journey south. She bought warm gloves, quilted shoes and silver gilt cutlery 'for travelling'. After staying at a 'very extravagant' hotel in Lyon and seeing Avignon, the Pont du Gard and the Roman antiquities at Nimes, they slept at Aix-en-Provence. At the beginning of November, Augusta, Emma and Mrs Deadman arrived in Nice, which had reverted to the Kingdom of Sardinia after the defeat of Napoleon. Consequently, Augusta arranged fifteen Italian lessons for Emma with the local abbé.

She recorded the rental of 'Monsr Avigdor's House, the best & most delightful of Nice, for which I am to pay £300' and when their baggage arrived from Paris they settled down to a warm and enjoyable winter. Augusta resumed her charitable habits and started making donations to the 'Monday beggar', an 'old woman' and other mendicants. She stocked her cellar buying bottles of Bourdeaux Médoc, La Fitte and a bottle of vin blanc de paysan, which they could drink both for enjoyment and medicinal purposes. She was pleased to find that Lady Bute was staying in Nice with her son, Lord Dudley Stuart, and his exotic new wife, Christine Bonaparte (Napoleon's niece, whom Stuart had secretly married in Rome). Augusta's stay in Nice was spoilt only when the ministrations of Lady Bute's doctor failed and 'dear Deady' died in early February.

Augusta and Emma visited Lakes Como and Maggiore and spent the summer of 1827 in Lausanne, from where they went to Geneva by steamboat. Augustus joined them at the end of June and his mother noted ruefully, 'My beloved arrived – not as soon as he ought – however he is come,' and rewarded him handsomely with a gift of £50. The three of them spent a fortnight in Venice in October, a perfect time of year to visit when the sun was still warm. Augusta enjoyed good health there and the combination of fine weather and the company of both her children encouraged her to hire a gondola for eleven days and throw herself into some energetic sightseeing.

Today's tourists would not recognise the order in which they tackled the sites ofVenice. One of the first places they visited is no longer well known. At the beginning of the nineteenth century the monastery on Isola di San Lazzaro near the Lido was an important centre of Armenian culture. Lord Byron had studied there in 1816 and its collections of manuscripts, books and paintings were popular with literary British visitors. Having purchased the poet's works before leaving Paris, Augusta found the rooms where Byron lived and worked of particular interest. John Ruskin's passion for Gothic architecture has made St Mark's Basilica the principal attraction in Venice but when Augusta was there in 1827, it was one of the last places that she visited. They went there two days before leaving and saw the four bronze horses looted by Napoleon, back in their rightful place, standing sentinel above the entrance.

The Jesuit church impressed Augusta with its baroque interior of 'verd antique inlaid all in marble of Carrera, the pulpit, the carpet of the altar, the columns, the paintings all worthy of attention'.[5] On consecutive days they went to the Palladian churches of Il Redentore and San Giorgio Maggiore. The former she found of 'very little worth', but acknowledged that St Francis and St Mark 'sculpté en bronze par Jerome Campagna' were 'beaux ouvrages'.

They stayed on the Grand Canal opposite the church of Santa Maria della Salute and Augusta was delighted with their hotel. It was reasonably priced, the staff were civil and she enjoyed playing cards with a fellow guest, Lady Charlotte Stopford, the Duke of Buccleuch's daughter. On leaving Venice they went to Padua and Bologna where Augusta tipped one of the servants 'for making my porridge in the rain.' They went to the museum in Bologna and saw, 'Raphael's beautiful *St Cecilia*, Réné Guido's *Murder of the Innocents* and many more magnificent pictures.'[6] They were in Florence at the beginning of November. The last time Augusta was there, she was hot, pregnant and disgruntled; she had felt so poorly that she had done little sightseeing. This time, on their short stay she did not miss the Michelangelo tombs in the Medici Chapel at San Lorenzo and on 8 November went to the Strozzi Chapel in Santa Maria Novella 'pour voir les tableaux' – Filippino Lippi's frescoes of the lives of the apostles, Philip and James, completed in 1502.

What were Augusta's feelings when she returned to Rome for the first time with both her children in November 1827? She must have shown the children all the places in which she had been wooed so intensely by their father. Surely they went to the fateful steps of the Chiesa di San Giacomo where she met the Prince and surely they looked at the exterior of Hotel Sarmiento, where she was married, but it is poignant that, unlike all the other places they toured, she does not note a single place that they visited. Her memories of Rome were perhaps too painful.

After spending the winter there, they travelled to Tuscany via Pisa, where Augusta admired the 'inclining tower'. They visited Leghorn, the 'very handsome town' in which she had spent so many anxious weeks waiting for a convoy in 1793. Payments to doctors, apothecaries and pharmacies now appear with more frequency in Augusta's accounts. She still had faith in the curative properties of water and she and Emma went to Bagni di Lucca, where the sulphur and saline springs were renowned. Augusta hoped that the warm water spa, once a summer residence of Napoleon, would prove beneficial and she took a house there. She was still in Tuscany on Emma's birthday, 'a welcome day' when Augusta gave her 'dear loved girl £20'.[7] During a fortnight back in Florence she gave her daughter who 'is so kind to me' £25 as well as a pelisse like the one belonging to Lady Burghersh, the fashionable wife of the British minister in Florence and favourite niece of the Duke of Wellington. Continuously grateful to her daughter for her solicitude during their trip, Augusta also gave Emma a diamond necklace. They spent Christmas in Rome and on 4 May 1829, two weeks after royal assent was given to the act for the Emancipation of the Roman Catholics in Britain, Augusta and Emma left the eternal city.

From Genoa they went by sea to Marseilles. Travelling overland to Bordeaux, they boarded a vessel and steamed down the Garonne and across the Bay of Biscay to Dublin. In Liverpool they stocked up with silver, buying a teakettle, lamp, candlesticks, two chased bowls and a cream jug. They took a house in Leamington in August, trusting that the spa's salty waters might cure Augusta, but her strength was failing and on 1 October she and Emma began to make their way home slowly. After travelling for three years Augusta was able to write on Sunday, 20 October, 'My dear Ramsgate where we arrived to my great satisfaction … the day quite magnificent.'

Augusta had always filled in her account books neatly but by the end of 1829 numerous mistakes disfigure the columns and Emma's helping hand is discernible. A payment for housekeeping expenses and brandy on 1 March was Augusta's final entry and poignantly her blotting paper remains in situ between the pages. Emma noted that 'my beloved Mother' died on Thursday, 4 March 1830. *The Gentleman's Magazine*, which had not noticed her birth in 1761, published a short obituary with details of her two marriages, the birth of her children and the granting of the royal licence to use the name de Ameland. It also carried two mistakes. She did not die on 28 February and she was the second daughter of the Earl of Dunmore, not the fourth. A week after the death of her mother, Emma went to London and bought a black parasol and an expensive mourning shawl, costing £8 10*s*, of which her mother would surely have approved. Much loved by the people of Ramsgate, their 'Duchess' was interred at St Lawrence Church on 13 March: it was the only burial that day.

34

Sir Augustus D'Este and Mademoiselle D'Este

King George IV's death on 26 June three months later might have heralded an era of royal acceptance for the D'Este children. The late King had lost patience with Augusta at the beginning of the century and his relationship with the Duke of Sussex had broken down in 1814 after an altercation over his treatment of his daughter, Princess Charlotte. There had been little chance of George IV welcoming Emma and Augustus into the royal fold.

With the accession of well-meaning William IV and kindly Queen Adelaide, the situation changed. The relationship between the Duke of Sussex and the new monarch was warm and William's attitude to Augustus and Emma was influenced by the fact that he himself had ten illegitimate children. The new King regarded his nephew and niece sympathetically and conferred a knighthood and a pension on Augustus and offered Emma the rank and title of the daughter of a marquess. While grateful to the King, Emma knew from whom she was descended and if she could not be acknowledged as the daughter of a royal Duke and the granddaughter of the King, she was unwilling to be ranked in any other way. To the approval of many, she refused the offer and continued to be known as Mademoiselle D'Este until she was married. Like her brother, she was forced to adopt certain social habits to prevent awkwardness. The problem of precedence and the style of her announcement were solved at dinner parties by Emma slipping into the dining room while the guests were being seated, rather than being announced in the drawing room at the beginning of the evening.[1]

Augusta had worked hard for years to have her children recognised as royal and it was her misfortune that she did not live to see her daughter accepted at the court of King William and Queen Adelaide. Emma stayed at Windsor Castle and Brighton Pavilion with the King and Queen and she was a bridesmaid at the wedding of William's youngest daughter, Amelia, to Lord Falkland. We should not be surprised that Lady Holland commented spitefully that the Queen 'only sees Ld Howe, Ly Brownlow, Miss D'Este & a few of that trempe'.[2]

When not at court, Emma spent much of her time visiting friends like the Brownlows at Belton in Lincolnshire and the Jerseys at Middleton Park in Oxfordshire. In the autumn of 1833 during a Scottish odyssey to see her relations, she stayed in chilly splendour with her cousins at Hamilton Palace. She visited a round of Murray cousins at Blair Atholl and Scone Palace and concluded her tour by spending a few days with her uncle George at Dunmore Park. She spent most of the spring of 1837 at Windsor Castle, where the monarch's health was declining and was there on 20 June when her 'beloved King' expired at twenty past two in the morning.[3] Two days later she went to Sewell & Cross, the drapers in Soho, and spent more than £12 on mourning.

Her brother's relationship with William IV had not been easy. As he grew older, Augustus became more and more obsessed with his lack of status and in 1831 filed a chancery bill to validate his parents' marriage. To the Duke of Sussex's embarrassment and without his permission, Augustus included all his parents' love letters as evidence. This attempt at ensuring his legitimacy was partly a reaction to the news that after the death of Lady Augusta, the Duke had remarried privately outside the terms of the Royal Marriages Act.

The Duke's new wife was a widow, Lady Cecilia Buggin, the daughter of the Earl of Arran and his countess, who had been governess to Lord Arran's older children. Lady Cecilia had travelled about with the Duke of Sussex after her husband's death in 1825, using her mother's maiden name, Underwood. According to the granddaughter of the Duke's friend Lord Leicester, 'Many people were still inclined to look coldly upon her, but at Holkham they knew that she really had been married to the Duke, (though only after she had lived with him), as the marriage ceremony was performed by a friend of my grandfather, Archdeacon Glover.'[4]

The Duke of Sussex had not sought permission to marry because he knew that any issue he and the Duchess might have would demote the children of his younger brother, the Duke of Cambridge, in the line of succession. A marriage to Cecilia within the terms of the Royal Marriages Act would also have prompted calls for posthumous legalisation of his marriage to Augusta. This the Duke would not countenance as it would promote Sir Augustus D'Este above his nephew, Prince George of Cambridge. D'Este's chancery bill was unsuccessful and its only result was a breakdown of his relationship with his father and the King. The accession of his young cousin, Victoria, heaped misery on Sir Augustus and in the summer of 1838 he recorded in his pocket journal that his father had had the 'Little Queen' to dine with him and that she went in state. He added bitterly that neither he nor Emma was invited.

In 1840 Lady Cecilia was created the Duchess of Inverness in her own right and was received at court. Many people echoed the thoughts of the Lord Leicester's granddaughter that it seemed 'strange that, whilst Lady Augusta Murray, who had in every way a better right, was never acknowledged by the Royal Family as the Duke's wife, Lady Cecilia Underwood was not only acknowledged, but was created a Duchess with the Duke's Scottish title of Inverness'.[5] Augustus D'Este was tormented. He saw the elevation of Lady Cecilia as an unbearable slight on his mother's memory and immediately expressed his resentment to his father. It was made worse by the fact that Lady Cecilia's title was Scottish. Henry Murray, Augusta's nephew, also took up his late aunt's cause. He asked the Duke of Hamilton to intercede on her behalf, reminding him that Augusta's 'honor & memory are put to open shame & her children are dishonoured & her Husband silent!!!'[6]

The Duke of Sussex however, had kept his word to Augusta. He never broke the marriage vows that he made in Rome and waited until Augusta died before he took a second wife. Soon after her death, he wrote sadly to the Duke of Hamilton, 'when one looks back to events of thirty seven years ago one can not do it without a sigh. My intentions were and always have been honest and for the best, I could not fight more than I did against established Laws and a Power greater than my own.' He added warmly 'peace to her soul do I say from the bottom of my heart'.[7]

The combination of D'Este's chancery bill and the Duke's second marriage caused a complete collapse in the relationship between father and son but D'Este remained close to his mother's family, maintaining contact with his Murray cousins, uncles and aunts. He was kind to Lady Virginia and often sent her monetary gifts. He made an annual visit to his lunatic cousin, John Tharp, resident at the private asylum in the former bishop's palace at Much Hadham, and he remembered Augusta's old retainers such as Mrs Jordan, her milk woman, whom he helped with pecuniary 'assistances'.

While kind and considerate to others, his health was deteriorating. He began to feel unwell in 1822 after a relation with whom he was to stay in Scotland had died suddenly. The shock brought on the beginnings of a debilitating disease of the nervous system and although he did not know it, he had contracted multiple sclerosis. By January 1826, with the termination of his short affair with Princess Feodora, his eyes began to bother him. Unaware of the cause of his incapacity and beset by afflictions affecting his mobility, he tried a number of remedies including galvanisation, massages and vapour baths or 'shampooing' at Mahomed's Turkish Bath in Brighton. His condition, steadily worsening, was aggravated by the mental anguish caused by his father's second marriage. When the Duke of Sussex died of erysipelas on 21 April 1843, he had not been reconciled with his son and made no provision for D'Este in his will. The Duke's relationship with his daughter had been different; he had bought her a house in South Street, Mayfair, described her as his 'delight' and bequeathed her £10,000.

The Gentleman's Magazine obituarist mentioned both of the Duke's children.[8] The writer railed against the Royal Marriages Act, which according to Lord Brougham was 'the most unfortunate of all acts, the very worst of all human laws'. He remarked that of 'all the sons of George III, the Duke of Sussex was, after the Duke of York, the most popular; and, next to his eldest brother, the most accomplished'. The writer also acknowledged that Augustus's 'career at the University of Göttingen, and his subsequent sojourn at Rome, gave him opportunities … denied to his brothers. Of these advantages he fully availed himself; and during his Continental tour he acquired that art of social intercourse, no less than that familiarity with the topics of the day, which made his conversation at once easy and pleasing.' The obituarist applauded his roles as grand master of the Freemasons, and as president of the Society of Arts and of the Royal Society. He commented on the Duke's liberality in the causes of the abolition of the slave trade and parliamentary reform. Unlike his father, George III, and his brother, George IV, Augustus had supported Roman Catholic Emancipation.

The Duke of Sussex was buried, according to his wishes, in the public cemetery at Kensal Green so that when her time came, the Duchess of Inverness could be interred with him. In the account of the funeral in *The Gentleman's Magazine*, the ceremony took place in the cemetery chapel.

The illegitimate son of the deceased, Colonel Sir Augustus Frederick D'Este, KCH, was listed, in the best tradition of Victorian euphemism, as one of the 'Personal Friends of his late Royal Highness'.

The year after the Duke's death, D'Este lodged a claim to succeed to his father's English peerage. Its failure increased his bitterness:

> The scurrilous satire upon justice called the Committee of Privileges of the House of Lords reported my claim not to be proved, but certain Law Lords declared that it was an injustice of the greatest degree to me, and in consequence of a Law *which should never have been passed*; and that Parliament, by making a Provision for me, should seek to make to me some amends. Sir Robt Peel would bring no message from the Crown to that effect; and no member in either House from a noble love of justice, brought my case under consideration: so, after the honours which had been conferred on the Duchess of Inverness, I remained NEGLECTED – in the MIRE.[9]

Sir Robert did, however, advise Queen Victoria to give Augustus and Emma a pension. Both accepted her offer with gratitude, although Emma stated that, 'My Brother certainly had a better *excuse* for accepting Her Majesty's liberality than I have; owing to my Father's neglect of making the slightest provision for his son – & that that son's ill health makes many *Luxuries* (which I can do without) *necessaries* to him.'[10] The last years of Augustus's life were wretched. Incontinent and immobile, he was 'an afflicted and thwarted man, the victim of the slings and arrows of outrageous fortune, bald, becoming deaf and with a spasticity of such severity that locomotion was only possible by clinging to the shoulder of his manservant or using his "chair on wheels."'[11] His mental health was similarly compromised.

Fired with resentment and stung by the preferment of the Duchess of Inverness, Augustus resolved to give Augusta the recognition that had eluded her in life. He commissioned Edward Haynes, the Ramsgate builder, to build a Gothic mausoleum in the form of a Greek cross 'to receive the mortal remains of his venerated and loved mother' in St Lawrence churchyard. Augustus agreed a sum of £212 with Haynes for the 'Sepulchre' and spent the autumn of 1847 supervising its progress. D'Este's health was deteriorating fast, so seven workmen were employed on his mother's monument and he encouraged them with generous tips.[12] He commissioned George White, who had recently finished repairing the chapter house at York Minster, to carve the stones and paid the respected 'Architectural Sculptor' handsomely. When the building was complete, the coffins of the Earl and Countess of Dunmore and their daughter, Augusta, were moved from a vault in the church and deposited inside. The inscription on the west side gave particulars of both Lady Augusta's marriages 'held invalid in England as contrary to an Act of Parliament, entitled "The Royal Marriages Act."'[13]

The mausoleum was completed just in time. Augustus died on 18 December 1848, a month before his 55th birthday. He bequeathed his 'dearly loved cousin Viscount Fincastle' his tartans, highland dress, broadswords, dirks and pistols. He also left him his books relating to Scotland 'particularly those [concerned with] the memorable year one thousand seven hundred and forty five' when Bonnie Prince Charlie raised his standard: a strong indication of the deceased's animosity towards the Hanoverian dynasty.[14]

After Augusta's death her son had rented rooms at 17 Wellington Terrace when he was in Ramsgate and as neither he nor Emma needed their childhood home, the Mount Albion estate was divided into lots and sold for development. Emma donated the shrubbery behind the house as a site for Holy Trinity church and Ramsgate's growing population welcomed an extra place of worship. The townspeople revered their 'Duchess' and preserved her memory three times in Augusta Road, Steps and Place. Mount Albion's kitchen garden became Arklow Square and D'Este Road now traverses what used to be Augusta's park. The walk separating her pleasure grounds from the park has become Truro Road, which commemorates Emma and her husband, Sir Thomas Wilde, who later became Lord Truro.

Emma's wedding took place at St Alphege, London Wall, on 13 August 1845. According to *The Freemasons' Quarterly*, the 'ceremony took place under circumstances which carried an air of great mystery, and manifested a desire, on the part of the bride and bridegroom, to keep the proceedings extremely secret' and whenever the possibility of the marriage was mentioned in the press, it was rejected. The 44-year-old bride was late. She arrived 'quite privately, was elegantly attired, and wore a profusion of jewels'. She was 'in excellent spirits, possessing a very commanding appearance' and 'looked exceedingly well'. Sir Stephen Lushington, Queen Caroline's other executor, gave her away and apart from the celebrant and clerk, there was no one else present.

Twice *The Freemasons' Quarterly* informed its readers that a special licence had been required, adding that the 'parties manifested great anxiety for the termination of the ceremony'. Emma's wedding sounds uncannily similar to that of her parents in December 1793. The masonic reporter, an assiduous journalist, ensured that he saw the marriage certificate, where he noticed that 'the Duke of Sussex' simply appeared in the box for the name of the father of bride 'without any honorary addition (such as his Royal Highness), declaring him to have been of the blood royal'. It was a dreadful irony that, although unrecognised as such, the bride was nevertheless a descendant of King George II and could have been subject to the Royal Marriages Act. By marrying her without Queen Victoria's consent, the groom, one of the country's foremost lawyers and a former attorney general, might be breaking the law. There were therefore good reasons why the happy couple had avoided publicity and wanted the ceremony completed.

The press concluded that the attachment between the two parties was formed after Sir Thomas had represented the bride's brother in his peerage claim. On his wedding day however, the groom recalled the August day in 1821 when he first met Emma, the young woman in the party that accompanied Queen Caroline's coffin to Brunswick.

When her husband was created Baron Truro of Bowes on his appointment as Lord Chancellor in 1850, Emma became Lady Truro. That November they stayed two nights with the Queen at Windsor Castle. Victoria was much amused by the Lord Chancellor's stories but the diminutive monarch found her 'very handsome' cousin a trifle overpowering.[15] Despite the nineteen-year age difference between Emma and her husband, their marriage, was happy but childless. Lord Truro died in 1855 after two years' illness.

Emma had inherited asthma from her father and in the autumn of 1865 went abroad for the benefit of her health. Three weeks after her return she died suddenly at her house in Eaton Square on the afternoon of 21 May 1866. The *Thanet Advertiser* recorded the demise of the Dowager Lady Truro 'with regret' and recalled her long connection with Ramsgate, where she was respected 'as a lady of strict business habits, and, though rather reserved in manner' lived 'in a very quiet and unostentatious way'.[16] A week later her remains were brought down to Ramsgate by train. When the body was removed from 13 Eaton Square and conveyed to Victoria Station there was a long line of private carriages including those of HRH the Duchess of Cambridge, HRH the Duke of Cambridge, the Duchess of Inverness, the Duchess of Marlborough and Lord and Lady Carrington.[17]

Her funeral took place on 28 May at St Lawrence church 'without the slightest parade of her high and honourable birth'. After the service, the cortège moved slowly across the churchyard to the D'Este mausoleum, followed by the chief mourner, Lord Truro, other members of the Wilde family and some of the deceased's servants. 'The whole of the mourners then entered the tomb where the burial service was impressively read by the Rev. G. W. Sicklemore' and Emma's coffin laid to rest with those of her husband, grandparents, brother and beloved mother.[18] Her cousin, the seventh Earl of Dunmore, was waiting on the Prince of Wales and could not attend.

Epilogue

Lady Augusta Murray's life neatly spanned the reigns of both George III and George IV, to whom she was inextricably linked. Her children had no descendants to perpetuate her memory and history has largely forgotten her. Her family seat at Dunmore Park lies in ruins and her portrait by George Romney is untraced, facts that have conspired to keep her story obscure.

When posterity does recall the unacknowledged wife of George III's least-known son, Augusta is portrayed as trapping an innocent prince into an illegal marriage. Augustus himself, however, vindicated Augusta 'of having practised any arts of circumventions or seduction'. Lonely and homesick, when he met her on the steps of a Roman church, he was beguiled. Ostracised by his father and disliked by his eldest brother, the Prince spent so long in exile that he is a shadowy figure. It is more than forty years since Mollie Gillen published her seminal biography, *Royal Duke*, on Prince Augustus Frederick.[1]

George III's failure to communicate a plan for his sickly son's future left Augustus floundering, alone and far from home. When he married Augusta Murray without asking his father's permission, his 'improper connection' became the first casualty of the Royal Marriages Act, a measure drawn up with the best of intentions by a disappointed and angry king. The Prince's marriage outraged George III's sense of duty, leaving Augustus incredulous at the harshness of his father's reaction. Having been absent during the early episodes of the King's illness, Augustus's understanding of his father's personality was so slight that he was ill prepared for his vindictiveness.

When Prince Augustus left for Lisbon in December 1800, he parted from Augusta on excellent terms, but in 1801 there was an unexplained and irrevocable split and they never met again. Although Lady Augusta's weddings were illegal under the terms of the Royal Marriages Act, her birth and ancestry made her a suitable consort for the sixth son of the King. Therein lay the irony of her life and one to which she was never reconciled. Proud of her royal forebears, the loss of status after her two marriages was a perpetual source of frustration and distress.

Excluded by the Royal Family, Lady Augusta made it her business to research her lineage and to pass on the information to her children, leaving them in no doubt of their distinguished origins. She always regarded herself as the Duchess of Sussex and to her family, friends and retainers she was never anything else. She only used her courtesy title, Baroness D'Ameland, when it was expedient to do so.

Her parents and siblings cherished 'Goosy'. Her relationship with her mother was close and her siblings' loyalty enduring and endearing. She was Virginia's 'dear Duchess'; Jack's expedition to Lisbon on Augusta's behalf was testimony to his affection for his eldest sister; George stood bail for her and Alexander travelled to Norfolk in an attempt to obtain her marriage certificate from the Reverend William Gunn. Augusta adored Catherine and doted on 'dear Susan', whom she nursed during her final illness and whose funeral expenses she paid. Three of Augusta's siblings – Alexander, Susan and Leveson – had daughters named 'Augusta' in her honour.

Augustus D'Este's attempt at erecting a sepulchre to his mother's lasting memory has ended in failure. Through no fault of his, the mausoleum is a melancholy sight today; its location, by the low wall at the western edge of St Lawrence churchyard, has left the sad little building unnoticed. It is vulnerable, knee-deep in nettles and surrounded by litter. Once a pleasing and airy spot, it is now dank and depressing. The yews, planted at each corner, have grown so high that the sepulchre is deprived of light. Vandals have ripped off its roof tiles and carvings lie discarded on the plinth. Graffiti disfigures two of the three commemorative plaques and all but one of the bosses has been smashed. Inside the blocked entrance, however, six coffins remain unmolested: two contain the unacknowledged grandchildren of King George III and a third their mother, the duchess he denied.

Bibliography

Adams, H.C., *Wykehamica: A History of Winchester College and Commoners*, (James Parker, 1878)

Allardyce, Alexander (ed.), *Letters from and to Charles Kirkpatrick Sharpe Esq*, 2 vols, (William Blackwood & Sons, 1888)

Aspinall, A. (ed.), *Letters of George IV*, 3 vols, (Cambridge University Press, 1938)

Aspinall, A. (ed.), *Letters of the Princess Charlotte 1811–1817*, (Home and Van Thal, 1949)

Aspinall, A. (ed.), *The Later Correspondence of George III*, 5 vols, (Cambridge University Press, 1962–1970)

Aspinall, A. (ed.), *Correspondence of George, Prince of Wales 1770–1812*, 8 vols, (Cassell, 1969)

Auckland, William, *The Journal and Correspondence of William, Lord Auckland*, 4 vols, (Richard Bentley, 1861)

Austen-Leigh, James Edward, *Memoir of Jane Austen*, (Richard Bentley & Son, 1926)

Baird, Rosemary, *Mistress of the House: Great Ladies and Grand Houses 1670–1830*, (Weidenfeld and Nicolson, 2003)

Bamford, Francis (ed.) and Wellington, Duke of (ed.), *The Journal of Mrs. Arbuthnot 1820–1832*, 2 vols, (London, Macmillan, 1950)

Bickley, Francis (ed.), *The Diaries of Sylvester Douglas (Lord Glenbervie)*, 2 vols, (Constable, 1928)

Black, Jeremy, *The British Abroad: The Grand Tour in the Eighteenth Century*, (Alan Sutton, 1992)

Brogan, Hugh, *The Penguin History of the USA*, second edition, (Penguin, 1999)

Brougham, Henry, *The Life and Times of Henry Lord Brougham*, 3 vols, (William Blackwood and Sons, 1871)

Brownlow, Emma Sophia, *Slight Reminiscences of A Septuagenarian from 1802–1815*, (John Murray, 1867)

Brownlow, Emma Sophia, *The Eve of Victorianism: Reminiscences of the Years 1802–1834*, (John Murray, 1940)

Busson, Charles, *The Book of Ramsgate*, (Barracuda Books, 1985)
Buxton Forman, H. (ed.), *The Complete Works of John Keats*, 4 vols (Gowars & Gray, 1901)
Caley, Percy Burdelle, *Dunmore: Colonial Governor of New York and Virginia 1770–1782*, 2 vols (Ph.D. diss., University of Pittsburgh, 1939)
Chapman, Guy, *William Beckford*, (Jonathan Cape, 1937)
Chapman, R.W. (ed.), *Johnson's Journey to the Western Isles of Scotland; and, Boswell's Journal of a Tour to the Hebrides with Samuel Johnson, L.L.D*, (Oxford University Press, 1970)
Coke, Mary, *The Letters and Journals of Lady Mary Coke*, 4 vols (David Douglas, 1889–96)
Commager, Henry Steele (ed.) and Morris, Richard B. (ed.), *The Spirit of 'Seventy-Six*, (Harper & Row, 1958)
Cook, A.K., *About Winchester College*, (Macmillan, 1917)
Cordingley, David, *Cochrane The Dauntless: The Life and Adventures of Admiral Thomas Cochrane, 1775–1860*, (Bloomsbury, 2007)
Cotton, Charles, *The History and Antiquities of the Church and Parish of St Laurence, Thanet*, (Simpkin, Marshall, Hamilton, Kent, 1895)
Craven, Wayne, *Colonial American Portraiture*, (Cambridge University Press, 1986)
David, James Corbett, *Dunmore's New World*, (University of Virginia Press, 2013)
David, Saul, *Prince of Pleasure: The Prince of Wales and the Making of the Regency*, (Little, Brown, 1998)
Dillon, John, *The Case of the Children of His Royal Highness the Duke of Sussex Elucidated*, (London: Saunders & Benning, 1832)
Ditchfield, G.M., *George III: An Essay in Monarchy*, (Palgrave Macmillan, 2002)
Doddridge, John Humphreys (ed.), *The Correspondence and Diary of Philip Doddridge, DD*, 5 vols, (Henry Colburn and Richard Bentley, 1831)
Dolan, Brian, *Ladies of the Grand Tour*, (Flamingo, 2002)
Eliott-Drake, Elizabeth (ed.), *Lady Knight's Letters from France and Italy 1776–1795*, (Arthur L. Humphreys, 1905)
Fitzgerald, Percy, *The Royal Dukes and Princesses of the Family of George III*, 2 vols, (Tinsley Brothers, 1882)
Fitzpatrick, John C. (ed.), *The Diaries of George Washington 1748–1799*, third impression, (Houghton Mifflin Company, 1925)
Fitzpatrick, John C. (ed.), *The Writings of George Washington from the Original Manuscript Sources 1745–1799*, (US Government Printing Office, 1931)
Fitzpatrick, Walter (ed.) and Bickley, Francis (ed.), *The Manuscripts of J.B. Fortescue, Preserved at Dropmore*, (HMSO, 1892–1927)
Forth, Douglas, *The Case of Augustus D'Este*, (Cambridge University Press, 1948)
Fraser, Flora, *Beloved Emma: The Life of Emma Lady Hamilton*, (Weidenfeld and Nicolson, 1986)
Fraser, Flora, *The Unruly Queen: The Life of Queen Caroline*, (Macmillan, 1996)
Fraser, Flora, *Princesses: The Six Daughters of George III*, (John Murray, 2004)

Fraser, William, *The Elphinstone Family Book of the Lords Elphinstone, Balmerino and Coupar*, 2 vols, (Edinburgh University Press, 1897)
Freeman, Douglas Southall *George Washington: a Biography; Vol. 3, Planter and Patriot*, (Charles Scribner's Sons, 1951)
Fulford, Roger (ed.), *The Autobiography of Miss Knight, Lady Companion to Princess Charlotte*, (William Kimber, 1960)
Fulford, Roger, *Royal Dukes, The Father and Uncles of Queen Victoria*, revised edition (Collins, 1973)
Garlick, Kenneth, *Sir Thomas Lawrence*, (Phaidon, 1989)
Gillen, Mollie, *Royal Duke: Augustus Frederick, Duke of Sussex (1773–1843)*, (Sidgwick & Jackson, 1976)
Gore, John (ed.), *Creevey's Life and Times*, (John Murray, 1934)
Granville, Castalia (ed.), *Lord Granville Leveson Gower, Private Correspondence 1781–1821*, 2 vols, 2 impression (John Murray, 1916)
Greville, Charles, *The Greville Memoirs: A Journal of the Reigns of King George IV, King William IV and Queen Victoria*, 8 vols (Longmans, Green, 1899)
Griffiths, Grace, *History of Teignmouth*, (ELSP, 2001)
Guide to Frogmore House and The Royal Mausoleum, revised edition (Royal Collection Enterprises, 2003)
Fischer, David Hackett, *Paul Revere's Ride*, (Oxford University Press, 1994)
Fischer, David Hackett, *Washington's Crossing*, (Oxford University Press, 2004)
Hadlow, Janice, *The Strangest Family: The Private Lives of George III, Queen Charlotte and the Hanoverians*, (William Collins, 2014)
Hepworth Dixon, William (ed.), *Lady Morgan's Memoirs: Autobiography, Diaries and Correspondence*, 2 vols (W.H. Allen, 1863)
Hibbert, Christopher, *The Grand Tour*, (Thames Methuen, 1987)
Hibbert, Christopher, *George III: A Personal History*, (Viking, 1998)
Hogg, Quintin, *The Purpose of Parliament*, (Blandford Press, 1946)
Hussey, Christopher, *English Country Houses: Late Georgian 1800–1840*, (Country Life, 1958)
Hutton, James (ed.), *Selections from the Letters and Correspondence of Sir James Bland Burges, Bart*, (John Murray, 1885)
Huxley, Gervas, *Lady Elizabeth and the Grosvenors: Life in a Whig Family, 1822–1839*, (Oxford University Press, 1965)
Ilchester, Earl of (ed.), *The Journal of Elizabeth Lady Holland (1791–1799)*, 2 vols, (Longmans, Green, 1908)
Ilchester, Earl of (ed.), *Elizabeth, Lady Holland to Her Son*, (John Murray, 1946)
Ingamells, John (ed.), *A Dictionary of British and Irish Travellers in Italy, 1701–1800*, (Yale University Press, 1997)
Jarrett, Derek, *Pitt the Younger*, (Weidenfeld and Nicolson, 1974)
Keay, Anna & Stanford, Caroline, *Landmark: A History of Britain in 50 Buildings*, (Frances Lincoln, 2015)
Kent, William (ed.), *An Encyclopaedia of London*, revised by Godfrey Thompson (J.M. Dent & Sons, 1970)

Laughlan, William F. (ed.), *A Companion and Useful Guide to The Beauties of Scotland by Sarah Murray*, (Hawick, Byways, 1982)
Lewis, Theresa (ed.), *Extracts from the Journals and Correspondence of Miss Berry*, 3 vols, (Longmans, Green, 1866)
Liscombe, R.W., *William Wilkins 1778–1839*, (Cambridge University Press, 1980)
Macdonald, John, *Memoirs of an Eighteenth-Century Footman: Travels (1745–1779)*, with an introduction by John Beresford, (London, George Routledge & Sons, 1927)
Malmesbury, Earl of, *Memoirs of an Ex-Minister: An Autobiography*, 2 vols, (Longmans, Green, 1884)
Maxwell, Herbert (ed.), *The Creevey Papers*, 2 vols, (John Murray, 1903)
Maxwell, Herbert, *The Honourable Sir Charles Murray KCB: A Memoir*, (W. Blackwood, 1898)
Middlekauff, Robert, *The Glorious Cause: The American Revolution 1763–1789*, (Oxford University Press, 1982)
Miers, Mary, *Highland Retreats: The Architecture and Interiors of Scotland's Romantic North*, (Rizzzoli, 2017)
Miller, Anna Riggs, *Letters from Italy*, 2 vols, 2 edition, (Edward and Charles Dilly, 1777)
Mowl, Timothy, *William Beckford: Composing for Mozart*, (John Murray, 1998)
Neale, J.P., *Views of Seats of Noblemen and Gentlemen in England, Wales, Scotland and Ireland*, 6 vols, 2 series, (Sherwood, Gilbert & Piper, 1826)
Oliver, J.W., *The Life of William Beckford*, (Oxford University Press, 1932)
Page, William (ed.), *The Manuscripts of the Duke of Somerset, the Marquis of Ailesbury and Sir T.H.G. Puleston*, (HMSO, 1898)
Pettit, Paul, *Devon, Cornwall and the Isles of Scilly*, (Michael Joseph, 1987)
Pickering, Spencer (ed.), *Memoirs of Anna Maria Wilhelmina Pickering*, (Hodder and Stoughton, 1903)
Plumb, J.H., *The First Four Georges,* (B.T. Batsford, 1956)
Pottle, Frederick (ed.), *Boswell's London Journal, 1762–1763. Together with Journal of my Jaunt, Harvest 1762*, (William Heinemann, 1951)
Richardson, Christopher Thomas, *Fragments of History Pertaining to The Vill, or Wille, or Liberty of Ramsgate*, (Fuller, 1885)
Riding, Jacqueline, *Jacobites: A New History of the '45 Rebellion*, (Bloomsbury, 2016)
Roberts, Henry D., *A History of the Royal Pavilion Brighton*, (Country Life, 1939)
Rush, Richard, *A Residence at the Court of London*, introduction by Philip Ziegler (Century, 1987)
Scarfe, Norman (ed.), *A Frenchman's Year in Suffolk, 1784*, (Boydell Press for the Suffolk Records Society, 1988)
Schama, Simon, *Rough Crossings: Britain, the Slaves, and the American Revolution*, (BBC Books, 2005)
Schecter, Barnet, *The Battle for New York: The City at the Heart of the American Revolution*, (Jonathan Cape, 2003)
Scott, Walter, *Peveril of the Peak*, 3 vols, (Robert Cadell, 1848)
Smith, E.A., *A Queen on Trial: The Affair of Queen Caroline*, (Alan Sutton, 1993)
Sproule, Anna, *Lost Houses of Britain*, (David & Charles, 1982)

Stirling, A.M.W. (ed.), *The Letter-Bag of Lady Elizabeth Spencer-Stanhope*, 2 vols, (The Bodley Head, 1913)

Strachey, Lady (ed.), *Memoirs of a Highland Lady, The Autobiography of Elizabeth Grant of Rothiemurchus Afterwards Mrs Smith of Baltiboys, 1797–1830*, (John Murray, 1911)

Thorne, R.G., *The House of Commons 1790–1820*, 5 vols, (Secker & Warburg, 1986)

Tillyard, Stella, *Aristocrats*, (Chatto & Windus, 1994)

Tillyard, Stella, *A Royal Affair: George III and His Troublesome Siblings*, (Chatto & Windus, 2006)

Tod, Andrew (ed.), *Memoirs of a Highland Lady*, 2 vols, (Canongate Classics, 1988)

Tomalin, Claire, *Mrs Jordan's Profession: The Story of a Great Actress and a Future King*, (Penguin, 1994)

Vickery, Amanda, *The Gentleman's Daughter: Women's Lives in Georgian England*, (Yale University Press, 1998)

Wain, John (ed.), *The Journals of James Boswell 1760–1795*, (Heinemann, 1990)

Walpole, Horace, *The Castle of Otranto*, (The Grey Walls Press, 1950)

Watkin, David, *Thomas Hope and the Neo-Classical Idea*, (John Murray, 1968)

Wraxall, N. William, *Historical Memoirs of My Own Time*, 2 vols, (T. Cadell and W. Davies, 1815)

Wylly, William, *A Short Account of the Bahama Islands, their Climate, Productions, etc.*, (London, 1789)

Young, Hilary (ed.), *The Genius of Wedgwood*, (Victoria & Albert Museum, 1995)

Notes

Introduction

1 Johanna Lausen-Higgins, *A Taste for the Exotic-Pineapple Cultivation in Britain*, Historic Gardens, 2010 www.buildingconservation.com

Chapter 1

1 PRO 30/93/1
2 Unless noted, the Prince's letters in this chapter are found in the Dunmore Family Papers
3 HLRO Peerage Claims, Vol. 12, Part 2, Southesk – Sussex, pp.23–25
4 NRS OPR Births 469/201 58 Airth
5 HLRO Peerage Claims, Vol. 12, Part 2, Southesk – Sussex, No. 29, p.64
6 Ibid., No. 34
7 PRO 30/93/1

Chapter 2

1 Jane Carson, *Lady Dunmore in Virginia*, Research Department, Colonial Williamsburg Foundation, January 1, 1962
2 Percy Burdelle Caley, *Dunmore: Colonial Governor of New York and Virginia 1770–1782*, (unpublished PhD thesis) Pittsburgh, Pennsylvania, 1939, Vol. 2, p.214
3 Compiled by Alistair and Henrietta Tayler, *The Book of the Duffs*, Vol. II, Edinburgh, 1914, p.315
4 Dunmore Mss., Series 1, Box 3, Folder 24

Chapter 3

1 Ed. Clementina Rind, *Virginia Gazette*, 3 March 1774, p.3
2 John Byrd to William Byrd, *Virginia Magazine of History and Biography*, 1930, XXXVIII, p.356
3 Ed. Clementina Rind, *Virginia Gazette*, 3 March 1774, p.3
4 John Summerson, *The Pelican History of Art: Architecture in Britain 1530–1830*, 1977, p.540
5 AO 13/28, PRO, London, transcript, CWF
6 Barbara Carson, *The Governor's Palace: The Williamsburg Residence of Virginia's Royal Governor*, Colonial Williamsburg Foundation, 1987, p.86
7 AO 13/28, PRO, London, transcript, CWF
8 Dunmore Mss., Series 1, Box 3, Folder 44
9 Ed. John C. Fitzpatrick, *The Diaries of George Washington 1748–1799*, Houghton Mifflin Company, 1925, Vol. I, p.27
10 Ibid., p.152
11 Douglas Southall Freeman, *George Washington, Planter and Patriot*, New York, 1951, p.350
12 Ibid., p.353
13 Ibid., p.354
14 Hugh Brogan, *The Penguin History of the USA*, Penguin, Second Edition, 2001, pp.103–104
15 Jane Carson, *Lady Dunmore in Virginia*, Research Department, Colonial Williamsburg Foundation, January 1, 1962, p.8
16 *John Quincy Adams' Diary*, The Adams Papers, John D. Rockefeller Jr. Library, Microfilm reel #32
17 Jane Carson, *Lady Dunmore in Virginia*, Research Department, Colonial Williamsburg Foundation, January 1, 1962, pp.6–7
18 PRO CO 5/1353
19 Ibid.
20 From George Washington to Richard Henry Lee, 26 December 1775, *Founders Online*, National Archives, accessed April 11, 2019, https://founders.archives.gov/documents/Washington/03-02-02-0568.

Chapter 4

1 David Adshead & Sally Jeffery, *John Erskine, Earl of Mar: A Gentleman Amateur in Twickenham*, The Georgian Group Journal, 2015, Vol. XXIII, p.13
2 J.W. Oliver *The Life of William Beckford*, Oxford University Press, 1932, p.85
3 Ibid., p.86
4 Timothy Mowl, *William Beckford Composing for Mozart*, John Murray, 1998, p.110
5 Arthur Chamberlain, *George Romney*, Methuen and Co., London, 1910, p.302. In 1910 the picture belonged to Charles Wertheimer and in the early 1970s it was sold to a Canadian buyer but remains untraced

6 RA GEO/ADD/51/1/18
7 Ibid.
8 Ibid.
9 Jane Austen's London, St James Palace, Pt II, 27.4.13, Internet Blog by Louise Allen
10 PRO 30/29/4/7 No.63
11 Ibid.
12 Dunmore Mss., Series 1, Box 3, Folder 14
13 RA GEO/ADD/51/1/45
14 RA GEO/ADD/51/3/135
15 *A Re-enactment of a Wealthy Woman Getting Dressed in 18th-century England* by Madeline Raynor, video from the Lady Lever Art Gallery and National Museums, Liverpool.
16 RA GEO/ADD/51/1/120
17 Dunmore Mss, Series 2, Bundle 14, E21
18 PRO 30/29/3/90
19 B. Longmate, *A Supplement to the Fifth Edition of Collins's Peerage of England*, London, 1784, p.43
20 Wiltshire & Swindon History Centre H/1946 MR bx 40/21
21 Timothy Mowl, *William Beckford Composing for Mozart*, John Murray, 1998, p.124
22 Ibid., p.133

Chapter 5

1 Ed. J.A. Home, *Letters and Journals of Lady Mary Coke*, Edinburgh, 1896, Vol. IV, p.178
2 RA GEO/MAIN/47834-5
3 RA GEO/ADD/9/5
4 Ibid., 6
5 Ibid., 41
6 Ibid., 8
7 Ibid., 9
8 Ibid., 19
9 Ibid., 42
10 Ibid., 47
11 Ibid., 48
12 Ibid., 49
13 Ibid., 52
14 Ibid., 58
15 RA GEO/MAIN/47846
16 RA GEO/ADD/9/60
17 Ibid., 61
18 Ibid., 65

19 Ibid., 70
20 RA GEO/MAIN/47860
21 Ibid., 47862
22 Ibid., 47871
23 Ibid., 47928-9
24 Ed. Lady Eliott-Drake, *Lady Knight's Letters from France and Italy 1776–1795*, London, 1905, p.166
25 RA GEO/MAIN/47950
26 Ed. James Hutton, *Selections from the Letters and Correspondence of Sir James Bland Burges, Bart.,* John Murray, 1885, pp.195–196
27 RA GEO/MAIN/47971
28 RA GEO/ADD/9/158

Chapter 6

1 PRO 30/29/4/7, f.65
2 Ibid., f.64
3 Ibid., f.66
4 PRO 30/93/3
5 PRO 30/29/4/7, f.68
6 Nigel Aston, 'Dillon, Arthur Richard (1721–1806)', *Oxford Dictionary of National Biography*, Oxford University Press, 2004
7 PRO 30/29/4/7, f.67
8 Ibid., f.68
9 Ibid., f.66
10 Ibid., f.67
11 Ibid., f.68
12 Ibid., f.64
13 Ibid., f.69
14 Brian Dolan *Ladies of the Grand Tour*, Flamingo, 2002, p.213
15 John Malcolm Bulloch, *The Earls of Aboyne*, Huntly, 1908, p.29
16 Ibid., f.69
17 Ibid., f.66
18 Ibid., f.69

Chapter 7

1 PRO 30/29/4/7, f.70
2 PRO 30/29/6/5/2
3 PRO 30/29/4/7, f.70
4 Ibid., f.71
5 RA GEO/ADD/9/76

6 PRO 30/29/4/7, f.72
7 Ibid.
8 Ed. Lady Eliott-Drake, *Lady Knight's Letters from France and Italy 1776–1795*, London, 1905, p.187
9 RA GEO/ADD/51/3/50

Chapter 8

1 Waddesdon Rothschild Collections online catalogue
2 Barker, G. (23 September 2004). Hamilton, Lord Archibald (1770–1827), politician. *Oxford Dictionary of National Biography*
3 RA GEO/ADD/51/3/73-74
4 Ibid., 169
5 Ibid., 173
6 Geoffrey V. Morson, 'Hamilton, Sir William (1731–1803)', *Oxford Dictionary of National Biography*, Oxford University Press, 2004
7 Ed. William Page, *The Manuscripts of the Duke of Somerset, the Marquis of Ailesbury and Sir T.H.G. Puleston*, London HMSO, 1898, p.250
8 Ibid.
9 Ed. James Hutton, *Selections from the Letters and Correspondence of Sir James Bland Burges, Bart.*, John Murray, 1885, p.285

Chapter 9

1 Mollie Gillen, *Royal Duke Augustus Frederick, Duke of Sussex (1773–1843)*, Sidgwick & Jackson, 1976, p.49
2 RA GEO/MAIN/47982
3 Ibid., 47984
4 Ed. Lady Elliott-Drake, *Lady Knight's Letters from France and Italy, 1776–1795*, London, 1905, p.187
5 *The Universal Magazine of Knowledge and Pleasure for March, 1794,* Vol. XCIV, p.181
6 Christopher Hibbert, *Rome, The Biography of a City,* Penguin, 1985
7 Ed. Lady Elliott-Drake, *Lady Knight's Letters from France and Italy, 1776–1795*, London, 1905, p.179
8 Unless noted, all references in this chapter are from PRO 30/93/1
9 RA GEO/ADD/51/3/182
10 RA GEO/MAIN/47989

11 Ed. A. Aspinall, *The Later Correspondence of George III*, CUP, 1962, Vol. I, p.643, 824
12 RA GEO/MAIN/47994

Chapter 10

1 Unless noted, all references in this chapter are from PRO 30/93/1
2 *The Universal Magazine of Knowledge and Pleasure for March, 1794,* Vol. XCIV, p.181
3 RA GEO/MAIN/47999

Chapter 11

1 Unless noted, all references in this chapter are from PRO 30/93/1
2 RA GEO/ADD/51/2/121
3 Ed. Earl of Ilchester, *The Journal of Elizabeth Lady Holland (1791–1799)*, Longmans, Green, 1908, Vol. I, p.147
4 Ibid., Vol. II, p.70
5 RA GEO/ADD/9/143
6 Mollie Gillen, *Royal Duke Augustus Frederick, Duke of Sussex (1773–1843)*, Sidgwick & Jackson, 1976, p.51
7 HL/PO/DC/CP/15/3, N-Z, 7, p.3
8 Ibid.
9 Ibid., p.1
10 HLRO Peerage Claims, Vol. 12 Part 2, Southesk – Sussex, pp.9–12
11 Ibid.

Chapter 12

1 HLRO Peerage Claims, Vol. 12, Part 2, Southesk – Sussex, pp.9–12
2 Mollie Gillen, *Royal Duke Augustus Frederick, Duke of Sussex (1773–1843)*, Sidgwick & Jackson, 1976, p.61
3 HLRO Peerage Claims, Vol. 12, Part 2, Southesk – Sussex, pp.58–63
4 Ed. Lady Eliott-Drake, *Lady Knight's Letters from France and Italy 1776–1795*, London, 1905, p.192
5 HLRO Peerage Claims, Vol. 12, Part 2, Southesk to Sussex, pp.13–20
6 Ibid., pp.6–9
7 Ibid., pp.13–20
8 Ibid., pp.58–63
9 PRO 30/93/1
10 HLRO Peerage Claims, Vol. 12, Part 2, Southesk – Sussex, pp.62–64, No. 28

11 Ibid., pp.21–22
12 Dunmore Mss., Series 2, Bundle 14, E8
13 Mollie Gillen, *Royal Duke Augustus Frederick, Duke of Sussex (1773–1843)*, Sidgwick & Jackson, 1976, p.66
14 PRO 30/93/1

Chapter 13

1 PRO 30/93/1
2 RA GEO/MAIN/48002
3 Unless noted, all references in this chapter are from PRO 30/93/2
4 Mollie Gillen, *Royal Duke Augustus Frederick, Duke of Sussex (1773–1843)*, Sidgwick & Jackson, 1976, p.74

Chapter 14

1 Unless noted, all references in this chapter are from PRO 30/93/3
2 Anna Riggs Miller, *Letters from Italy*, London, 1777, Vol. I, p.362
3 Mollie Gillen, *Royal Duke Augustus Frederick, Duke of Sussex (1773–1843)*, Sidgwick & Jackson, 1976, p.72
4 Dunmore Mss., Series 2, Bundle 14, E17
5 RA GEO/MAIN/48026
6 Dunmore Mss., Series 2, Bundle 14, E6
7 RA GEO/MAIN/48008
8 PRO 30/93/5
9 Ibid.
10 Simon Adams, 'Dudley, Sir Robert (1574–1649)', *Oxford Dictionary of National Biography*, Oxford University Press, 2004
11 RA GEO/MAIN/48009

Chapter 15

1 Unless noted, all references in this chapter are from PRO 30/93/3
2 Daniel A. Baugh, Michael Duffy, 'Hood, Samuel, first Viscount Hood (1724–1816)', *Oxford Dictionary of National Biography*, Oxford University Press, 2004
3 Chichester, H., & Beaumont, D. (8 January 2009). O'Reilly, Alexander, Count O'Reilly in the Spanish nobility (bap. 1723, d. 1794), army officer in the Spanish service. *Oxford Dictionary of National Biography*, Oxford University Press

Chapter 16

1 Unless noted, all references in this chapter are from PRO 30/93/3
2 RA GEO/ADD/9/166
3 HLRO Peerage Claims, Vol. 12, Part 2, Southesk – Sussex, p.43
4 Ibid., p.45
5 RA GEO/MAIN/48037
6 Ibid.
7 Ibid., 48035

Chapter 17

1 RA GEO/MAIN/48035
2 PRO 30/93/3
3 Ibid.
4 Ed. A. Aspinall, *The Later Correspondence of George III*, CUP, 1963, Vol. II, p.136, 987
5 PRO 30/93/3
6 RA GEO/MAIN/48015
7 RA GEO/ADD/43/3/4
8 Ibid., 10
9 Ibid., 12

Chapter 18

1 HLRO Peerage Claims, Vol. 12, Part 2 Southesk – Sussex, p.47
2 PRO 30/93/3
3 Ed. A. Aspinall, *The Later Correspondence of George III*, CUP, Vol. II, 1963, p.xxxix, n.1
4 HLRO Peerage Claims, Vol. 12, Part 2 Southesk – Sussex, pp.46–47
5 RA GEO/MAIN/48016
6 PRO 30/93/4
7 RA GEO/ADD/43/3/22

Chapter 19

1 Janice Hadlow, *The Strangest Family*, William Collins, 2014, p.148
2 RA GEO/MAIN/15938
3 Baugh, D. (3 January 2008). Byng, John (bap. 1704, d. 1757), naval officer. *Oxford Dictionary of National Biography*, Oxford University Press
4 RA GEO/ADD/43/3/22

Chapter 20

1 RA GEO/MAIN/48019-29
2 Ibid., 48019
3 Ibid., 48024
4 Ibid.
5 Ibid., 48025
6 Ibid.
7 Ibid.
8 Dunmore Mss, Series 2, Bundle 14, E49
9 RA GEO/MAIN/48029
10 Ibid.
11 RA GEO/MAIN/48030-42
12 Ibid., 48032
13 Ibid.
14 Ibid., 48038
15 Ibid., 48040
16 *Gentleman's Magazine*, London, Vol. LXIV, p.87
17 *The Case of The Children of HRH the Duke of Sussex Elucidated: A Juridical Exercitation by Sir John Dillon Knt.*, London, Printed for Saunders & Benning, 1832
18 Ed. A. Aspinall, *The Later Correspondence of George III*, CUP, Vol. II, 1963, pp.175–176, 1017
19 PRO 30/93/1

Chapter 21

1 E.A. Smith, 'Scott, John, first Earl of Eldon (1751–1838)', *Oxford Dictionary of National Biography*, Oxford University Press, 2004
2 R.A. Melikan, 'Scott, William, Baron Stowell (1745–1836)', *Oxford Dictionary of National Biography*, Oxford University Press, 2004
3 RA GEO/MAIN/7424
4 HLRO Peerage Claims, Vol. 12, Part 2 Southesk – Sussex, pp.48–50
5 Dunmore Mss, Series 2, Bundle 2, E13
6 Charles Dickens and the Law: (2) David Copperfield and Doctors' Commons, *Musings, Memories and Miscellanea*, Blog at Wordpress.com, Henry Brooke, December 20, 2015 in *Miscellanea*
7 HL/PO/DC/CP/15/3 No. 7, p.5
8 RA GEO/MAIN/48050-6
9 HL/PO/DC/CP/15/3 No. 7, p.18
10 Ed. Lady Eliott-Drake, *Lady Knight's Letters from France and Italy 1776–1795*, London, 1905, p.193
11 HLRO Peerage Claims, Vol. 12, Part 2 Southesk – Sussex, p.52
12 PRO 30/93/3

Chapter 22

1 HL/PO/DC/CP/15/3 No. 7, p.18
2 RA GEO/MAIN/48059
3 Henderson, T. (3 January 2008). Augustus Frederick, Prince, duke of Sussex (1773–1843). *Oxford Dictionary of National Biography*, Oxford University Press
4 HL/PO/DC/CP/15/3 No. 7, p.19
5 Ed. W. Fitzpatrick & F. Bickley, *The Manuscripts of J.B. Fortescue, preserved at Dropmore,* London, HMSO, 1892–1927, Vol. II, p.504
6 Dunmore Mss, Series 2, Bundle 14
7 RA GEO/MAIN/48063
8 Ibid., 48066
9 Ibid., 48068-9
10 Ibid., 48071
11 Ibid., 48073
12 Mollie Gillen, *Royal Duke Augustus Frederick, Duke of Sussex (1773–1843),* Sidgwick & Jackson, 1976, p.94
13 RA GEO/MAIN/48089-91
14 Ibid., 48098-9
15 Ibid., 48119-20
16 Ibid., 16712
17 Dunmore Mss, Series 2, Bundle 14, E15
18 RA GEO/MAIN/48096

Chapter 23

1 Mollie Gillen, *Royal Duke Augustus Frederick, Duke of Sussex (1773–1843),* Sidgwick & Jackson, 1976, p.86
2 Tobias Smollett, *Humphry Clinker*, Penguin Classics, 2008, pp.22 & 33.
3 Blair Adam Mss., Series 2, Bundle 562
4 David Wilkinson, 'Adam, William (1751–1839)', *Oxford Dictionary of National Biography*, Oxford University Press, 2004
5 Blair Adam Mss., Series 2, Bundle 562/1
6 Ibid., 12
7 Ibid., 11
8 HL/PO/DC/CP/15/3 Printed Cases, N-Z, 7, p.21
9 PRO 30/93/4
10 RA GEO/MAIN/1727
11 RA GEO/ADD/9/435
12 Ibid., 422
13 Ibid., 412
14 Ibid., 417
15 Ibid., 439
16 Ibid., 454
17 Ibid., 456

18 Ed. A. Aspinall, *The Later Correspondence of George III*, Cambridge, 1967, Vol. III, No. 1768, Chatham Papers, p.85
19 Dunmore Mss., Series 2, Bundle 14, E20
20 RA GEO/MAIN/48148-9
21 Dunmore Mss., Series 2, Bundle 14, E20
22 Ibid.
23 RA GEO/MAIN/9272-3
24 Ibid., 48140
25 Ibid., 48151
26 Ibid., 48155
27 Ibid., 48160
28 Ibid., 48161-2
29 Ibid.
30 Ibid., 48163
31 Ed. A. Aspinall, *The Correspondence of George, Prince of Wales 1770–1812*, Cassell, 1969, Vol. IV, No. 1482
32 Ibid.
33 Dunmore Mss., Series 2, Bundle 14, E20
34 Ibid.
35 RA GEO/ADD/51/5/70
36 RA GEO/MAIN/48156-7
37 Ibid., 9272-3
38 PRO 30/93/4

Chapter 24

1 RA GEO/MAIN/48167-9
2 Ibid., 48170
3 Ibid., 48174
4 Ibid., 48177
5 Ibid., 48181
6 Ibid., 48182-3
7 Ibid., 48192
8 Ibid., 48193
9 Ibid.
10 Ibid., 48197
11 Ibid., 48199
12 Ed. Roger Fulford, *Autobiography of Miss Knight*, William Kimber, 1960, p.78
13 Mollie Gillen, *Royal Duke Augustus Frederick, Duke of Sussex (1773–1843)*, Sidgwick & Jackson, 1976, p.111
14 James Edward Austen-Leigh, *Memoir of Jane Austen*, Oxford, 1926, p.68
15 HLRO Peerage Claims, Vol. 12, Pt. 2, Southesk – Sussex, p.74
16 RA GEO/ADD/51/2/4
17 Ibid., 11
18 Ibid., 26

19 HLRO Peerage Claims, Vol. 12, Pt. 2, Southesk – Sussex, p.77
20 Ibid.
21 Dunmore Mss., Series 2, Bundle 2, E61
22 RA GEO/MAIN/48206
23 Ibid., 48222
24 Ibid., 48219-20

Chapter 25

1 RA GEO/MAIN/48225
2 RA GEO/ADD/51/2/26
3 RA GEO/MAIN/48226
4 A. Bird, *The Damnable Duke of Cumberland*, London, Barrie and Rockcliff, 1966, p.220
5 Dunmore Mss., Series 2, Bundle 2, E56
6 RA GEO/MAIN/48226
7 Mollie Gillen, *Royal Duke Augustus Frederick, Duke of Sussex (1773–1843)*, Sidgwick & Jackson, 1976, p.117
8 Blair Adam Mss., Series 2, Bundle 562
9 PRO TS 11/389/1215
10 Blair Adam Mss., Series 2, Bundle 562
11 Ibid.
12 Ibid., Bundle 272/2
13 RA GEO/MAIN/48236
14 Blair Adam Mss., Series 1, Box 27, Folder A
15 Ibid.
16 Ed. Francis Bickley, *The Diaries of Sylvester Douglas*, Constable & Co Ltd London, Vol. I, pp.338–339
17 Douglas Firth, *The Case of Augustus D'Esté*, Cambridge, 1948, p.4
18 Christopher Hibbert, *George III A Personal History*, New York, 1998, pp.84–85
19 Douglas Firth, *The Case of Augustus D'Esté*, Cambridge, 1948, p.4
20 Ibid.
21 Ibid., p.5
22 Ibid.
23 Blair Adam Mss., Series 1, Box 31, Folder L
24 Ibid., Box 36, Folder L
25 Ibid.
26 RA GEO/ADD/51/2/152
27 Ed. A. Aspinall, *The Correspondence of George, Prince of Wales*, Cassell, 1969, Vol. VI, p.36, n.
28 Blair Adam Mss., Series 2, Bundle 562
29 Ed. A. Aspinall, *The Correspondence of George, Prince of Wales*, Cassell, 1968, Vol. V, p.374, n.(c)
30 Blair Adam Mss., Series 2, Bundle 562
31 RA GEO/ADD/9/178

Chapter 26

1 Charles Dickens, *Little Dorrit*, Collins' Clear-Type Press, p.638
2 East Kent RO R/U5/E2
3 Ed. Andrew Tod, *Memoirs of a Highland Lady*, Canongate Classics, 1988, Vol. 1, pp.182–183
4 Ibid., pp.183–184
5 RA GEO/ADD/51/3/104
6 Ibid., 118
7 Charles Busson, *Book of Ramsgate*, Barracuda Books, 1985, p.46
8 Ed. Andrew Tod, *Memoirs of a Highland Lady*, Canongate Classics, 1988, Vol. 1, p.184
9 PRO 30/93/6/5
10 PRO 30/93/8
11 Dunmore Mss., Series 2, Bundle 14, E86
12 Ed. A.M.W. Stirling, *The Letter-Bag of Lady Elizabeth Spencer-Stanhope*, London, 1913, Vol. I, pp.144–145
13 Ed. James Greig, *The Farington Diary*, London, 1923, Vol. II, pp.274–275
14 Ed. Andrew Tod, *Memoirs of a Highland Lady*, Canongate Classics, 1988, Vol. 1, p.184
15 Ibid., p.182
16 Ibid., p.183
17 Ibid., p.192
18 Herbert Maxwell, *The Honourable Sir Charles Murray, K.C.B. A Memoir,* Edinburgh, 1898
19 Ed. Frederick Pottle, *Boswell's London Journal 1762–1763 together with Journal of My Jaunt Harvest 1762*, William Heinemann, 1951, p.63
20 RA GEO/ADD/51/2
21 PRO 30/93/13
22 Ed. Andrew Tod, *Memoirs of a Highland Lady*, Canongate Classics, 1988, Vol. 1, p.192
23 Richard Rush, *A Residence at the Court of London*, Century, 1987, p.34
24 PRO 30/93/6
25 Juliet Learmouth, *The London Town House of Lady Isabella Finch,* The Georgian Group Journal, 2017, Vol. XXV, p.91

Chapter 27

1 RA GEO/ADD/51/2/61
2 Ibid., 144
3 Ed. Andrew Tod, *Memoirs of a Highland Lady*, Canongate Classics, 1988, Vol. 1, p.196
4 RA GEO/ADD/51/6/85

5 Moscucci, O. (24 May 2007). Denman, Thomas (1733–1815), man-midwife. *Oxford Dictionary of National Biography*, Oxford University Press
6 RA GEO/ADD/51/5/165/85
7 Harrow School Archives A2008/25/6(4)
8 Ed. Andrew Tod, *Memoirs of a Highland Lady,* Canongate Classics, 1988, Vol. 1, p.196
9 NRS 2177, Bundle 1667
10 NRS C4/954/5

Chapter 28

1 Harrow School Archives A2008/25/6
2 PRO 30/93/8 - 17
3 Harrow School Archives A2008/25/6
4 PRO 30/93/09
5 Ed. Andrew Tod, *Memoirs of a Highland Lady*, Canongate Classics, 1988, Vol. 1, p.197
6 PRO 30/93/14
7 Ed. Andrew Tod, *Memoirs of a Highland Lady*, Canongate Classics, 1988, Vol. 1, p.184
8 Ibid., p.197
9 PROB 31/1012/128
10 PRO 30/93/13

Chapter 29

1 RA GEO/ADD/51/2/37
2 PRO 30/93/5
3 RA GEO/ADD/51/5
4 Ibid.
5 PRO 30/93/5
6 Ibid.
7 RA GEO/ADD/51/5/106
8 RA GEO/ADD/51/5/70
9 Ibid.
10 RA GEO/ADD/51/5/57
11 Mollie Gillen, *Royal Duke Augustus Frederick, Duke of Sussex (1773–1843)*, Sidgwick & Jackson, 1976, p.138
12 Ed. Andrew Tod, *Memoirs of a Highland Lady*, Canongate Classics, 1988, Vol. 1, p.182
13 Ibid., p.184
14 Ibid., p.197
15 Ibid.

16 RA GEO/ADD/51/3/85
17 Douglas Firth, *The Case of Augustus D'Esté*, Cambridge, 1948, p.6
18 Ibid., p.7
19 Ibid., p.11
20 PRO 30/93/6/9
21 Douglas Firth, *The Case of Augustus D'Este*, Cambridge, 1948, p.13
22 Winchester College Archives, WCM:23593A
23 David Turner, *The Old Boys*, Yale University Press, 2015, p.63
24 PRO 30/93/12
25 PRO 30/93/19
26 Ibid.
27 Ibid.
28 Ibid.
29 Ibid.
30 Elizabeth Grant of Rothiemurchus, *Memoirs of a Highland Lady 1791–1827*, Albemarle Library, John Murray, Revised and Edited by Angus Davidson, Second Impression, 1960, pp.238–239

Chapter 30

1 PRO 30/93/6 No. 17
2 Ibid.
3 *Gentleman's Magazine,* London, 1804, Vol. LXXIV, pp.1174–1175
4 PRO 30/93/6 No. 18
5 Ibid., No. 21
6 Ibid., No. 24
7 Emma Sophia Brownlow, *Slight Reminiscences of A Septuagenarian from 1802–1815*, John Murray, 1867, pp.166–167
8 Ibid.
9 *The New Monthly Magazine*, Henry Colburn, 1817, Vol. VII, p.23
10 Emma Sophia Brownlow, *Slight Reminiscences of A Septuagenarian from 1802–1815*, John Murray, 1867, p.169
11 PRO 30/93/6 No. 19
12 Ibid., p.22
13 Ed. A. Aspinall, *Letters of Princess Charlotte 1811–1817*, London, 1949, p.15, n.4
14 Ibid., p.105
15 Ibid., p.204
16 Ed. A. Aspinall, *The Letters of King George IV 1812–1830,* Cambridge, 1938, Vol. II, No. 717, p.222
17 PRO 30/93/22
18 Ibid.
19 Ibid.

Chapter 31

1 PRO 30/93/10
2 PRO 30/93/13
3 Ibid.
4 PRO 30/93/20
5 PRO 30/93/13
6 Ed. The Earl of Ilchester, *Elizabeth, Lady Holland to Her Son 1821–1845*, John Murray, 1946, p.76, n.2
7 Ibid.

Chapter 32

1 Dunmore Mss., Series 2, Bundle 14, E49
2 Flora Fraser, *Beloved Emma*, Weidenfeld and Nicolson, 1986, p.310
3 Ed. Andrew Tod, *Memoirs of a Highland Lady*, Canongate Classics, 1988, Vol. 1, p.197
4 PROB 11/1611
5 *Gentleman's Magazine*, London, 1818, Vol. LXXXVIII, p.640
6 Richard Rush, *A Residence at the Court of London*, Century, 1987, p.80
7 Ibid., p.81

Chapter 33

1 Dunmore Mss, Series 2, Bundle 14, E19
2 Ibid., E53
3 Ibid.
4 Ibid.
5 PRO 30/93/16
6 Ibid.
7 Ibid.

Chapter 34

1 Mollie Gillen, *Royal Duke Augustus Frederick, Duke of Sussex (1773–1843)*, Sidgwick & Jackson, 1976, p.203
2 Ed. Earl of Ilchester, *Elizabeth, Lady Holland to Her Son 1821–1845*, John Murray, 1946, p.120
3 PRO 30/93/17
4 Ed. Spencer Pickering, *Memoirs of Anna Maria Wilhelmina Pickering*, Hodder & Stoughton, 1903, p.255
5 Ibid.

6 NRS 2177/Bundle 704
7 Mollie Gillen, *Royal Duke Augustus Frederick, Duke of Sussex (1773–1843)*, Sidgwick & Jackson, 1976, p.202
8 *Gentleman's Magazine*, London, 1843, pp.645–652
9 Douglas Firth, *The Case of Augustus D'Esté*, Cambridge, 1948, p.47
10 Mollie Gillen, *Royal Duke Augustus Frederick, Duke of Sussex (1773–1843)*, Sidgwick & Jackson, 1976, p.241
11 Douglas Firth, *The Case of Augustus D'Esté*, Cambridge, 1948, p.58
12 PRO 30/93/24
13 Charles Cotton, *The History and Antiquities of the Church and Parish of St. Laurence, Thanet, in the County of Kent,* London and Ramsgate, 1895, p.151
14 PROB 11/2086
15 Mollie Gillen, *Royal Duke Augustus Frederick, Duke of Sussex (1773–1843)*, Sidgwick & Jackson, 1976, p.242
16 *Thanet Advertiser*, Saturday, 26 May, 1866
17 Ibid., Saturday, 2 June 1866
18 Ibid.

Epilogue

1 Mollie Gillen, *Royal Duke Augustus Frederick, Duke of Sussex (1773–1843)*, Sidgwick & Jackson, 1976

Index